QUICKBOOKS FOR PROFIT: MAKING THE NUMBERS WORK

QUICKBOOKS FOR PROFIT: MAKING THE NUMBERS WORK

David Campbell and Mary Campbell

Osborne **McGraw-Hill**

Berkeley New York St. Louis San Francisco
Auckland Bogotá Hamburg London Madrid
Mexico City Milan Montreal New Delhi Panama City
Paris São Paulo Singapore Sydney
Tokyo Toronto

Osborne **McGraw-Hill**
2600 Tenth Street
Berkeley, California 94710
U.S.A.

For information on translations or book distributors outside of the U.S.A., please write to Osborne **McGraw-Hill** at the above address.

QuickBooks for Profit: Making the Numbers Work

Copyright © 1993 by McGraw-Hill. All rights reserved. Printed in the United States of America. Except as permitted under the Copyright Act of 1976, no part of this publication may be reproduced or distributed in any form or by any means, or stored in a database or retrieval system, without the prior written permission of the publisher, with the exception that the program listings may be entered, stored, and executed in a computer system, but they may not be reproduced for publication.

1234567890 DOC 99876543

ISBN 0-07-881934-2

Publisher
Kenna S. Wood

Acquisitions Editor
Elizabeth Fisher

Associate Editor
Scott Rogers

Technical Editor
Campbell and Associates

Project Editor
Kelly Barr

Copy Editor
Judith Brown

Proofreader
Mick Arellano

Indexer
Valerie Robbins

Computer Designer
Lance Ravella

Illustrator
Marla J. Shelasky

Cover Designer
Studio Silicon

Information has been obtained by Osborne **McGraw-Hill** from sources believed to be reliable. However, because of the possibility of human or mechanical error by our sources, Osborne **McGraw-Hill**, or others, Osborne **McGraw-Hill** does not guarantee the accuracy, adequacy, or completeness of any information and is not responsible for any errors or omissions or the results obtained from use of such information.

CONTENTS AT A GLANCE

I BASIC SKILLS
1. Overview and Startup Activities 3
2. Setting Up QuickBooks for Your Business 21
3. Writing Checks and Maintaining Records ... 55
4. Making Register Entries 89
5. Preparing Budget Reports 117

II MANAGING ACCOUNTS RECEIVABLE
6. Invoicing Customers 137
7. Recording Payments and Managing Accounts Receivable 167

III MANAGING PAYABLES
8. Payroll 191
9. Mortgages, Credit Cards, and Other Liabilities 219

IV GETTING INFORMATION FROM YOUR SYSTEM
10. Refining Your Financial Picture 245

| 11 | Creating Standard and Custom Reports | 275 |
| 12 | Year-End Reports and Special Activities | 305 |

V APPENDIXES

A	Installing QuickBooks	327
B	Backing Up and Merging Files	333
C	Glossary	339
D	Converting Quicken Files for Use in QuickBooks	347
E	Customizing QuickBooks	351
	Index	359

CONTENTS

Acknowledgments xvii
Introduction xix

I BASIC SKILLS

1 Overview and Startup Activities 3
    QuickBooks Overview 5
        Recording Financial Transactions 5
        Writing Invoices and Processing Payments 8
        Writing Checks and Paying Bills 9
        Reporting Options 10
        Customizing QuickBooks 11
        QuickBooks Help Features 14
    Starting Your First QuickBooks Session 15
        Starting a New Company 15
    Getting Around in QuickBooks 15
        Using the Menus 16
        Using QuickBooks Windows 18
        Using Quick Keys 18

2 ▰ Setting Up QuickBooks for Your Business 21
  Setting Up Your Company 23
    Establishing the Company Files 23
    Setting Up an Account 24
    Setting Up a Printer 25
    Looking at the Sample Company Data 26
    Accessing Help 27
    Working Effectively with QuickBooks 27
  Taking a Look at What Lists Offer 30
  Creating Your First List with Customer Types 33
    Deleting Customer Types 34
    Adding Customer Types 35
    Performing List Maintenance 36
    Printing a List 37
  Working with Other Company Lists 38
    Using the Payment Terms List 38
    Using the Employee List 39
    Using the Customer List 40
    Adding Customer Notes 42
    Working with the Vendor and Vendor
      Types Lists 44
    Working with the Payment Methods List 46
    Working with the Project List 46
    Working with Items/Parts/Services 48
    Adding Shipping Methods 51
    Adding Invoice Memos 52

3 ▰ Writing Checks and Maintaining Records 55
  Ordering Check Stock 56
  Writing Checks 56
    Fields in the Write Checks Window 58
    Entering Basic Information 59
    Completing the Voucher 61
    Making and Recording Corrections 63
    Taking a Look at the Register Entries 63
    Voiding Checks 64

Printing Checks	65
Printing Sample Checks First	65
Selecting Checks to Print	70
Correcting Mistakes in Checks	72
Reconciling Your Account	73
QuickBooks' Reconciliation Process	74
Preparing the Printer for Reconciliation	76
Steps to Follow for a Successful Reconciliation	76
QuickBooks' Reconciliation Reports	79
Additional Reconciliation Issues and Features	81
Updating Your Opening Balance	81
Correcting Errors in Reconciliation	86

4 ■ Making Register Entries   89

Maintaining a Register	90
Recording Your Transactions in the Register	94
Adding Accounts as You Record a Transaction	96
Catching Up with Entries	97
Reviewing Register Entries	97
Scrolling Through the Register	98
Using the Find Feature	99
Using the Go to Date Feature	102
Revising Transactions	102
Changing a Transaction	103
Voiding a Transaction	104
Deleting a Transaction	104
Reinstating a Transaction	104
Reversing Transactions	105
Using Projects	105
Defining Projects	105
Entering Transactions with Subprojects	106
Splitting Transactions	106
Using Subaccounts	107
Entering a New Subaccount	108

Memorized Transactions	108
Memorizing a Register Entry	109
Memorizing a Check	111
Working with Transaction Groups	111
Defining a Transaction Group	111
Changing a Transaction Group	112
Having QuickBooks Remind You to Record Transactions	114
Recording a Transaction Group	114

5 ▬ Preparing Budget Reports 117

Developing a Financial Management Program	118
Preparing a Business Plan	119
Sources of Funding	120
Budget Planning	121
QuickBooks' Budgeting Process	122
Specifying Budget Amounts	123
Entering Monthly Detail for Budget Categories	125
Creating and Printing a Budget Report	126
Modifying a Budget Report	127
Filtering Transactions for Budget Reports	128
Report Discussion	131
Wide-Screen Reports	131

II ▬ MANAGING ACCOUNTS RECEIVABLE

6 ▬ Invoicing Customers 137

Types of Invoices	138
Creating an Invoice	140
The Invoice Window	142
Transactions Created By an Invoice	146
Line Items in the Item List	146
Special Checks Made While Entering an Invoice	151
Entering an Invoice You Have Already Sent Out	153

Reviewing Completed Invoices	154
Fixing Invoice Errors	154
Memorized Invoices	155
Deleting an Invoice	156
Credit Memos	156
Printing an Invoice	157
Options for Printing Invoices	158
Printing an Invoice Again	161
Printing Mailing Labels	162
Options for Printing Mailing Labels	163

7 Recording Payments and Managing Accounts Receivable ... **167**

Receiving Payments	168
Receive Payments Window	170
Applying a Discount	171
Matching Payments to Invoices	172
Overpayments	174
Entries Created When You Enter a Payment	175
Fixing Errors in Payments	177
Making Deposits	178
Deposits Prepared by QuickBooks	179
Depositing Cash Sales	181
Transactions Created When You Make a Deposit	183
Customer Information	183
Looking at Aging	186

III MANAGING PAYABLES

8 Payroll ... **191**

The QuickBooks Payroll System	192
Payroll Forms	194
Federal Payroll Forms	194

State and Local Government Payroll Information	195
Writing a Payroll Check	196
Register Entries for Payroll Transactions	197
Recording IRS Deposits	199
IRS Deposit Rules	201
Memorizing Payroll Transactions	202
Establishing Transaction Groups	202
Payroll Reports	204
Payroll Report Overview	204
Dates for Filing Federal Payroll Tax Returns	205
Employer's Quarterly Federal Tax Return	206
Other Quarterly Reports	209
Preparing W-2 Forms	210
Other Annual Tax Forms and Reports	212

9 — Mortgages, Credit Cards, and Other Liabilities — 219

Short- Versus Long-term Liabilities	220
Accounts Payable	220
Entering Bills	221
Recording Payments	226
Other Short-term Liabilities	231
Sales Taxes	231
Payroll Taxes	234
Deposits and Gift Certificates	234
Credit Card Accounts	236
Paying the Credit Card Bill	237
Mortgages and Other Long-term Liabilities	239

IV — GETTING INFORMATION FROM YOUR SYSTEM

10 — Refining Your Financial Picture — 245

Inventory Valuation	246
Entering the Inventory's Initial Value	249

Recording Inventory	249
What Are the Items Worth?	249
Updating the Inventory Balance	251
Producing the Inventory	252
Asset Depreciation	253
Depreciation Methods	254
Entering Assets and Depreciation into QuickBooks	257
Looking at Your Equity	263
Creating a Profit and Loss Statement	263
Equity Accounts in QuickBooks	264
Sole Proprietorships	267
Partnerships	270
Corporations	272

11 Creating Standard and Custom Reports 275

Creating a Standard Report	276
Viewing a Report on the Screen	279
Printing a Report	279
Options for Customizing Reports	280
Filtering Report Data	280
Using F8 for Customize or Options	282
Cash Versus Accrual Basis Accounting	283
Cash Versus Accrual Methods	285
Memorizing Reports	286
Recalling a Report You Have Memorized	286
A Closer Look at Some of the Reports	287
Balance Sheet	287
Changing the Standard P&L Report	288
Monitoring Accounts Receivable	291
Creating Payables Reports	294
Analyzing Cash Flows	295
Taking a Summary Look	295
Creating a Transaction Report	297
Looking at Income and Expense Transactions	299
Monitoring Projects	299

12 Year-End Reports and Special Activities 305
    The Business Cycle 306
    Accounting Steps at the End of the Cycle 307
    Avoiding the Typical Year-End Closing Process
        with QuickBooks 307
        Accounting for Prepaid Expenses 308
        Adjusting the Equity Account for Earnings 309
    Performing Year-End Maintenance Tasks 310
        Backing Up the Year's Transactions 311
        Protecting Your Data with Passwords 312
    Getting the Data You Need to
        Complete Year-End Tax Forms 315
        Schedule C, Profit or Loss from Business 315
        Form 1099 for Independent Contractors 320
        Payroll Taxes 321
        Form 1120, U.S. Corporation Income Tax
            Return 322

V APPENDIXES

A Installing QuickBooks 327
    Installing QuickBooks on a Hard Drive 328
    Registering QuickBooks 329
    Setting Up Printers in QuickBooks 330

B Backing Up and Merging Files 333
    Backing Up Your QuickBooks Files 334
    Restoring Your QuickBooks Files 335
    Merging QuickBooks Files 336

C Glossary 339

D Converting Quicken Files for Use in
    QuickBooks 347
    Performing the Conversion 348

E Customizing QuickBooks 351
Customizing the Company for Your Use 352
Company Information 352
Options 353
Passwords 355
Password Table 356
Customizing QuickBooks for All Companies 356
Options 356
Screen Colors 358
Monitor Refresh Speed 358
Setting the Data Directory 358

Index 359

ACKNOWLEDGMENTS

We wish to thank the many individuals at Intuit and Osborne/McGraw-Hill for their help with this project. Special thanks to Ridgely Evers at Intuit for all of his ideas that QuickBooks incorporates. His contagious enthusiasm about the product helped convince us to write this book. Liz Fisher and Scott Rogers at Osborne also contributed a great deal to this book. They helped to shape the approach that would best meet the needs of business users by reading many drafts of the manuscript and making constructive suggestions. Others at Osborne who helped us to complete this book include project editor Kelly Barr, illustrator Marla Shelasky, and the entire production department. Thanks are due as well to Judith Brown, who did a great job of copyediting.

We would also like to thank Gabrielle Lawrence for her help with the project. Her knowledge of accounting and many bright ideas helped to make this a better book. Special thanks also go to Elizabeth Reinhardt, who helped with the payroll chapter and checked other chapters to ensure that they were without errors.

INTRODUCTION

If you are trying to run a business *and* deal with all the financial issues, QuickBooks can make your job more manageable. Whether your business is a home-based enterprise or one with several offices and employees, QuickBooks provides the capabilities you need to manage expenses, analyze your cash flows, look at the profit and loss picture, or put together a budget. QuickBooks' ability to handle the recording of payroll information makes it easy to monitor your federal and state tax withholding, FICA, and other payroll-related costs. You can use QuickBooks with QuickPay for an even more sophisticated approach that will handle all of your payroll computations. Although it is not quite the same as having an accountant on your payroll, QuickBooks makes an otherwise unmanageable job manageable by allowing you to perform all of the necessary tasks without learning accounting jargon or complicated procedures.

About This Book

QuickBooks for Profit: Making the Numbers Work is designed to get you started using QuickBooks features immediately so you can apply them to your own business needs. The book covers the essential features that you will need, regardless of the type of business you are running. As you work through the chapters you will find many tips and practical examples to make you feel as though you have seasoned computer pros and fellow business users guiding you each step of the way.

QuickBooks for Profit: Making the Numbers Work

The book offers more than instruction on using QuickBooks features; the examples given are based on the authors' actual business transactions. Although the names of banks, customers, employees, and suppliers have been changed, all of what you read is based on transactions similar to the ones that you will need to record for your own business. You must, of course, evaluate each suggestion to determine its usefulness for *your* business.

Throughout the book you will find numerous tips. When we started our business twelve years ago, we had to learn many things the hard way. We also invested a considerable amount of time trying to find information on federal and state tax filing requirements. We have included as much of this information as possible to save you time and frustration.

How This Book Is Organized

This book is divided into five parts that allow you to focus on basic skills, accounts receivable, payables, reporting, or miscellaneous topics. Part I covers topics that you will use throughout the rest of the book, such as setting up the program, writing checks, making register entries, and working with budgets. If you have never used QuickBooks you will want to begin here to build a base of skills with which to master other areas of the product.

Chapter 1 introduces the product and explains the basics of its use from the user's standpoint. It lets you know what the product can do for you. Chapter 2 explains the basic techniques for working with the package. Also, this chapter explains the importance of selecting the correct chart of accounts and tells you how to create lists for vendors, employees, customers, and other information. You will use these lists throughout your work in QuickBooks. Chapter 3 covers writing and printing checks, as well as the end-of-month reconciliation procedure. Chapter 4 teaches you how to record transactions for quick entries and how to split transactions to record as much detail as possible. Chapter 5 shows you how to make budget entries and adjustments and how to print a budget report.

Part II provides the information you need to handle your accounts receivable. In Chapter 6 you learn how to create invoices and the labels to mail them out. Chapter 7 teaches you how to match payments with

Introduction

xxi

invoices as they are received and how to manage your collectibles using QuickBooks' reports.

Part III focuses on the management of payables. You learn how to use your cash as long as possible yet still pay within a discount period where applicable. Chapter 8 provides all the detail you need to set up the required payroll accounts and write payroll checks. Chapter 9 shows you how to set up liability accounts for mortgages and vendor accounts and also how to monitor account activity and keep track of what you owe.

Part IV shows you how to get information from your system. Inventory valuation, asset depreciation, and owners' equity are covered in Chapter 10. All of these adjustments are necessary to allow you to see an accurate picture of how the company is doing. In Chapter 11 you learn how to create QuickBooks' standard and custom reports. Chapter 12 discusses year-end activities and tells you how to complete them. You learn how QuickBooks' reports can provide the information you need to complete state and federal tax forms required at the end of the year.

Part V contains appendixes that cover installation, backup procedures, a glossary of terms, Quicken conversion, and customizing options.

Conventions Used in This Book

Throughout the book you will find many procedures for accomplishing QuickBooks tasks. The same conventions are used in all of these procedures to make them easy for you to follow. Menu selections are shown with the number of the menu option preceding the selection, for example:

Choose 7 Setup/Customize from the Main Menu.

This makes it easier to make the correct selection using either the keyboard or the mouse.

The names of keys, such as [F2], [Enter], and [Tab], are shown in key capsules. In situations where two keys must be pressed at the same time, they are joined by a hyphen, as in [Ctrl]-[Enter].

QuickBooks for Profit: Making the Numbers Work

Information that you should type in is shown in **boldface**. In addition, the names of menus, windows, and reports are shown using the same capitalization as QuickBooks for consistency.

In some cases you will find that there are several ways to accomplish the same task. Rather than confuse you with several approaches, we have selected the approach that is most efficient for a beginner.

QuickBooks and Your Business

QuickBooks provides the help you need to organize all of your business finances. With it, you can establish accounts for monitoring your business checking account, as well as other assets and liabilities. You can record all of your financial information with QuickBooks, and you will quickly master features like the ones used for monitoring your accounts receivable and accounts payable. QuickBooks can also assist you with gathering information for tax preparation, budgeting, and assessing the financial health of your firm.

It is hoped that some of the tips and ideas you find in this book will help to spur your problem-solving creativity as you develop strategies to meet the challenges of your business. Consult your accountant to ensure that what you want to do adheres to conventional accounting practices.

PART 1

BASIC SKILLS

CHAPTER

1 OVERVIEW AND STARTUP ACTIVITIES

Whether you are running a retail business, offering consulting services, or managing a farm, maintaining adequate business records is essential. Regardless of the type of business you are running, the accounting records that you keep let you analyze income and expenses, compute the worth of the business, and permit you to fulfill government reporting requirements for tax and regulatory reporting needs.

4

QuickBooks for Profit: Making the Numbers Work

Since there are many other activities that compete for your time, you need a system that maintains up-to-date records with minimal time spent. QuickBooks can provide the solution that you are looking for. QuickBooks lets you record financial events with a single entry. You save time, since you do not have to record double entries in journals as you would with a manual system, or take weeks to master a sophisticated accounting package. QuickBooks maintains each entry that you make, integrating all of the information and allowing you to group it and present it in different ways.

Once you master a few basics, you'll find QuickBooks is faster and easier than manually recording information.

You have probably grown accustomed to the manual methods of recording your business information even if you do not like the time it requires. If you are going to switch to another approach, you want a solution that is both easier and faster. QuickBooks offers this solution. You can use the list selection features in QuickBooks to partially automate the entry of your information. You will be able to record frequently used information on employees, customers, shipping methods, and other things into lists, and then reuse the data rather than retyping it each time. QuickBooks can write a check for you to sign, create an invoice for products or services, or record your bills while organizing and managing the information for you. You will be pleased with how much of your work you can have QuickBooks do for you.

If you are a Quicken user, you will be pleased to find that QuickBooks was developed by Intuit, the makers of Quicken, and shares some of its features. The similarity between QuickBooks and Quicken makes it easy for you to upgrade from Quicken to QuickBooks. But QuickBooks offers more than Quicken, with features such as enhanced accounts receivable and accounts payable. QuickBooks is more attuned to business terminology and provides expanded reporting and password features. You might decide to continue using Quicken for personal finances and investment management and use QuickBooks for all of your business finances. You will quickly learn the new terminology in QuickBooks and will appreciate its many business-oriented features. If you have never used Quicken, don't worry. You will find all the information you need in this book to put QuickBooks to work for you.

This chapter's overview looks at some of the main components of the package. You will learn how to start QuickBooks for your company and a few essential features of the program. You do not need to sit at your computer to read and understand this chapter. It provides what you need to begin a more in-depth investigation of specific features.

QuickBooks Overview

QuickBooks is designed to automate financial tasks for your company. When you start QuickBooks, you need to set up a company or set of files in which to store your information. As part of this process you tell QuickBooks what type of company you have, choosing from a list of 22 possibilities. Your answer determines the standard set of accounts that QuickBooks provides for recording information. This standard set of accounts is called a *chart of accounts* and is tailored for the type of business you are in. A wide variety of business types are supported, such as agricultural, accounting, medical, legal, not-for-profit, religious, and consulting.

> **NOTE:** A chart of accounts is essential for organizing your data. Without one, all of your financial entries would be lumped together, and it would be difficult to get a handle on how your business was doing at any particular time.

Each of the accounts in the chart of accounts can be classified as either a balance sheet account or an income and expense account. *Balance sheet accounts* are used to record a company's assets, liabilities, and the difference between these two amounts—the owner's equity in the firm. Think of a balance scale with assets on one side and liabilities on the other. The amount needed to make the sides balance is the *owner's equity*. *Income and expense accounts* are used to record the revenue that the firm generates and the expenses that it incurs in generating this revenue.

Recording Financial Transactions

If you are tired of making manual entries in a journal for every financial transaction, you will appreciate what QuickBooks can do for you. There is no need to worry about neatness even if you have to correct mistakes a few times. Also, the math calculations are always perfect, since QuickBooks does all of them for you.

QuickBooks for Profit: Making the Numbers Work

Within a company, accounts are the organizational unit that QuickBooks uses. Any financial activity that you record affects the balance in a QuickBooks account. You can establish checking and savings accounts, credit card accounts, liability accounts, and asset accounts—in short, any account that you are already using, as well as some new ones that can help you make sense of all your data. You can even transfer funds from one account to another using the Transfer feature. Every account is stored in your company file to make it easy to access all of your data no matter how sophisticated your business finances are.

The information on a financial event is called a *transaction*. QuickBooks can record the details of each of your financial transactions, whether it is money your business earns (revenue) or what you spend to keep the business going (expenses). It also records transactions that affect your business resources (assets) and your financial commitments (liabilities). Your ownership in the business (equity) can also be monitored with QuickBooks.

You have probably been using a manual register like the one shown in Figure 1-1 to record your checks and other transactions. When you

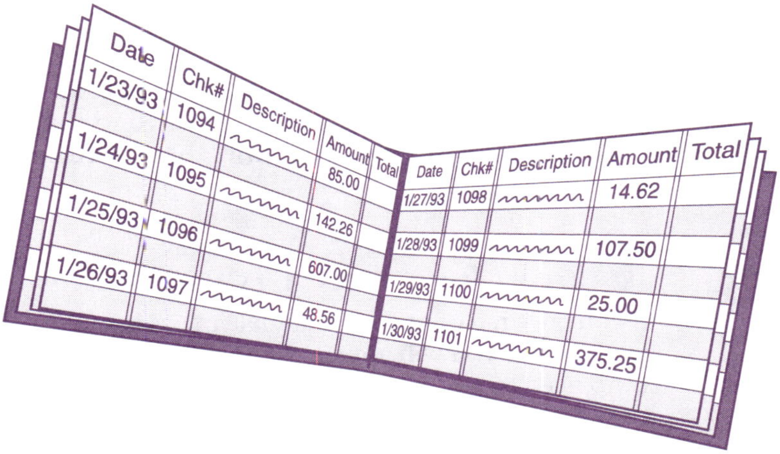

Sample manual check register
Figure 1-1.

Overview and Startup Activities

begin working with QuickBooks, you'll find that every balance sheet account that is part of your chart of accounts will also have a register. (A QuickBooks register is a lot like a manual register because it lets you record all the elements of a financial transaction. The electronic version that QuickBooks offers has other advantages, as you will see later.) This means that there is a register for every checking or savings account that you have. There is also a register for your assets to allow you to record depreciation of these assets. QuickBooks also provides an alternative to direct register entries for many transactions and allows you to focus on the document that you want to produce as you write a check or issue an invoice. You can simply complete the check or invoice that you need, and QuickBooks will create the underlying register entry for you automatically, as shown in Figure 1-2. Focusing on the check or invoice can save time and is an easy process to master, since you do not need to concern yourself with which account you need, only the document that you are trying to create.

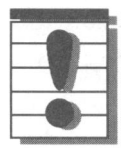

TIP: To create professional-looking checks and invoices, you can acquire supplies directly from Intuit in several styles. Intuit has checks and invoices for both tractor-feed and laser printers.

If you have written a check by hand and want to record it, you will need to use the register for your entry. If it is a check that you issue periodically, QuickBooks can memorize it and allow you to recall it from a list of memorized transactions easily.

QuickBooks automatically creates some register entries for you
Figure 1-2.

Writing Invoices and Processing Payments

With QuickBooks, you no longer need to type invoices individually. The program provides the layout and some of the entries for you. QuickBooks supports three different invoice styles that are selectable by company. You can choose from a product, service, or professional invoice. A *product invoice* is normally used by businesses that sell parts or materials. A *service invoice* is used by businesses that bill for services that are labor-based, for example, computer repair. A *professional invoice* would be used by a doctor, lawyer, accountant, or dentist.

Figure 1-3 shows a product invoice being completed. The diamonds that you see on this invoice mark the fields that can be completed by selecting from a list of possibilities. The *'s for the invoice number are replaced with an assigned number when the invoice is printed.

QuickBooks provides a screen like the one shown in Figure 1-4 for receiving customer payments. As you make your entries the payment will be applied to an open invoice and the accounts receivable balance will be reduced. Allowable discounts and credits are also handled.

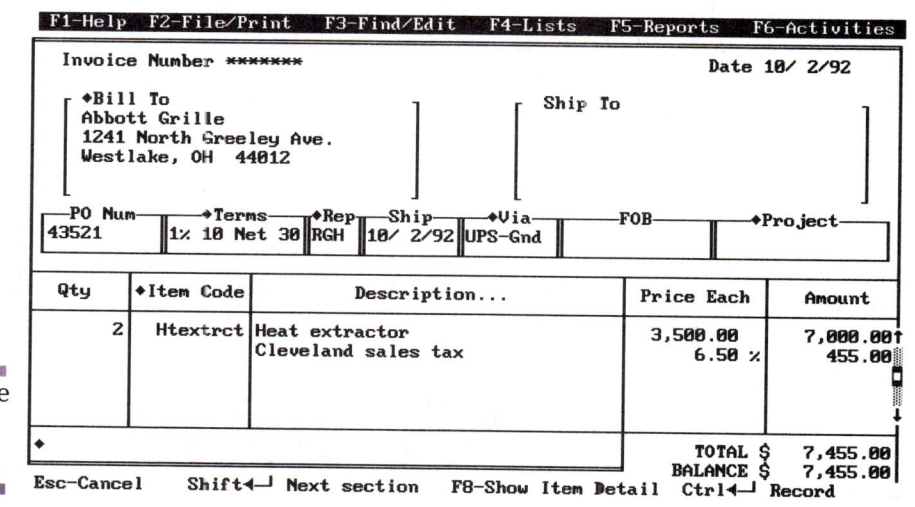

Product Invoice window
Figure 1-3.

Overview and Startup Activities

```
                    R E C E I V E    P A Y M E N T S
   ◆Customer  :                            Amount rec'd:
   Date rec'd : 10/ 6/92                 Existing credits
   ◆Pmt method:
   Pmt number :                           Total to apply

   ┌──────────┬──────────┬──────────┬──────────┐
   │ Invoice  │ Due Date │ Balance  │ Payment  │
   │          │          │          │          │
   │          │          │          │          │
   │          │          │          │          │
   │          │ TOTALS   │          │          │
   └──────────┴──────────┴──────────┴──────────┘
                            Unapplied (to credit memo)

   Esc-Cancel    F8-Apply Discount     F9-Paid in Full/Unpaid  Ctrl⏎ Done
   law (Receivables)
```

Receive
Payments
window
Figure 1-4.

Writing Checks and Paying Bills

Every time you write a check manually, you have to record it in your checkbook register. If you write your checks with QuickBooks, you can streamline this process to one step, since QuickBooks automatically records the check *when* you write it.

QuickBooks automatically displays a voucher-style check when you tell it that you want to write a check. Only the first few lines of the voucher area are visible on your screen, but you can enter as many as 31 different accounts for payments that must be allocated to numerous accounts.

Completing a QuickBooks check is easy since the process is identical to writing a check manually.

QuickBooks makes writing checks easier since much of the information that you need to complete on a check, like the one shown in Figure 1-5, is entered by making selections from lists. QuickBooks automatically dates a check with the current date, saving you an entry unless you want to change it. When you complete the digits for the dollar amount, QuickBooks automatically writes it out in words on the next line. Even the address is completed for you if you choose a name from the payee list that QuickBooks constructs from entries in its vendor, customer, and employee lists. Nothing could be easier to complete, since the only

QuickBooks for Profit: Making the Numbers Work

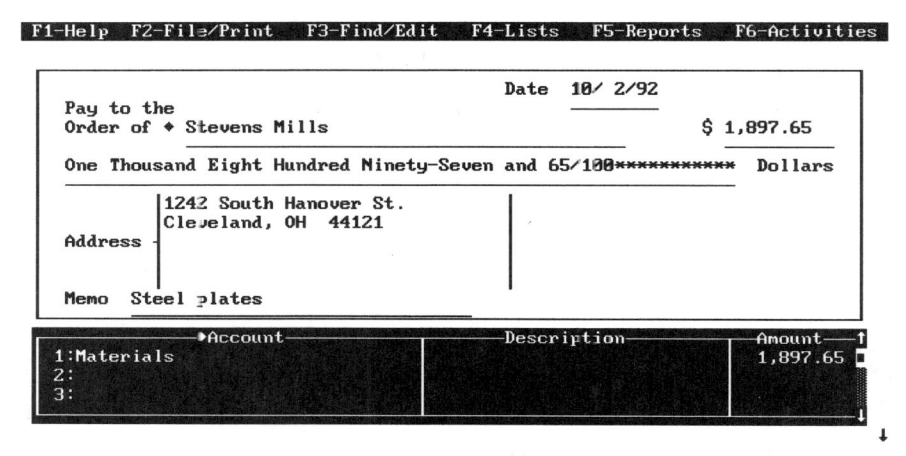

```
F1-Help  F2-File/Print  F3-Find/Edit  F4-Lists  F5-Reports  F6-Activities

                                    Date   10/ 2/92
   Pay to the
   Order of ♦ Stevens Mills                          $ 1,897.65

   One Thousand Eight Hundred Ninety-Seven and 65/100************  Dollars

              1242 South Hanover St.
              Cleveland, OH  44121
   Address

   Memo   Steel plates

         ←Account            Description              Amount
      1:Materials                                     1,897.65
      2:
      3:

   First Cardinal                        Checks to Print: $     1.00
   Esc-Leave   Ctrl↵ Record              Ending Balance:  $21,049.00
```

QuickBooks check
Figure 1-5.

other fields you must type if you want them are the Memo and Description entries.

Printing the checks that you have written is also easy, and you can go back and view them in the register at any time. After printing, the *'s in the check number field are replaced with a check number. The following register entry corresponds to the check that was just written but has not yet been printed:

```
10/02 |*****|Stevens Mills      | 1,897|65|      | |19,152|35
 1992 |Memo:|Steel plates       |      |  |      | |      |
 -----|♦Acct|Materials          |      |  |      | |      |
```

Reporting Options

If you are using a manual accounting system, your only reports are probably the regulatory reports that you must submit. You probably never have the time to create anything else. QuickBooks can provide reports that will help you manage your business finances better, with almost no additional time needed to create them.

Overview and Startup Activities

QuickBooks' reports present the data from your financial activities in either detailed or summarized form. There are 13 predefined reports and 2 generic options, for a total of 15 reports. These can be further customized to allow you some control over their format and the amount of data that they contain.

QuickBooks provides reports for almost any situation. You can customize the 13 standard options for even greater flexibility.

The 13 predefined reports include a standard balance sheet and profit and loss statement, which show the balance sheet account balances at any given time and allow you to take a look at how well revenues have covered expenses for a period of time (month, quarter, or year, for example).

QuickBooks provides several reporting options for both accounts payable and accounts receivable. You can use these reports to monitor cash flow, monitor the aging of your receivables, and determine the latest possible payment dates. You can also print out a report to use in contacting customers with delinquent accounts. In addition, you can create a 1099 report and a sales tax report.

Other reports include payroll, budgeting, and a report to help you forecast your cash flow. You can also create a project report, a transaction report, a summary report, and an itemized income and expense report. Figure 1-6 shows a cash flow report, which can help you pinpoint times when the projected cash coming in is less than your scheduled cash going out.

Customizing QuickBooks

Although you may be attracted to the low price of QuickBooks (which is made possible in part by its wide appeal to many business users), you probably also want a package that is tailored to your business needs. QuickBooks provides customizing options that allow you to change some features of the package to more closely meet your business needs, while allowing all users to capitalize on the basic features of the package.

The first decision you must make in using QuickBooks is what type of company file you want to create. This selection provides the accounts that you will use to record your information. If none of the options exactly meets your needs, choose the closest match possible and then customize the options provided, or choose to set up company accounts on your own.

QuickBooks for Profit: Making the Numbers Work

```
           CASH FLOW FORECAST REPORT AT 7-DAY INTERVALS
                       3/ 1/92 Through 3/30/92
Sample Data Company-All Checking/AR/AP Accounts                  Page 1
3/ 3/93
                         Accts       Accts     Checking     Net      Projected
       Date Range         Recv       Payable     Accts    Inflow      Balance
       ------------    ---------   ---------  ---------  ---------  -----------

Checking balance                               34,382.00
Past due A/R & A/P      7,710.57     -723.63
                        ---------   ---------  ---------
       As of   2/29/92  7,710.57     -723.63  34,382.00              41,368.94

     3/ 1/92 - 3/ 7/92  1,980.85   -6,712.00  -4,255.37  -8,986.52   32,382.42
     3/ 8/92 - 3/14/92      0.00   -3,835.84    -672.07  -4,507.91   27,874.51
     3/15/92 - 3/21/92      0.00  -20,173.74       0.00 -20,173.74    7,700.77
     3/22/92 - 3/28/92      0.00   -1,700.00       0.00  -1,700.00    6,000.77
     3/29/92 - 3/30/92      0.00   -2,925.00       0.00  -2,925.00    3,075.77
                        ---------   ---------  ---------  ---------

     3/ 1/92 - 3/30/92  1,980.85  -35,346.58  -4,927.44 -38,293.17

                                   ---------   ---------  ---------
       As of   3/30/92  9,691.42  -36,070.21  29,454.56               3,075.77
```

**Cash flow report
Figure 1-6.**

QuickBooks offers a number of other opportunities for customizing the package. You can set up the lists of information needed to complete register entries, checks, and invoices. Just as each company may have its own unique chart of accounts, it may also have its own unique list of customers, vendors, employees, shipping methods, and other data. The various lists and the procedure for making additions and deletions are covered in Chapter 2.

Customizing QuickBooks lets you tailor the program so it does just what you need.

In addition to selecting the type of company and creating lists of frequently needed data, QuickBooks has a number of menu screens that allow you to define exactly how the program, your company, and your hardware will work.

Customizing the Program

As you learn to use QuickBooks you are likely to develop preferences about how you use the program. Some of these options can be defined as *program options*. This allows you to set them once and keep them in effect—even if you work with several programs. Program options include whether or not the Bizminder utility is used to display reminder messages when you start QuickBooks and nine other options available on a Program Options menu, shown in Figure 1-7. Notice that each option requires only the selection of a single letter like **Y** or **N**, or the entry of a digit. You use these options to control the number of lines of text that appear on your screen, to determine the date format, and to control how far in advance you receive reminders about bills and invoices.

Customizing Your Company

QuickBooks provides 15 different customization options for each company. Even if you only have one company file you will probably want to customize some of the settings to better meet your needs. When you change company options, those that you set for an earlier company are no longer in effect. You can use these options to select the style of invoice that you want to use or to flag the reuse of a check or invoice number.

Program Options window
Figure 1-7.

```
                      Program Options

     1. QuickTrainer lag: Short/Long/Off  (S/L/O): O
     2. Beep when recording and memorizing (Y/N): Y
     3. Request confirmation (for example,
           when changing the Register)     (Y/N): Y
     4. MM/DD/YY or DD/MM/YY date format    (M/D): M
     5. Days in advance to remind of scheduled
           bills, invoices, and groups    (0-30): 3
     6. Bizminder active                    (Y/N): Y
     7. 43 line register/reports (EGA,VGA) (Y/N): N
     8. On new checks/invoices, start with the
           Payee/customer or Date field    (P/D): P
     9. Double-click speed for mouse (0 turns
           mouse off)                      (0-9): 4
    10. Warn to deposit payments received  (Y/N): N

    Esc-Cancel        F1-Help         Ctrl⏎ Done
```

Setting Up Your Hardware

QuickBooks offers a variety of different monitor settings. If you have a color monitor, you can choose a screen color combination that is appealing. You can also change the screen refresh speed for most monitors.

Probably the most important hardware settings you will change are those affecting your printer. You can set up two different printers for use with QuickBooks, in case you want to use one for checks or invoices and the other for reports.

QuickBooks Help Features

The help system in QuickBooks has two components: a QuickTrainer feature and a standard onscreen help facility. The QuickTrainer is help that pops up on screen when you are slow to respond to requests for information that QuickBooks presents. The QuickTrainer feature is designed to stay on the screen as you work, to guide you through the current task. The standard onscreen help is displayed only on request. You can ask for it rather than trying to find additional information in your QuickBooks manual. Figure 1-8 shows one of the QuickBooks help screens.

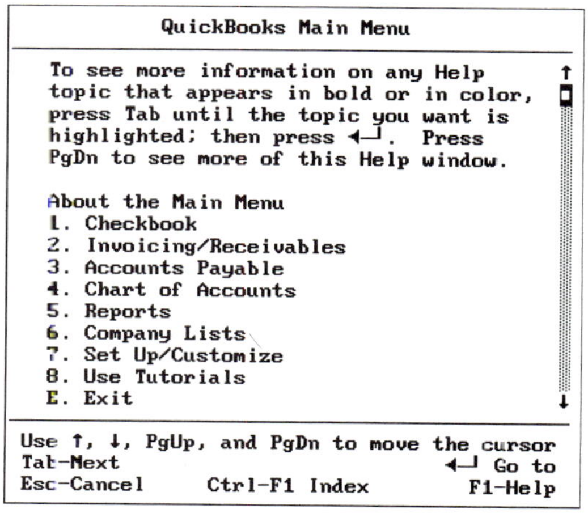

Help screen for QuickBooks Main Menu
Figure 1-8.

Overview and Startup Activities

Starting Your First QuickBooks Session

Appendix A covers QuickBooks installation. In this chapter you learn how easy it is to set up QuickBooks on your system. If you have not installed QuickBooks, skip to Appendix A to complete the necessary steps.

The first time you start QuickBooks you will have a few essential tasks to perform. Be certain that you register your copy of the program before you forget. This lets Intuit know that you are a valid user, lets you use their support line, and ensures the continued operation of your program. You will also want to set up your company files at this time and get your printer ready so that it can produce reports when you need them. In Chapter 2 you will learn how to setup your printer and tailor QuickBooks to your needs.

Starting a New Company

You can create a new company for each division or region within a company, if you wish. You are not restricted to starting only different companies.

When you set up a company in QuickBooks, you are providing a name and set of accounts for QuickBooks to use in maintaining your company's "books" or financial records. You can set up a company for any type of business organization, whether it's a corporation, sole proprietorship, or partnership. You can even set up a company name for a division within a company. You can choose to use a cash basis system or attempt to match revenue and expenses in an accrual system.

QuickBooks stores all of the company books that you create in a subdirectory called QBDATA. You can create other directories before starting QuickBooks and make any of them the active directory; then add your new company files to this location. In Chapter 2 you will learn all the specifics for starting QuickBooks and setting up your own company.

Getting Around in QuickBooks

QuickBooks provides an easy-to-use menu system. At any time you can press `Esc` a sufficient number of times to return to the Main Menu and start again if you are not in the right place. Many screens also have pull-down menus that let you choose an activity without returning to the Main Menu. You use the function keys to activate these menus. In addition to the menus there are numerous *Quick Keys* that allow you to make a selection by pressing a special key combination.

QuickBooks for Profit: Making the Numbers Work

You will also need to move about in QuickBooks windows, and you will learn which keys to use in case you prefer the keyboard over the mouse.

Using the Menus

Menus present you with a list of choices. QuickBooks has several different types of menus depending on the type of activity you are performing with the program.

QuickBooks' menus present all your choices.

The Main Menu presents a list of choices that are an overview of all the features offered by the program, as shown in Figure 1-9. From the Main Menu you can choose to write checks or invoices, update accounts receivable or payable information, create reports, add data to company lists, customize QuickBooks settings, use the built-in tutorial, or exit from the program. You can select the Main Menu options three ways: type the letter or number that precedes the selection, highlight the selection and press [Enter], or double-click the selection with your mouse.

NOTE: *Double-clicking* requires you to move the mouse pointer to the desired option and then press the left mouse button twice in rapid succession.

For most of the Main Menu selections, QuickBooks displays another window that contains a menu of further selections to help refine your first selection. You can select from the secondary menu using the same methods that worked with the Main Menu options.

```
         QuickBooks
         Main Menu

      1. Checkbook
      2. Invoicing/Receivables
      3. Accounts Payable
    ▶ 4. Chart of Accounts
      5. Reports
      6. Company Lists
      7. Set Up/Customize
      8. Use Tutorials
      E. Exit
```

QuickBooks Main Menu Figure 1-9.

Overview and Startup Activities

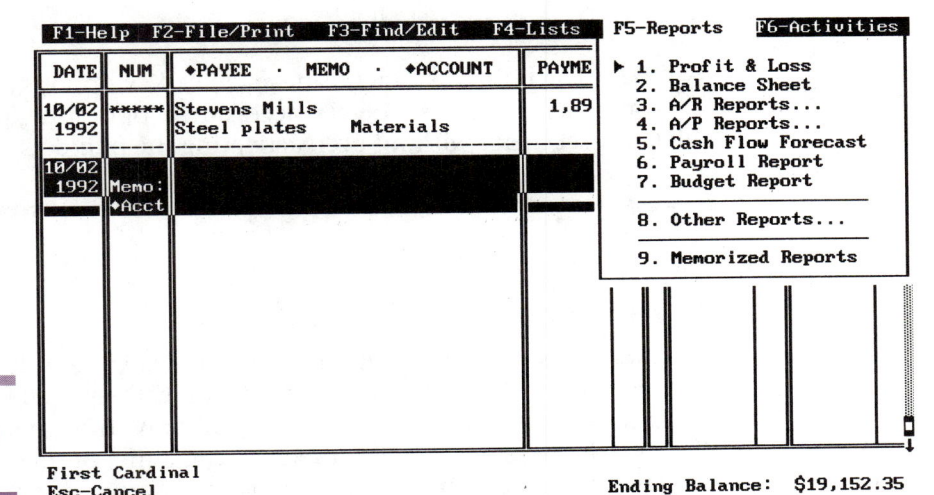

```
 F1-Help  F2-File/Print  F3-Find/Edit  F4-Lists  F5-Reports   F6-Activities
┌──────┬─────┬──────────────────────────────────┬───────┬────────────────────────┐
│ DATE │ NUM │ ◆PAYEE  ·  MEMO  ·  ◆ACCOUNT     │ PAYME │ ▶ 1. Profit & Loss     │
├──────┼─────┼──────────────────────────────────┼───────┤   2. Balance Sheet     │
│10/02 │*****│Stevens Mills                     │ 1,89  │   3. A/R Reports...    │
│ 1992 │     │Steel plates      Materials       │       │   4. A/P Reports...    │
├──────┼─────┼──────────────────────────────────┼───────┤   5. Cash Flow Forecast│
│10/02 │     │                                  │       │   6. Payroll Report    │
│ 1992 │Memo:│                                  │       │   7. Budget Report     │
│      │◆Acct│                                  │       │                        │
│      │     │                                  │       │   8. Other Reports...  │
│      │     │                                  │       │                        │
│      │     │                                  │       │   9. Memorized Reports │
│      │     │                                  │       └────────────────────────┤
│      │     │                                  │       │
│      │     │                                  │       │
 First Cardinal
 Esc-Cancel                                       Ending Balance:   $19,152.35
```

Pull-down Reports menu
Figure 1-10.

QuickBooks provides specialized menus when you are in the process of writing a check, working in a register, and creating an invoice. These menus are different from the Main Menu since they pull down from the top of the screen. These menus are activated with a function key listed in the menu bar at the top of the screen. Figure 1-10 shows the Reports menu that displays when you press [F5] from a register window. The options in a pull-down menu can be selected by using all the techniques that worked for Main Menu selections.

The last type of menu that you will see in QuickBooks is the Action menu that appears when you are working with a company list. You can press [F7] to see this menu anytime one of the company lists is displayed on the screen. Although the options vary with the list you are working on it might look something like this:

```
        ┌─────F7-Actions──────┐
        │▶ 1. Add New  Ctrl-Ins│
        │  2. Delete   Ctrl-Del│
        │  3. View/Edit Ctrl-E │
        │  4. Print    Ctrl-P  │
        └──────────────────────┘
```

> **NOTE:** The pull-down menus have Quick Key options at the right of some menu options. You can access these options by pressing the Quick Key sequence without even activating the pull-down menu.

Using QuickBooks Windows

QuickBooks displays many different windows or screens depending on what activity you are performing. For example, the screen for writing checks looks very different from the screen for writing an invoice. Likewise, the register screen is different from either of these two. There are a number of keys that you can use to move around in these windows no matter which one you are in.

In some windows you will want to make entries in every field. You can type your entry and press `Enter` or `Tab` to move to the next field. QuickBooks provides efficient options no matter what you want to do next in a window. You can use the mouse and click on a desired field or the scroll boxes at the side to change your position on a screen, or you can use a variety of special key options that you will learn about in Chapter 2.

Using Quick Keys

Quick Keys let you complete tasks faster than the related menu selections.

Quick Keys are key combinations that provide a shortcut to a feature on one of QuickBocks' pull-down menus. Instead of activating the menu and selecting the desired option, you can use key combinations to access the feature directly. Because the same pull-down menu options are not available on all screens, the key combinations will depend on which QuickBooks window you are in. For example, the action provided by pressing `Ctrl`-`Y` will take you to Pay Bills if you are in the Accounts Payable register, Receive Payments if you are in Accounts Receivable, and Reconcile if you are working in the check register. Although you should not try to memorize all of these options, you might start taking a look at the menus for the commands you use frequently. With some repetition you will learn the most important Quick Keys for your tasks.

Overview and Startup Activities

In this quick overview of the main features of QuickBooks you have seen some options that can help you maintain your business records. You are now ready to take a closer look at each of the main areas of QuickBooks. Begin with Chapter 2, where you can establish a company and make some customizing changes to meet your needs. Once you start using QuickBooks you will wonder why you have waited so long to automate your business record keeping.

CHAPTER

2 SETTING UP QUICKBOOKS FOR YOUR BUSINESS

You are probably anxious to save as much time as possible with QuickBooks, and would like to begin entering transactions immediately. Although you can do this as soon as you enter your company information, you can save yourself more time in the long run if you invest the time now in registering your copy of the program and defining your business carefully.

QuickBooks' lists let you make an entry once and use it as often as needed without typing.

To define your business in QuickBooks you enter some of the data that you use all the time into lists.

Even though it will be a little while before you are ready to make your first transaction entry, the preparation time will be more than offset by the continued time savings you will experience when you record your financial information in QuickBooks. For example, company lists contain entries that can be used to complete fields on checks and invoices. The fields that use the information from company lists are called *diamond fields* since they are marked by a diamond. When you need to enter data in a diamond field, you press [Ctrl]-[L] and select the desired option from the list rather than typing it. These lists also form a valuable base of information that can be printed for reference in different activities.

Remember, when you use QuickBooks you are building an information base that can assist you in making profitable decisions. This means that your information must be accurate, consistent, and available when you need it. To help you meet these goals for your information, QuickBooks uses company lists. When you start, the only thing that QuickBooks knows about your business is the chart of accounts that you have selected. By teaching QuickBooks a few things about your customers, suppliers, invoices, and shipping methods, it can actually assist you in recording information. Although you can enter this information as needed, you can save time by recording at least some of the commonly used entries in the lists that QuickBooks maintains.

Using lists can help save you time in many ways. First of all, you can pick an entry quickly and accurately. Also, because lists can contain information such as addresses and preferred shipping methods, you can pick a name from a list and have QuickBooks add the address and preferred shipping method automatically.

NOTE: If you do not want to set up lists for your company you can skip to the next chapter, although you could benefit from skimming through this material to see how easy it is to get QuickBooks set up before you start entering transactions.

Setting Up QuickBooks for Your Business

Setting Up Your Company

You must set up a company before using QuickBooks features. For many users one company is sufficient as they are only running one business. Other users might have several business entries, several departments that they wish to keep separate records for, or a number of clients that they do the record keeping for. QuickBooks stores each company that you create in a separate set of files. Your company files will be stored in the QBDATA directory unless you change the directory.

You will want to set up a checking account as soon as you set up your company. You will also want to set up a printer so that it will be ready when you want to print a report later. It would also be worth your time to take a quick look at the sample company data provided with QuickBooks. Learning how to switch to this data gives you a readily available test facility for any new feature that you want to check out before using it with your own company data.

Establishing the Company Files

When you set up a company in QuickBooks you give it a name and choose a set of accounts to use in recording your financial information.

CAUTION: The business type you choose is one of the few things that cannot be changed once it is selected. If you choose a business type where the accounts do not match your needs, you will have to change them individually or set up a new company.

These steps for adding a new company will work whether you are creating your first QuickBooks company or your tenth:

1. Choose 7 Set Up/Customize from the Main Menu.
2. Choose 1 Select/Add a Company, press (F7) and choose 1 Add New.
3. Type a name using as many as 30 characters and press (Enter). Avoid the use of the following characters in the name:
    [ ] ~ /

4. Press [Ctrl]-[L] to display the list of options and select the one that closely matches your business type. If you want to add each account yourself, choose None.
5. Press [Ctrl]-[Enter] or [F10] to finalize your choice.

NOTE: If you have data in Quicken that you want to use with QuickBooks, you use a different approach to setting up your business. Your Quicken data can be converted to QuickBooks for you. Your Quicken data will be available after the conversion, although any reports that have been memorized by Quicken will not be available. For the details on how to convert your Quicken data to QuickBooks see Appendix D.

Setting Up an Account

Although QuickBooks sets up a few balance sheet accounts when you choose a company type, it does not add a business checking account. This is because you must enter an account balance when you set up an account like this.

QuickBooks automatically takes you to the chart of accounts when you set up your first company. If this is not your first company, you need to go to this screen by selecting 4 Chart of Accounts from the Main Menu. From the Chart of Accounts follow these steps to add a new account:

1. Press [F7] to open the Actions menu.
2. Choose Add New.
3. Select the type of account to add.

   To set up a checking account, choose Checking, then fill in the Add New Checking Account window shown in the following:

Setting Up QuickBooks for Your Business

```
              Add New Checking Account
    Name for this account:

    Account balance: 0.00      as of: 10/ 6/92
    ─────────────── (Optional Information) ───────────────
    Description:

    Notes/Account number:

    Esc-Cancel          F1-Help          Ctrl↵ Done
```

> **CAUTION:** If you choose None rather than a company type, you will have to add every account yourself, including those needed for payroll entries.

4. Press [Ctrl]-[Enter] when finished.

Setting Up a Printer

Although you may not be ready to print just yet, you will want to set up your printer now. Later when you are ready to print checks or a report, you can print right away. You can install two different printers; then use one for reports and one for check writing.

Setting up two different printers lets you use one for check writing and the other to print reports.

To set up a printer follow these steps:

1. Choose 7 Set Up/Customize from the Main Menu.
2. Choose 6 Set Up Printers and select either printer 1 or 2.
3. Highlight your brand of printer and press [Enter].
4. Change any options you want to change and then press [Ctrl]-[Enter].
5. Press [Esc] until the Main Menu displays.

Looking at the Sample Company Data

Although you are probably anxious to enter your own company data into QuickBooks, there are times when it is preferable to use the sample company data that Intuit provides with the product. This data allows you to try a feature before entering your real data into your actual company files. You can easily switch to the sample company data to try a few features, then with the benefit of the experience you've gained, return to your own data to implement a new feature. You can also use the techniques presented in this section if you create several companies of your own and want to switch among them.

The sample data provided with QuickBooks is placed in a file named QBSAMPLE. The default location for the sample file is C:\QBOOKS\QBSAMPLE. To use QBSAMPLE you must first make this directory active and then select the QBSAMPLE file. These are the required steps from the Main Menu:

1. Choose 7 Set Up/Customize from the Main Menu.
2. Choose 7 Change Data Directory.
3. Change the directory displayed to C:\QBOOKS\QBSAMPLE, or any other directory name where you may have placed the sample data, and press [Enter].
4. Choose 1 Select/Add a Company.
5. Select the filename SAMPLE from the list and press [Enter].

TIP: Keep the sample company data in mind when you want to try out a new feature that you are not ready to implement with your company files.

After working with the sample company data, you can switch back to the data for your company and use the same series of steps, just changing the active directory back to QBOOKS and selecting the file that contains your real data.

Accessing Help

QuickBooks provides QuickTrainer screens to help guide you through tasks when you are slow to provide information. After you have mastered the basic tasks you might find this help annoying and wish to turn it off. To turn QuickTrainer off, do the following:

1. Choose 7 Set Up/Customize from the Main Menu.
2. Choose 5 Customize QuickBooks.
3. Choose 1 Options, then type an **o** to turn off QuickTrainer, and press `Ctrl`-`Enter`.

You can press `Esc` to remove QuickTrainer data from the screen.

TIP: If you disable QuickTrainer, you can always bring up a message with `Ctrl`-`Q` if you are stuck.

Pressing `F1` activates QuickBooks' Help feature. If you want to browse through the range of options shown, you can access the index of help topics by pressing `Ctrl`-`F1`.

Working Effectively with QuickBooks

In the few tasks that you have tried so far, you needed only a few keys such as `Tab` or `Enter` to get the job done. QuickBooks supports a variety of key combinations that can make your job easier. QuickBooks provides a solution for almost every action you might want to take as you are making entries—whether you want to move from field to field or finalize your response after only one entry. You can use a mouse and click on the desired field to make the next entry or use the combinations shown in Table 2-1 to proceed.

In Chapter 1 you learned that QuickBooks also provides a series of key combinations known as Quick Keys that provide shortcuts to accessing

Key	Action
Ctrl-End	Moves to the last check or invoice
Ctrl-Enter	Finalizes the current window
Ctrl-Home	Moves to the first check or invoice
Ctrl-Pg Dn	Moves to the next check or invoice
Ctrl-Pg Up	Moves to the previous check or invoice
Ctrl-←	Moves left one screen on reports
Ctrl-→	Moves right one screen on reports
Ctrl-S	Moves to the voucher area on a check
End	Moves to the end of a field
End, End	Moves to the end of the transaction
Enter	Moves to the next field
Home	Moves to the beginning of the field
Home, Home	Moves to the beginning of the transaction
Pg Dn	Moves down one screen
Pg Up	Moves up one screen
Shift-Tab	Moves to the previous field
Tab	Moves to the next field
↓	Moves down one transaction
↑	Moves up one transaction

Keys Used to Move Around in QuickBooks
Table 2-1.

features on the QuickBooks pull-down menus. Rather than activate the menu and then select the desired option, you can select it directly by pressing a Quick Key. Table 2-2 provides a list of all the Quick Keys used with QuickBooks. Though you may not want to memorize all of these, if you pay attention to the Quick Key combinations when you activate a menu, you will begin to use them automatically.

Setting Up QuickBooks for Your Business

Key Combination	Options	Works In
Ctrl-A	Select/Set Up Account	Register, Invoice, Check Writing
Ctrl-B	Backs Up File	Main Menu only
Ctrl-C	Calculator	Works in all locations
Ctrl-D	Delete Line Item	Invoice
Ctrl-E	Edits Highlighted Field	Register, Invoice, Check Writing
Ctrl-F	Find	Works in all locations except Main Menu
Ctrl-H	Transaction History	Invoice
Ctrl-I	Insert Line Item	Invoice
Ctrl-J	Transaction Group Invoice Group	Register Invoice
Ctrl-L	Show List	Register, Invoice, Check Writing
Ctrl-M	Memorize Transaction Memorize Invoice	Register Invoice
Ctrl-N	Notepad	Register, Invoice, Check Writing
Ctrl-P	Print	Register, Invoice, Check Writing
Ctrl-R	Register	Invoice, Check Writing
Ctrl-S	Split Transaction	Register
Ctrl-T	Recall Transaction	Register, Invoice, Check Writing
Ctrl-V	View Customer Record	Invoice
Ctrl-W	Write/Print Checks	Register
Ctrl-X	Go To Transfer	Register, Invoice, Check Writing
Ctrl-Y	Reconcile Receive Payment	Register, Check Writing Invoice
Ctrl-Del	Delete Transaction	Register, Invoice, Check Writing
Ctrl-↓	Repeat Find Next	Register, Invoice, Check Writing
Ctrl-↑	Repeat Find Back	Register, Invoice, Check Writing

Quick Keys
Table 2-2.

Taking a Look at What Lists Offer

QuickBooks has 11 different company lists. There are lists for the following types of information: customers, vendors, shipping methods, employees, invoice memos, customer type, vendor type, payment terms, payment methods, items/parts/services, and projects. One additional list, payee, contains all the entries placed in the vendor, customer, and employee lists. From the Main Menu you can choose 6 Company Lists to choose a list from the Select List window shown here:

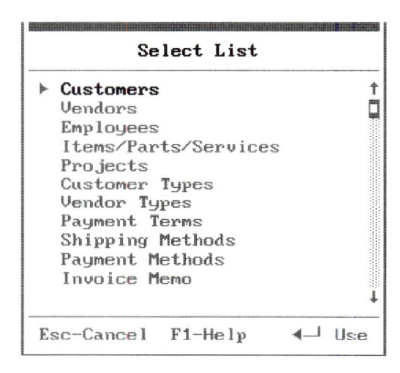

```
              Select List
    ▶ Customers                    ↑
      Vendors
      Employees
      Items/Parts/Services
      Projects
      Customer Types
      Vendor Types
      Payment Terms
      Shipping Methods
      Payment Methods
      Invoice Memo
                                   ↓
    Esc-Cancel  F1-Help   ←┘ Use
```

Regardless of which list you want to work with you can select it from this menu and then press F7 to add, delete, or modify entries. The fields that you enter for each list vary. Table 2-3 shows each list type and the locations where you use the data it contains. The table also lists some of the benefits of each list type.

QuickBooks also supports lists of memorized transactions. The fields where these lists are used are not marked by diamonds and they cannot be completed using a company list option.

Some lists contain standard entries when you start QuickBooks and others are empty. Standard entries are already in the customer types, payment methods, vendor types, and invoice memo lists. The entries provided may or may not meet your needs, but you can make changes, deletions, or additions to any list.

Before learning how to place entries in lists, let's jump ahead for a minute and look at the way lists are used. If you like, you can use the sample application that ships with QuickBooks to try this, since the

Use the standard company list options if they meet your needs. If they don't, delete them and add your own.

Setting Up QuickBooks for Your Business

lists for this application are already completed. This data is in a directory called QBOOKS\QBSAMPLE\, unless you have placed it in a different location. Just follow the next steps.

List	Location Used	Benefits of Use
Customers	Invoice	Consistent spelling of name
	Checks	Consistent address for a customer
		Automatic completion of address and shipping terms
Vendors	Check writing	Consistency in spelling
		Error-free vendor coding
Employees	Check writing	Consistent use of rep name and initials
	Register	Ability to filter by rep
	Rep field on invoices	Assurance that entry matches an employee
Items/Parts/Services	Invoice	Automatic computation of tax and subtotal
		Automatic invoice extension
Projects	Invoice	Grouping and reporting
	Register	
Customer Types	New customer	Grouping and reporting
Vendor Types	New vendor	Grouping and reporting
Payment Methods	Receive payments	No need to type method on each transaction
Payment Terms	New customer	No need to type in a new invoice
	Invoice	No need to enter in each invoice
Shipping Methods	Invoice	Limits shipment types available
Invoice Memo	Invoice	Provides ability to add a short personalized message

Uses for Lists
Table 2-3.

1. Choose 7 Set Up/Customize from the Main Menu.
2. Choose 7 Change Data Directory, change the data directory to C:\QBOOKS\QBSAMPLE\, and press [Enter].
3. Choose 1 Select/Add a Company from the Set Up/Customize menu and choose the filename SAMPLE. Press [Enter] to finalize.
4. Press [Esc] until the Main Menu is displayed.
5. Choose 2 Invoicing/Receivables and then 1 Write/Print Invoices.

You complete the Bill To, Project, Item Code, and Invoice Memo fields by pressing [Ctrl]-[L] and selecting from a list. Your selection causes the Address, Terms, Description, Rate, Amount, and Total to be filled in. Take a look at the invoice screen shown in Figure 2-1, which was created using the entries from the QBSAMPLE lists. If your lists are empty you will need to type every entry instead of just the Qty and PO Num.

These entries can be completed with the information entered in customer and items/parts/services lists by simply pressing [Ctrl]-[L] while

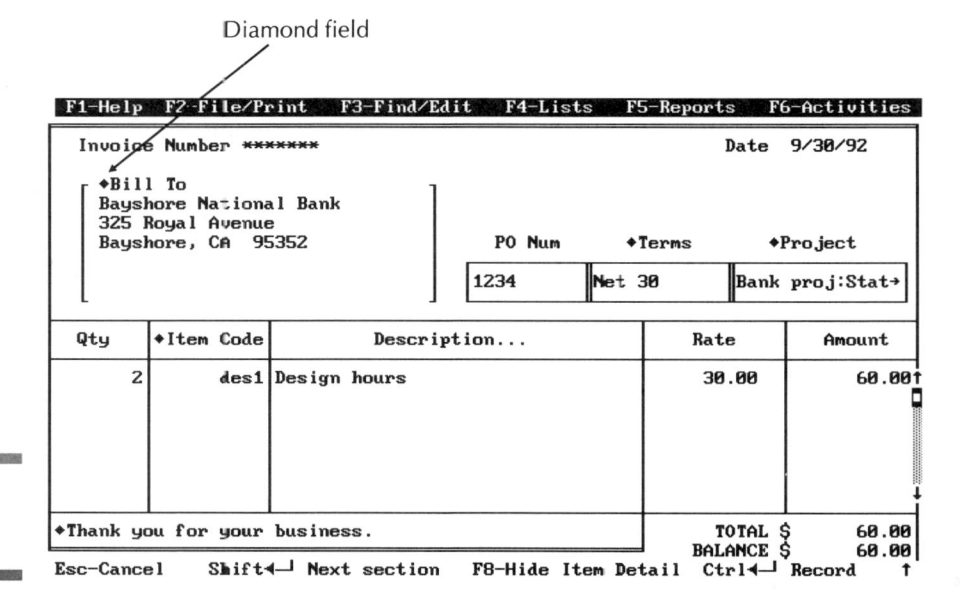

QuickBooks invoice
Figure 2-1.

Setting Up QuickBooks for Your Business

you are writing an invoice with QuickBooks and selecting a customer, sales rep, and the appropriate line items. The address and payment method are supplied automatically when a customer is selected from the list.

Creating Your First List with Customer Types

The customer types list is used to specify a customer type when you enter a new customer record. Although this is an optional field, its use lets you categorize customers for reporting purposes.

QuickBooks has four customer types already in the list when you set up your company. These are Dealer, Distributor, Manufacturer, and Wholesaler. These entries might be appropriate if you are a manufacturer but may not be appropriate for service and other types of businesses.

TIP: Think about how you would like to categorize your customer base when choosing your entries for customer types. Remember, you can group reports by customer type or pull a report for a single customer type.

If the existing customer types do not provide the classification you need, delete them and add your own. The categories that you use depend on what type of business you have. Table 2-4 provides some ideas about ways to use this field for different types of businesses.

TIP: Using the Customer Type field to help track sales by customer type lets you know if you need to focus on increasing the diversity of your customer base. Although specialization helps you capitalize on your strengths, diversity can be helpful in any type of business. This is especially true in times of economic downturns, when certain segments of the economy tend to be harder hit than others. A company whose only customers are car manufacturers, for example, faces tight times when sales of cars are sluggish. Most businesses can benefit from some diversity in their customer base in terms of both numbers and sales volume.

The information that you enter for each list differs, but the basic procedure is about the same. You will have the opportunity to take a close-up look at customer type lists in the next sections. Once you have mastered the procedure you can apply it to the other lists that QuickBooks offers.

Deleting Customer Types

If you are not planning to use standard list entries or would like to delete entries from any existing list, QuickBooks provides a Delete feature that is easy to use. If you are looking at the standard list types in your new company, follow these steps to delete the standard customer type entries:

1. Select 6 Company Lists from the Main Menu.
2. Select Customer Types.
3. Highlight the customer type that you no longer need in the list.
4. Press [F7] and select 2 Delete.

    As a shortcut you can also press [Ctrl]-[Del].
5. Press [Enter] to confirm the deletion or press [Esc] to cancel.

Uses of Customer Types for Different Businesses
Table 2-4.

Business	Example of Use
Agriculture	Differentiate the type of account, such as co-op or retail
Accounting	Indicate industry segment or size of business
Construction	Indicate minority-owned firm if company solicits government contracts
Consulting	Indicate industry segment or type of services performed for client
Legal	Indicate industry segment
Manufacturing	Differentiate industry segment, such as auto, construction, and so forth
Medical	Indicate type of insurance coverage
Service	Differentiate home versus commercial customers

Setting Up QuickBooks for Your Business

If you do not want any of the customer types shown initially you can repeat the process until they are all deleted.

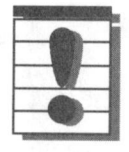

> **TIP:** You will want to delete any unwanted customers and customer types at least once a year, although a quarterly housecleaning might be a good idea. You do not have to worry about purging a customer with a balance—QuickBooks prevents you from doing this.

Adding Customer Types

You can be as creative as you want in setting up customer types. The feature is designed to allow you to categorize customers as you need to.

You should try to add all the customer types you will need before you start recording entries in your customer list. This provides a clearer picture of the organization. Of course, if your business expands, you can add more customer types to provide a category for each customer entry. For instance, if you are in the medical profession and become a participating physician in the Purple Medal Insurance plan you will want to add a customer type for Purple Medal. When you land your first government contract for your consulting practice you will want to add a customer type of government.

Follow these steps to add a new company to the blank customer types list where you have deleted all the existing entries:

1. Choose 6 Company Lists from the Main Menu.
2. Choose Customer Types from the Select List menu.
3. Press [F7] and choose 1 Add New to display this window:

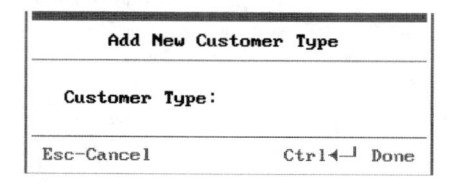

```
         Add New Customer Type

       Customer Type:

       Esc-Cancel           Ctrl↵  Done
```

4. Type a new customer type and press [Ctrl]-[Enter] to finalize your entry.

Figure 2-2 shows the customer types that were added to the sample company. Remember, to look at data for the sample company you must

QuickBooks for Profit: Making the Numbers Work

select 7 Set Up/Customize from the Main Menu. Then choose Change Directory, set the directory to QBSAMPLE, and select the sample company as you did earlier.

NOTE: As you complete the windows, to add entries to lists use `Tab` to move to the next field and `Shift`-`Enter` to move to the next section of a window.

If you notice a spelling error in a customer type entry you can correct it without deleting and reentering the customer type. All you need to do is select the customer types list and highlight the entry that requires change. Press `F7`, select 3 View/Edit, make the change, and then press `Ctrl`-`Enter`.

Performing List Maintenance

Even if you try to be thorough when you initially create your company lists, there will be changes. If your company is growing you are likely to have new customer types. You can use QuickBooks' features to maintain your company lists once you enter them.

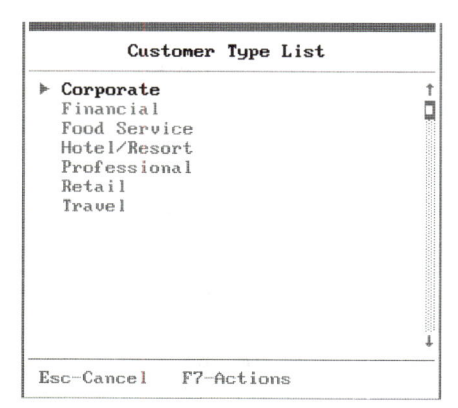

```
                Customer Type List
          ▶ Corporate
            Financial
            Food Service
            Hotel/Resort
            Professional
            Retail
            Travel




            Esc-Cancel    F7-Actions
```

Customer type list for sample company
Figure 2-2.

Setting Up QuickBooks for Your Business

The package allows you to delete entries, add new entries, and edit entries. When you are working with the project file you can even rearrange the entries. You can also print a list at any time to see what it looks like.

Printing a List

A listing of some of the QuickBooks lists is handy for training new employees or for reference. Keep it posted by your computer to look up options for customer types or shipping methods. The instructions in the previous sections for the customer types list will work for any list that QuickBooks supports; however, most lists do not offer all the choices that the customer lists do. For most lists your only option is to select a print destination. If you have not set up a printer for QuickBooks, you need to do so before trying to print a list, using the instructions in the previous section, "Setting Up a Printer."

To print the customer list while it is displayed on the screen follow these steps:

1. Press [F7].
2. Choose 4 Print. The Print Vendor List window displays.
3. Type a **Y** in the first field to tell QuickBooks you want to selectively include or exclude customers after filling in the current window; then press [Tab].
4. Type an **N** in the second field to display a full set of customer information including the Notepad entries; then press [Tab].
5. Type a **Y** in the third field to include a customer's transaction history; then press [Tab].
6. Select a printer location for Print To. Use .TXT File as an option when you want to use the entries with your word processor or spreadsheet.
7. Press [Ctrl]-[Enter] to finalize the window. The Date Range window appears.
8. Type the first date and press [Tab], then type the ending date.

   These dates control which transactions in the customer's transaction histories are included in the printout.
9. Press [Enter] to finalize the Date Range window.

10. In the Customer List window, highlight the customers you do not want included in the printout and press the [Spacebar] to remove the word "Print" from the Print field.

11. After specifying which customers you want included in the printout, press [Ctrl]-[Enter] to start the printing process. You will be prompted for the filename if you are using a .TXT file.

Working with Other Company Lists

You will need to decide how many of the 11 company lists are useful for you. Lists make the most sense when you can use the entries in them repeatedly. Multiple uses of the same entry save time and ensure consistency. If you find that you have unique negotiated payment terms with each of your customers, a list of payment terms does not offer much of an advantage. The same might be true of invoice memos where you have a small number of customers and want to personalize the message on each invoice. Take a quick look at each of the options before deciding if it is useful in your business.

Using the Payment Terms List

Payment terms define your payment expectations from a customer. They may allow customers to apply a discount to their payment or require prepayment before shipment. The payment terms included for a new company are as follows:

A change in payment terms in tight economic times can help you expand your customer base if you can afford to carry the receivables a little longer.

1% 10 Net 30
2% 10 Net 30
Due on recpt
Net 10
Net 30
Prepaid

After selecting Payment Terms from the Select List window and pressing [F7], select 1 Add New. The Add New Terms window is shown in Figure 2-3. You enter three fields that define the terms, and the terms are displayed at the top of the screen. Follow these steps to define a new payment term:

Setting Up QuickBooks for Your Business

1. Type a description of the payment term up to a limit of 12 characters and press `Tab`.
2. Type a number representing the number of days the customer has to pay the net amount and press `Tab`.

   This may be 10 days, 30 days, or even 0 days when you expect a prepayment or a payment upon receipt.
3. Type a number representing the discount payment and press `Tab`.

   This is entered as a number, where 1 represents 1 percent and 5 represents 5 percent, for example.
4. Type the number of days to pay and still get the discount and press `Ctrl`-`Enter`.

Entering 10 means that within the first 10 days, a 10 percent discount should be subtracted. After 10 days, the net amount is paid.

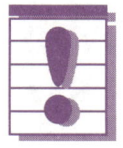

TIP: Since cash flow problems often plague new businesses, carefully consider the payment terms that you allow. You may need to consider terms such as Due on receipt, 1% 10 Net 30, or even partial prepayments if you have large out-of-pocket costs that you must cover. Check to see what terms your competition offers so you do not lose business by being more restrictive.

Using the Employee List

QuickBooks allows you to add entries to an employee list. Entries from this list can be used when you complete a new customer record to

Add New Terms window
Figure 2-3.

```
            Add New Terms
  Terms:
  Net due in how many days? 0
  Discount percentage (%): 0
  Discount if paid within how many days? 0
  Esc-Cancel                    Ctrl⏎ Done
```

specify the customer's sales representative. You can also use these entries in the Rep field on a product invoice if another sales representative is responsible for the sale. Lastly, employee list entries are found in the payee list when you record transactions or checks.

After selecting Employees from the Select List window, follow these steps to add a new employee:

1. Press [F7] and choose 1 Add New.

    An Add New Employee window that looks like Figure 2-4 displays.
2. Type the employee's initials and press [Tab].
3. Type the employee's name and press [Enter].
4. Type each line of the address, pressing [Enter] after each line except the last line.
5. Press [Ctrl]-[Enter] to finalize the entry.

Using the Customer List

If you have just started a new company in QuickBooks your customer list is empty. You will want to add entries to it to ensure that the customer's name is always spelled the same way. You can also use the list to access the payment terms, sales representative, and customer type.

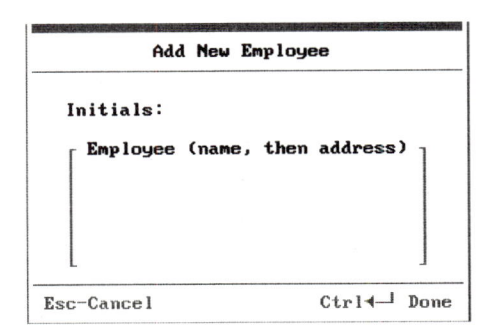

Add New Employee window
Figure 2-4.

Setting Up QuickBooks for Your Business

If you happen to be looking at the sample company instead and choose Company Lists, and then Customers, you will see a long list like the one in Figure 2-5. Use the scroll bar to move through this list quickly.

You can add customers to the list for the sample company or switch back to your directory and company and add them there. The basic procedure is the same once the company file is open and the customer list is displayed. The only required information is the customer name and bill-to address. You can leave the shipping address blank if it is the same as the billing address. Each field below this is optional, although filling in fields such as Customer Type will help you categorize data. The Credit (limit) field can be important to ensure that you do not overextend credit and incur bad debts. Follow these steps to add a new customer:

1. Choose 6 Company Lists from the Main Menu.
2. Choose Customers.
3. Press [F7] and choose 1 Add New.

   An Add New Customer window like the one shown in Figure 2-6 displays on the screen.

4. Type the company name and press [Enter].
5. Type the address and press [Enter] after each line.
6. Press [Tab] repeatedly to move to the Customer Type field and press [Ctrl]-[L] to make a selection from the list.

Customer list from sample company
Figure 2-5.

Customer List	
Customer	Balance
▶ Bayshore Book Nook	500.75
Bayshore National Bank	0.00
BaySoft, Inc.	0.00
Catering by Stephanie	0.00
Catherine L. Ellis Interiors	866.30
D. J.'s Cafe	0.00
Doell and Walters Realty	0.00
Dwight Joseph Asset Management	3,863.73
Fly Away Travel	0.00
Franzen Communications	1,469.88
Gee Whiz Toy Shop	504.39
Harrison's Home Furnishings	0.00
Esc-Cancel F7-Actions	

QuickBooks for Profit: Making the Numbers Work

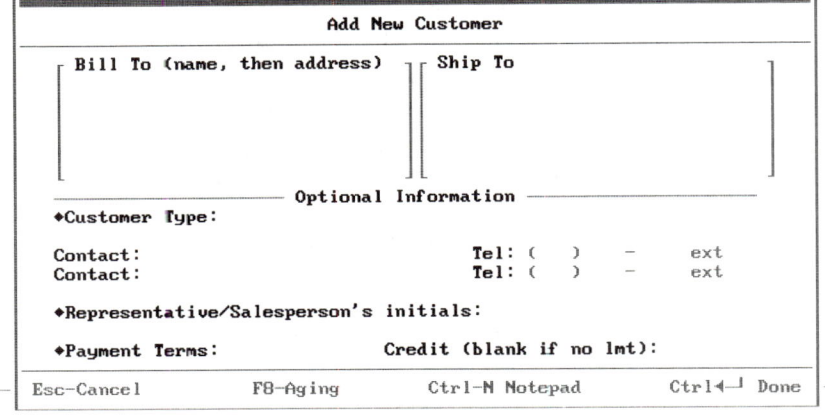

```
┌─────────────────────── Add New Customer ───────────────────────┐
│ ┌─ Bill To (name, then address) ─┐ ┌─ Ship To ──────────────┐ │
│ │                                │ │                         │ │
│ │                                │ │                         │ │
│ │                                │ │                         │ │
│ │                                │ │                         │ │
│ └────────────────────────────────┘ └─────────────────────────┘ │
│ ─────────────────── Optional Information ───────────────────── │
│ ◆Customer Type:                                                │
│                                                                │
│  Contact:                          Tel: (   )  -      ext      │
│  Contact:                          Tel: (   )  -      ext      │
│                                                                │
│ ◆Representative/Salesperson's initials:                        │
│                                                                │
│ ◆Payment Terms:           Credit (blank if no lmt):            │
│                                                                │
│  Esc-Cancel      F8-Aging      Ctrl-N Notepad    Ctrl⏎ Done   │
└────────────────────────────────────────────────────────────────┘
Sample Data Company
```

Add New Customer window
Figure 2-6.

7. Complete as many other optional fields as desired; then press Ctrl-Enter to finalize the entry.

NOTE: You can enter a note when you add a customer. You will see how in steps 3 to 5 in the following section.

TIP: Purge customer records that are inactive for a long time. Don't worry about deleting an active record since QuickBooks will not let you accidentally delete a customer with a balance.

Adding Customer Notes

The customer list offers a note-keeping capability along with the regular fields. Up to 15 lines of text can be recorded in the note without losing any of your earlier entries in the note. The customer notes that

Setting Up QuickBooks for Your Business

QuickBooks provides can be used in any way that you like. There is no way to extend the 15 line limit.

Since QuickBooks supports many different types of businesses, there are many different uses for customer notes. If you are a salesperson making sales calls on the same customers repeatedly you might want to record some pertinent information on the note card.

Use your creativity to decide how to use the Note feature to best meet your needs. If you have a medical or dental practice you might want to record special insurance information on the Notepad or add a reminder about when you want to see the patient again. Some of the other things that QuickBooks users record in this field are alternate contact numbers, such as a car phone number or weekend retreat number. A real estate agent might keep a description of a client's dream home, a veterinarian could note a patient's recent show awards, and a beautician might keep a record of a client's hair color and preferred permanent solution.

> **TIP:** It is important to show customers that you take an interest in them beyond the size of their order. Checking on little things like events their family members participate in is as important as checking on the quality of their last order. If you use the Note feature, you will not forget that your customer's son is a Little League All-Star.

To add a note about a customer with the customer list displayed follow these steps:

1. Highlight the desired customer and press [F7].
2. Choose 3 View/Edit.
3. Press [Ctrl]-[N].
4. Type the text of the note. Use the keys in Table 2-5 when you need to insert text or a date, or delete a line or characters.

    Your entry might look like Figure 2-7.

5. Press [Ctrl]-[Enter] to record the note or press [Esc] to discard it.

QuickBooks for Profit: Making the Numbers Work

Key	Effect
Ctrl-I	Inserts a blank line
Ctrl-D	Deletes the current line
Enter	Moves to the next line
F9	Inserts the current date
Ins	Turns on insert mode

Keys Used for Entering Notes
Table 2-5.

TIP: You can also access customer notes from the Write Checks and Write Invoices window by highlighting the name and pressing Ctrl-N. You use Ctrl-Enter to record the Notepad entries.

Working with the Vendor and Vendor Types Lists

Vendor lists are similar to customer lists except they represent the companies where goods and services are acquired. The vendor list is empty when you start a new company. You will want to add all of your regular vendors to this list since they will be useful for credit card and accounts payable transactions. The vendors that you add will also appear in the payee list that appears when you write checks.

The vendor type list is a separate list that allows you to categorize vendor entries. You can use the vendor type code from this list when you add a new vendor. The vendor type list for a new company contains 1099 Contractor, Food Service, Medical, Real Estate, Retail,

Customer note entry
Figure 2-7.

```
                         Notepad
9/29/92 Customer called about defective shipment. Rep will
visit site and expedite delivery of replacement materials.
```

Setting Up QuickBooks for Your Business

and Travel. Depending on the different types of purchases that you make you might want to add many more specialized entries. You can also use the vendor type classification to indicate minority-owned firms, women-owned firms, firms committed to aiding the handicapped, or firms committed to conservation or environmental safety.

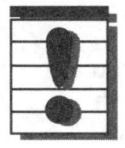

> **TIP:** The most useful grouping for most businesses is to classify vendors by the types of goods or merchandise they supply. However, some contractors who want to bid on government jobs may find the classification for minority-owned firms useful since they may need to support their claims concerning the use of such firms.

To add a vendor type code select 6 Company Lists from the Main Menu and then choose Vendor Types. Press `F7` and choose 1 Add New. All you need to enter is the category name when you add to the list.

To add a new vendor the procedure is basically the same except that you choose Vendors from the Select List window. When you press `F7` and choose 1 Add New, the Add New Vendor window displayed in Figure 2-8 appears. In addition to the Pay To name and address field,

```
                         Add New Vendor
    ┌ Pay To (name, then address) ┐
    │                              │
    │                              │
    │                              │
    │                              │
    └                              ┘
    ─────────────── Optional Information ───────────────

    ♦Vendor Type:
        (press F1 for common uses of vendor type)

    Account number/notes:
    Taxpayer ID Number:

    Contact:                          Tel: (    )  -      ext

    Esc-Cancel            Ctrl-N Notepad            Ctrl↵ Done
```

Add New Vendor window
Figure 2-8.

optional fields for a vendor type, account number or note, taxpayer ID number, and a contact name and phone number exist. You can press `Ctrl`-`L` for the Vendor Type field and select an entry from the vendor types list.

Working with the Payment Methods List

Payment method can include cash, check, or credit card. Like other lists, you can put this one to more creative use if you want to.

The entries from the payment methods list can be used when you are working in the Make Deposit window. Categorizing deposits with entries from this list allows you to print deposit slips by payment method. As you add new payment methods to the existing list you are limited to ten characters for each entry.

Working with the Project List

Like some of the other lists the main purpose of the project list is to provide broader capabilities for classifying data on a report. When completing transactions or invoices, you can use the entries in this list as a way of keeping track of costs for a job or project. Contractors might use this field for the address of a property, and commercial lease agents might use it to keep track of specific lease locations. Figure 2-9 shows some of the projects in the project list for the sample company that comes with QuickBooks. Note how the project names are close matches with some of the customer names that you saw earlier, to remind the user who each project is for. The indented entries are the subprojects.

TIP: You can use the project entries to provide a job order costing capability. It is possible for a service-type business to have many jobs for one customer, and the ability to implement job order costing to keep track of charges by project and subproject will make the statements easier to read and understand.

QuickBooks does not have any predefined projects. You will need to add your own if this more detailed approach to reporting is of interest to you.

Setting Up QuickBooks for Your Business

```
                    Project List
          Project                  Description
   ►                           Add New Parent Project
       Bank proj              Bayshore Nat Bank proj
         Brochure
         Dir Mail             Direct mail piece
         Stationery           Stationery, etc.
       Baysoft proj           Baysoft projects
         Dir Mail             Direct mail piece
         Mug                  Custom mug
         Newsletter
         Slide                Slide presentation
         Stationery           Stationery, etc.
         Sweat                Custom sweatshirt

   Esc-Cancel              F7-Actions
```

Project list from sample company
Figure 2-9.

Creating a Project

You will probably need to create a project entry for each major job or client. The exception would be a small one-time job with no possibility of additional business. Projects are essential if you want to be able to report on costs and revenues by project.

To add a project follow these steps:

1. Choose 6 Company Lists from the Main Menu.
2. Choose Projects.
3. Highlight the first entry.
4. Press [F7] and choose 1 Add New from the following menu:

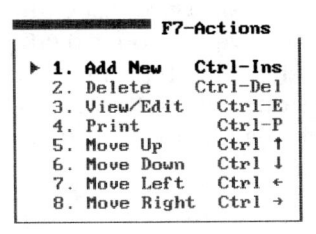

```
              F7-Actions
   ► 1. Add New      Ctrl-Ins
     2. Delete       Ctrl-Del
     3. View/Edit    Ctrl-E
     4. Print        Ctrl-P
     5. Move Up      Ctrl ↑
     6. Move Down    Ctrl ↓
     7. Move Left    Ctrl ←
     8. Move Right   Ctrl →
```

You can also press the Quick Key, [Ctrl]-[Ins], for the same effect.

5. Complete the project name and description and press [Ctrl]-[Enter].

Creating a Subproject

Creating a subproject allows for better control of costs for large projects.

A subproject is the next lower level from a project. It breaks the project down into smaller pieces to allow you to report costs and revenues at this lower level. A project might be a client, and the subprojects might be the various activities performed for the client. For a contractor, the project could be a construction site and the subprojects the various activities, such as electrical work, plumbing, dry wall, and so forth. For a doctor the project could be a patient and the subprojects the various visits and procedures performed for the patient.

To add a subproject, position your cursor on the project that it will be under and repeat the procedure described in steps 4 and 5 of the preceding section.

Reorganizing Projects

You can change the order of projects and subprojects. You can change a project into a subproject and a subproject into a project. Each action you take requires the use of the [Ctrl] key. If you press [Esc] while still holding down [Ctrl], QuickBooks will undo the effect of your last change.

To change a subproject to a project, highlight it and press [Ctrl]-[←]. To change a project to a subproject, press [Ctrl]-[→]. To move projects or subprojects up and down in the list press [Ctrl]-[↑] or [Ctrl]-[↓].

Working with Items/Parts/Services

The items/parts/services list contains the building blocks, or lines, that make up an invoice. You can enter lines for services or products into this list rather than type an entry each time you need it. You can also use lines from this list to compute taxes or subtotals on an invoice. If you assign the line items in this list to accounts you can report sales by account.

The type of the line item you use in an invoice is what tells QuickBooks how to handle the entry. QuickBooks supports eight different line item types. Some, like Part, Service, and Other Charges, are designed to help you organize detail line items. QuickBooks calculates the Amount field for these items after you enter a number in the Qty field, since the Price Each is part of the line item in the list. Some types cause QuickBooks to perform calculations using the previous line item. These include Sales Tax,

Setting Up QuickBooks for Your Business

Subtotal, and Discount if it is a percent. If you use a Payment line item the amount that you enter is made negative and subtracted from the invoice amount. The use of a Refund line item causes QuickBooks to prepare a check. Figure 2-10 shows some of the items from the Item List in the SAMPLE data file.

Adding a Line Item

The windows that QuickBooks uses for adding line items vary depending on the type of item you are entering. You can follow these basic steps for all types of line items:

1. Choose 6 Company Lists from the Main Menu.
2. Choose Items/Parts/Services.
3. Press [Ctrl]-[Ins] to add an item.
4. Choose the type of item that you want.

   Figure 2-11 shows the Add New Part Item window. Table 2-6 provides additional information about each type of line item.

5. Complete the Add window for the item and press [Ctrl]-[Enter] to finalize the entry.

```
                        Item List

       Item Code   Type        Description         Price Each

    ▶  sub         Subt    Subtotal of taxable items
       sub2        Subt    Subtotal
       total       Subt    Total charges
       BCPKG       Part    500 Business Cards with 1    175.000
       matl        Part    Materials used                 0.000
       mug         Part    Custom mugs                    4.500
       pen         Part    Custom ballpoint pens          0.950
       slide       Part    Custom slide transparenci      3.750
       swt         Part    Custom sweatshirts             7.500
       tbag        Part    Custom travel bag              6.500
       tshirt      Part    Custom T-shirts                3.000
       bcard       Service Printing 500 business car     65.000

       Esc-Cancel              F7-Actions
```

Item list from sample company
Figure 2-10.

Add New Part Item window
Figure 2-11.

```
┌─────────────────────────────────────────────────────────────┐
│                       Add New Part Item                     │
│  Code:                    ♦Account:                         │
│  Price each: 0.00              (if a percentage, type '%' after price) │
│  ┌─ Description to show on invoice ──────────────────────┐  │
│  │                                                       │  │
│  │                                                       │  │
│  └───────────────────────────────────────────────────────┘  │
│  Esc-Cancel                                    Ctrl⏎ Done   │
└─────────────────────────────────────────────────────────────┘
```

> **NOTE:** Item codes can be up to ten characters.

Using Numbers for Item Codes

Codes for items can be numeric if you prefer, but you will want to come up with a scheme that continues to order the items by type. The Subtotal type is assigned to the first group, and the others are assigned

Type	Use
Part	Record sales of inventory
Service	Record sales of services
Other Charges	Record miscellaneous charges such as freight
Discount	Specify dollar or percentage discounts
Sales Tax	Specify a tax rate
Payment	Indicate payment receipt at the time the invoice is issued
Refund	Record a check refund to a customer
Subtotal	Compute a subtotal of all previous line items

Line Item Types
Table 2-6.

Setting Up QuickBooks for Your Business

in the following order: Part, Service, Other Charges, Discount, Payment, Refund, and Sales Tax, as shown in this sample:

Range of Entries	Type
00001 to 09999	Subtotal
10000 to 19999	Part
20000 to 29000	Service
30000 to 39999	Other Charges
40000 to 49999	Discount
50000 to 59999	Payment
60000 to 69999	Refund
70000 to 79999	Sales Tax

You must assign a sequence of numbers to a type and each type must have a unique digit in the first position. Depending on the number of codes you need, you can have 100, 1,000, 10,000, or more codes for each type of item. This means that you can use 0001 to 0099, 00001 to 09999, 000001 to 099999, 0000001 to 0999999, or 00000001 to 09999999 for the Subtotal type. Then use 100, 1000, 10000, 100000, or 1000000 to begin the Part type, and so on.

Adding Shipping Methods

The shipping methods list provides a number of options for shipping: Airborne, DHL, Emery, Fed Ex, UPS-Blue, UPS-Gnd, UPS-Red, and U.S. Mail. The information from this list is used when you press Ctrl-L to display the list of options on the Via field in an invoice. If you work with other freight carriers or private couriers you can add them to the list shown in Figure 2-12.

As long as the costs for shipping are covered by customers you can leave the full range of shipping options in the list. If you must cover shipping costs before making a profit you may want to remove any shipping methods that are too expensive. For example, you may want to eliminate the overnight couriers and keep UPS-Gnd and the U.S. Mail only.

```
                Shipping Method List
        ▶ Airborne
          DHL
          Emery
          Fed Ex
          UPS-Blue
          UPS-Gnd
          UPS-Red
          US Mail



        Esc-Cancel    F7-Actions
```

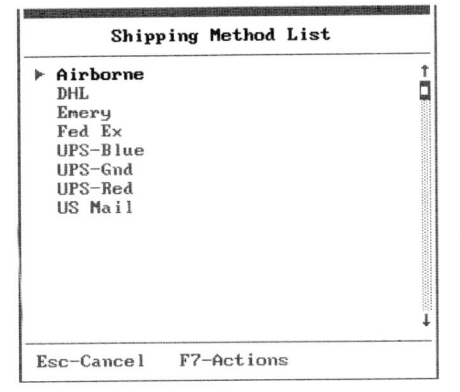

Shipping method list
Figure 2-12.

Adding Invoice Memos

You can create a set of messages to appear on invoices with the invoice memo list. These messages can thank customers for their business, request prompt payment, or threaten the use of a collection agency if payment is not received promptly.

The invoice memo list already contains entries when you start a new company. The messages provided are as follows:

    Please remit to above address
    Please remit. Past due!
    Please return one ... with payment
    Taxpayer Identification number
    Thank you for your business
    Thank you!

After displaying the list, you can use `F7` to add a phone number that customers can call with questions, or add a stronger reminder for payments on past due balances.

CHAPTER

3

WRITING CHECKS AND MAINTAINING RECORDS

With your company information entered into QuickBooks company lists, you are ready to make use of some of the work you have done and write checks using some of your entries. You will find QuickBooks' approach to check writing as simple as writing a check manually but with many advantages: you can correct mistakes before printing, choose a payee name and address from a list, enter numeric digits and have the

Using QuickBooks to write your checks saves time because you use entries that you have already made rather than writing everything out.

check amount spelled out automatically, and complete a voucher allocating the check amount to as many as 31 different accounts or projects. If you prefer, you can continue to write checks manually and enter the information into a QuickBooks check register. You will learn how to do this in Chapter 4. However, writing checks manually prevents you from enjoying one of QuickBooks' helpful features: when you use QuickBooks for writing your checks, the register entries are created for you automatically.

In order to use QuickBooks for check writing and printing, you must order special check stock that corresponds to the QuickBooks layout. You can order these checks in different styles. Also, you can select from laser printer or tractor-feed paper. You will find that banks, credit unions, and savings and loans all accept this check stock since it has the account number and check number on each check.

Ordering Check Stock

Intuit offers check stock for both continuous-form printers and laser or inkjet models. On all types of printers you can select either standard checks or a check with a voucher, which is ideal for accounts payable and payroll. The voucher check for the laser printer even comes in a pre-collated duplicate version that lets you print an extra copy for your records. Intuit offers other accessories such as window envelopes, forms leaders to prevent wasted checks, and deposit slips. Figure 3-1 shows a sample standard check for a laser printer. The voucher design (seen with tractor feed) is shown in Figure 3-2.

You can order supplies from Intuit by calling 800-433-8810. You may find that their prices are slightly higher than those charged by your bank, but you will save time if you use theirs. Also, Intuit lets you choose from hundreds of standard logos to add to your check at no extra charge.

Writing Checks

You have probably been writing checks manually for years. Writing a check in QuickBooks requires the same entries as a manual check except that QuickBooks records the check in the register automatically. This gives you a much better chance of getting your registers totally in

Writing Checks and Maintaining Records

Sample standard check
Figure 3-1.

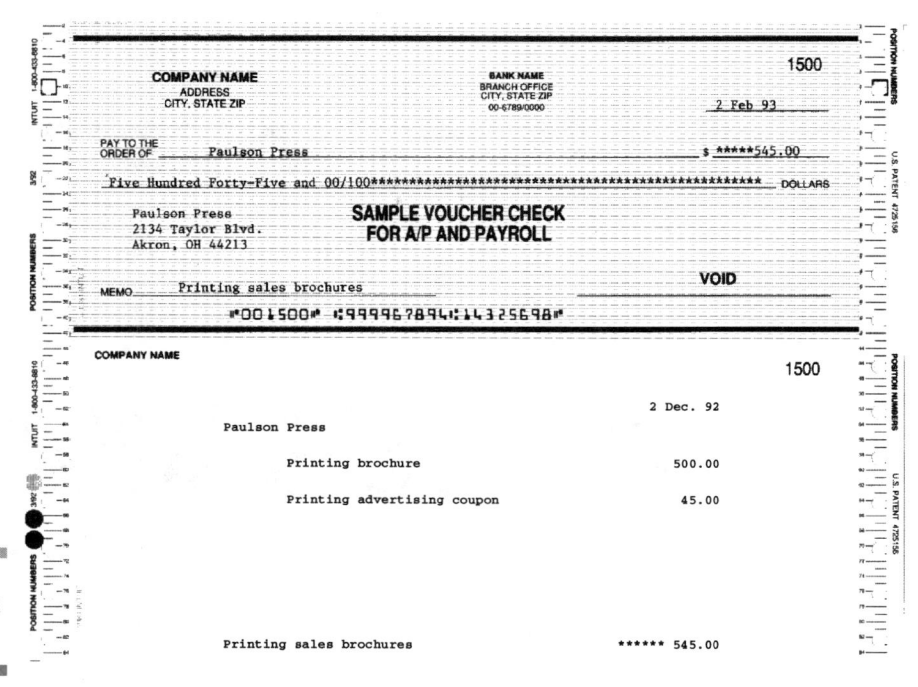

Sample voucher check
Figure 3-2.

sync with the bank. To display the Write Checks window choose 1 Checkbook from the Main Menu, then choose 1 Write/Print Checks.

Fields in the Write Checks Window

You should already be familiar with most of the fields on the Check Writing window, since they are the same types of information that you enter on handwritten checks (name, dollar amount, and so forth). However, there are some entries at the bottom of the QuickBooks Write Checks window that will be new to you. As many as three monetary amounts may appear in the bottom-right corner of the screen, as shown in Figure 3-3. These are the Checks to Print, Current Balance, and Ending Balance fields.

The Checks to Print field holds the total dollar amount of all the checks written but not yet printed. This will not appear until you fill in the first check and record the transaction. Current Balance is a field that appears only if you write checks with dates after the current date, called

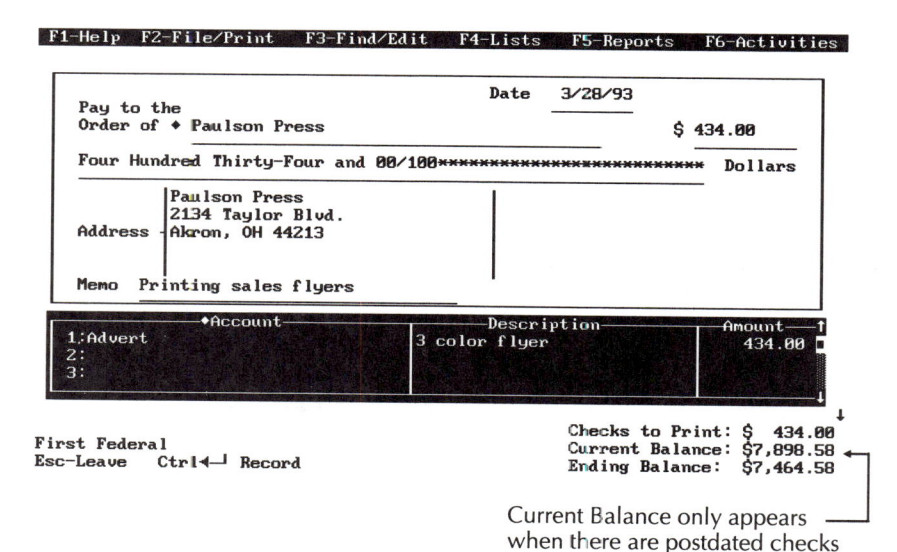

Write Checks window
Figure 3-3.

```
F1-Help   F2-File/Print   F3-Find/Edit   F4-Lists   F5-Reports   F6-Activities

                                          Date     3/28/93
        Pay to the
        Order of ♦ Paulson Press                            $ 434.00
        Four Hundred Thirty-Four and 00/100*************************** Dollars

                    Paulson Press
                    2134 Taylor Blvd.
        Address     Akron, OH 44213

        Memo    Printing sales flyers

               ◆Account            Description                 Amount
        1: Advert                3 color flyer                  434.00
        2:
        3:

First Federal                        Checks to Print: $   434.00
Esc-Leave   Ctrl⏎  Record            Current Balance: $7,898.58
                                     Ending Balance:  $7,464.58
```

Current Balance only appears when there are postdated checks

Writing Checks and Maintaining Records

The basic information you enter in QuickBooks to write a check is the same information you enter when you write a check by hand.

postdated checks. Postdated checks are written to record future payments. For instance, if you enter a check on September 10 for a December 24 payment, the check is postdated. All checks entered after the current date are considered postdated checks and do not affect the current balance. They will, however, alter the ending balance. QuickBooks allows postdated entries so you can schedule future expenses and write the check entry while you are thinking of it. Keep in mind that it is not necessary to print postdated checks when you print current checks.

The Ending Balance is the balance in the account after checks, current and postdated, have been deducted. Without postdated checks, the Current Balance and Ending Balance are the same and there is no need for QuickBooks to display both fields. However, if you have postdated checks, the Current Balance will be displayed.

Entering Basic Information

You use [Tab] or [Enter] to move from field to field on the check form. QuickBooks' default setting starts with the Payee field, although you can alter it to start with the date if you typically enter checks with different dates. If you want to move back to a previous field, use [Shift]-[Tab]. Press [Ctrl]-[S] to move to the voucher area at any time. When you finish entering the check information and are ready to record it, press [Ctrl]-[Enter] to automatically record the transaction.

At a minimum you must supply a payee name and an amount when you complete a QuickBooks check. Depending on the settings for your company, you may need to supply an account for each check. Or you may need to change the setting in Require account on all transactions found in the Customize Current Company window. This window is accessible if you choose 7 Set Up/Customize, then select 4 Customize Current Company, and 2 Options.

You can minimize your typing as you write QuickBooks checks if you use the company lists to provide a payee and account name. When you press [Ctrl]-[L] and select a payee, QuickBooks completes the address area of the check for you as well as the payee entry. Figure 3-4 shows a check with the payee and address supplied by a simple selection from the payee list. If you elect to type a payee, you can copy the payee name down to the address area by pressing the key with " on it. If you change

QuickBooks for Profit: Making the Numbers Work

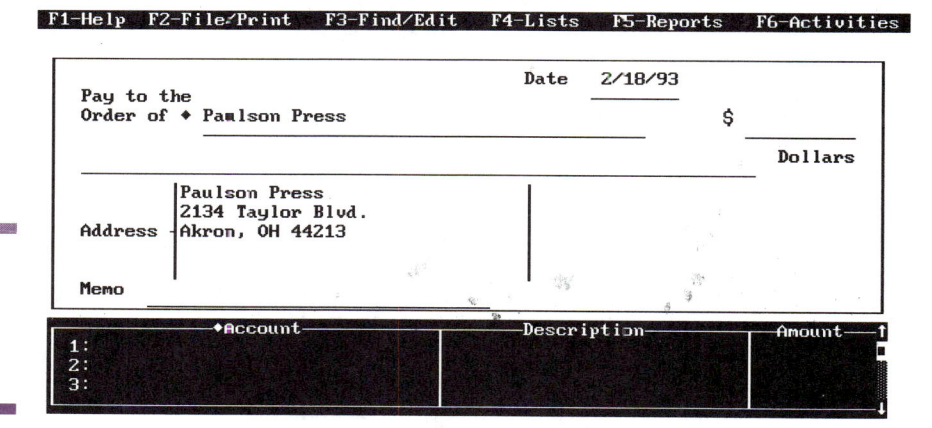

```
F1-Help  F2-File/Print  F3-Find/Edit  F4-Lists  F5-Reports  F6-Activities
```

```
                                          Date   2/18/93
Pay to the
Order of ♦ Paulson Press                                   $
                                                              Dollars

           Paulson Press
           2134 Taylor Blvd.
Address    Akron, OH 44213

Memo

          ♦Account              Description          Amount
1:
2:
3:
```

Check with address and payee information
Figure 3-4.

the custom settings for the current company you can display an extra message line with as many as 24 characters next to the address.

TIP: You do not need to use the (Shift) key when you want to copy the payee with ", even if this symbol is located on the top of the key.

Type the digits representing the amount and QuickBooks will add the written amount automatically. This ensures that the written description matches the digits entered.

TIP: If you are paying several invoices with one check, leave the Amount field blank and type the amounts in the voucher area to have QuickBooks total them for you. As you add each new amount on a voucher line, the amount of the check at the top of the screen changes.

The default entry for the Date field is the current date. It can be changed if you are writing a postdated check which shouldn't be

Writing Checks and Maintaining Records

61

printed until the bill is due. Use the Memo field to type a reminder of the reason for writing the check.

> **TIP:** For easier tracking later, use the Memo field to record the invoice number(s) that you are paying with the check. Later, in Chapter 9, you will learn about accounts payable features that will add these invoice numbers for you.

Completing the Voucher

Selecting accounts in the voucher area organizes your expenses so QuickBooks can later summarize the amounts you have paid for different types of expenses.

The voucher area is used for assigning the amount of the check to one or more accounts. There are three fields on each line of the voucher: Account, Description, and Amount. The voucher area appears on the Write Checks screen even if you plan to print the checks on standard check stock and will not be able to include the information on printed checks. You can use the voucher area to assign the check to one or more accounts, as shown in Figure 3-5. If you enter a description for the account, QuickBooks records the transaction as a *split transaction* (a transaction whose amounts are allocated among several accounts) even if you only select one account in the voucher area. To see the account assignment of a split transaction when you look at the check registers, you must open a Split Transaction window ([Ctrl]-[S]).

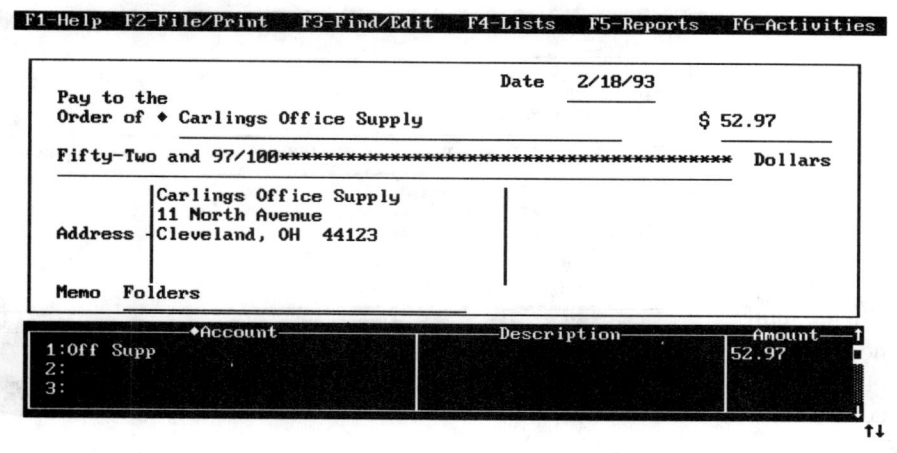

```
F1-Help   F2-File/Print   F3-Find/Edit   F4-Lists   F5-Reports   F6-Activities

                                          Date   2/18/93
        Pay to the
        Order of ♦ Carlings Office Supply              $ 52.97
        Fifty-Two and 97/100*********************************  Dollars

                  Carlings Office Supply
                  11 North Avenue
        Address  Cleveland, OH  44123

        Memo   Folders

        ────♦Account──────────────Description──────────Amount──
        1:Off Supp                                    52.97
        2:
        3:

First Federal                           Checks to Print: $  590.00
Esc-Leave   Ctrl┘ Record                Ending Balance:  $7,904.32
```

Voucher with one entry
Figure 3-5.

TIP: Even though voucher stock is more expensive than regular stock, it should be considered an essential expense when paying multiple vendor invoices or producing payroll checks. The extra cost is more than offset by the time you save by providing clear information to suppliers and employees and not having to look up the allocation among various accounts.

You can use `Ctrl`-`L` to list the various accounts that can be used for the account entry in each line of the voucher. Up to 31 lines can be entered, although only 16 will print. Figure 3-6 shows voucher entries that allocate the amount of a check to two different accounts.

NOTE: You can use the Description field in the voucher to keep additional notes on the payment as long as you use lines 16 and above, since these do not print on the check.

Voucher with check split between two accounts
Figure 3-6.

```
F1-Help  F2-File/Print  F3-Find/Edit  F4-Lists  F5-Reports  F6-Activities

                                      Date   2/18/93
        Pay to the
        Order of  ♦ Paulson Press                            $ 545.00

        Five Hundred Forty-Five and 00/100**************************  Dollars

                  Paulson Press
                  2134 Taylor Blvd.
        Address   Akron, OH 44213

        Memo   Printing sales brochures

        ──────◆Account──────────────Description──────────Amount──
        1:Brochures              Printing brochure              500.00
        2:Advert                 Printing advertising coupon     45.00
        3:
                                                                  ↑↓
        First Federal                          Checks to Print: $  642.97
        Esc-Leave    Ctrl⏎ Record              Ending Balance:  $7,851.35
```

Writing Checks and Maintaining Records

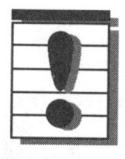

> **TIP:** To track expenses by project set the Custom Company Settings to turn on project tracking, and an extra field will display next to the Account field. This feature is essential for contractors, consultants working on several projects for one client, and others who want to keep track of expenses by job.

Making and Recording Corrections

When you are finished entering a check, press `Ctrl`-`Enter` to record the transaction. Although QuickBooks moves you to the next check, you can press `Ctrl`-`Pg Up` to see the check you just entered. You can enter as many checks as you want in one session.

Corrections can be made to a check before or after completing the transaction. Although it is easiest to make them before completion, the most important thing is catching the error before printing the check. To prevent problems, you will always want to review your transactions before printing. If you notice a mistake, correct it, and press `Ctrl`-`Enter` to record the corrected transaction.

Taking a Look at the Register Entries

The QuickBooks check register is just like a manual check register, except that QuickBooks automatically creates a register entry based on the information you write in a check.

The checks that you write automatically create entries in the account register for your checking account. In fact, the register is the only permanent place where you can see these entries. As you type each check, QuickBooks automatically adjusts your checking account balance by deducting the amount of the check. Once a check has been printed correctly it no longer appears in the Write Checks window. If you want to look at the entries for checks that you have written in the Register window press `F6` to activate the Activities menu and choose 1 Register, or press the Quick Key, `Ctrl`-`R`, for a shortcut approach. Figure 3-7 shows the register entry for a check. These entries correspond with the check shown in Figure 3-5. When you are ready to return to the Write Checks window, press `Ctrl`-`W` or make the proper selection from the Activities menu.

The account entry reflects the account assignment in the first line of the voucher area. The date of the register entry is the same as the check

Register entry for check
Figure 3-7.

```
2/18 ***** Carlings Office Supply      52 97           8,396 35
1993 Memo: Folders
     ◆Acct Off Supp
```

date. The check number will appear as asterisks (*) until the check is printed and a number is assigned. The payee entered for the check supplies the payee in the register entry. The entry for the check supplies everything needed to complete the register entry.

Figure 3-8 shows a register entry that corresponds to the check shown in Figure 3-6. Ctrl-S was pressed after displaying this transaction to open up the Split Transaction window.

Voiding Checks

Occasionally you may make a mistake in writing a check, or a check may be lost on the way to the payee. You can void the transaction associated with the check by moving to the check register. QuickBooks

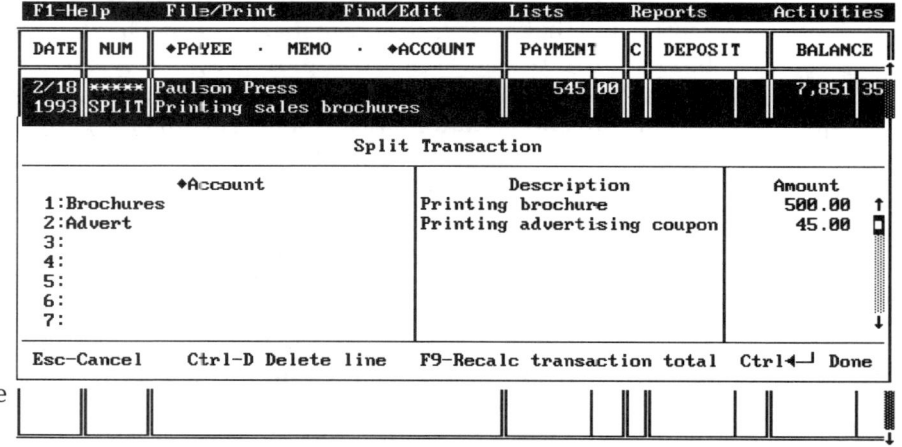

Register entry for check shown in Figure 3-6
Figure 3-8.

```
F1-Help      File/Print      Find/Edit      Lists      Reports      Activities
DATE   NUM   ◆PAYEE   ·   MEMO   ·   ◆ACCOUNT   PAYMENT  C  DEPOSIT   BALANCE
2/18  *****  Paulson Press                       545 00                7,851 35
1993  SPLIT  Printing sales brochures
                              Split Transaction
              ◆Account                        Description              Amount
      1:Brochures                      Printing brochure                500.00
      2:Advert                         Printing advertising coupon       45.00
      3:
      4:
      5:
      6:
      7:
      Esc-Cancel    Ctrl-D Delete line    F9-Recalc transaction total   Ctrl⏎ Done

      First Federal
                                                   Ending Balance:   $7,851.35
```

Writing Checks and Maintaining Records

adjusts your account balance to increase it by the amount of the voided check. Follow these steps to void a check:

1. Press `F3` to activate the Find/Edit menu.
2. Choose 6 Void Transaction.

   Void will be added in front of the payee name and an X will be placed in the Cleared column as QuickBooks displays the register entry.
3. Press `Ctrl`-`Enter`.

In Chapter 4 you will learn how to enter reversing entries to deal with situations such as a bad check that you have already recorded as a deposit to your account.

4. Press `F6` to activate the Activities menu and select 1 Write/Print Checks to return to the Write Checks window.

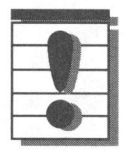

TIP: Before printing, you can delete a check written in error; after printing, a check should always be voided. This way you can account for all check stock. Deleting a check will leave a missing number in your sequence of checks and does not provide adequate information when you look at the account later.

Printing Checks

Printing checks with QuickBooks is easy. The only part of the task that might be a little difficult is lining up the check stock. Once you make use of the help that QuickBooks offers to simplify this part of the effort you will find the whole process easy.

You can choose to print some or all of your checks as soon as you write them or wait until later. Some users will print all the checks, then file them until it is time to pay them. Other users elect to wait until the bill is due to print the check.

Printing Sample Checks First

It is important to print sample checks to ensure that the text lines up correctly with the check stock. This will help you avoid wasting a large quantity of check stock. The procedure is different for tractor-feed and laser or inkjet printers. Tractor-feed printers use continuous-form paper with perforated edges that are stripped away after printing. Laser and inkjet printers use single sheets of paper that are normally loaded from a tray much like a copy machine.

Printing Samples with a Tractor-Feed Printer

To print a sample check from the Write Checks window with a tractor-feed printer, follow these instructions from the Write Checks screen:

1. Insert the sample checks in the tractor-feed as you do with any printer paper.

You can purchase Forms Leader pages from Intuit that assure proper alignment of the checks in the printer and allow you to use the first check. This way you won't waste a check at the beginning of each check writing session.

2. Turn on your printer and make sure that it is online and ready to begin printing.
3. Press F2 to activate the File/Print menu and select 2 Print Checks to display a Print Checks window that looks similar to the one shown in Figure 3-9.

Print Checks window

Figure 3-9.

```
                        Print Checks
                   There are 2 checks to print.
          Print checks dated through:  2/18/93
          Print All/Selected checks (A/S): A
          ♦Print to: HP LaserJet III/IIId, 10 cpi, Portrait, LP
          ♦Type of check:          Additional copies (0-9): 0
          To print a sample check to help with alignment, press F9.
                           F9-Print sample
          Esc-Cancel          F1-Help              Ctrl⏎ Print
```

Writing Checks and Maintaining Records

You can also press `Ctrl`-`P` rather than opening the menu. The Print Checks window appears.

4. Press `Enter` twice to accept the defaults of checks dated through the current date and all checks.
5. Press `Ctrl`-`L` if you need to change the selected printer, then select a printer from the list, and press `Enter`.
6. Press `Ctrl`-`L` to select the type of check (Standard or Voucher) and press `Enter`.
7. Press `F9` to select Print Sample; then, after reading QuickBooks' sample check note, press `Enter`.

   QuickBooks prints your sample check. Check the vertical alignment by observing whether the "XXX" for date and amount, the word "Payee" for "Pay to the Order of," and the phrase "This is a void check" for the memo are printed just above the lines on the sample check.

NOTE: You should not move the check up or down after printing; QuickBooks does this automatically.

8. Press `Enter` if the sample check has aligned properly. If not, continue with the remaining steps.
9. (Use this step only if your sample check did not align properly.) Look at the pointer line printed on your sample check. The arrow at each end points to a number on your tractor-feed sheet; this is your printer *position number*.

CAUTION: If your pointer line is not on one continuous line, you must check your printer settings to see that the pitch is 10 and the indent value is 0. You cannot continue with the following steps to achieve the correct results until you change the printer settings. Note the correct alignment position and consult Table 3-1. Press `Esc` to leave the print process for now.

QuickBooks for Profit: Making the Numbers Work

Printer Problem	Solution
Print lines are too close	Printer is probably set for eight lines to the inch—change to six
Print lines wrap and the date and amount are too far to the right	Pitch selected is too large—change to ten pitch
Print does not extend across the check; date and amount print too far to the left	Too small a pitch is selected—change to ten pitch
Print does not align with lines on check	Checks are not aligned properly—realign using the instructions in this chapter
Print seems to be the correct size but is too far to the left	Reposition checks from right to left
Printer is spewing paper or producing illegible print	Wrong printer was selected—change the selected printer
Printer does not print	Printer is not turned on, is not online, the cable is loose or is not selected
Print looks correct but it is indented	Change Indent setting to zero in the Print Settings window

Correcting Printer Errors **Table 3-1.**

10. Type the position line number and press Enter.

    QuickBooks automatically causes a form feed and prints another sample check. This time your check should be properly aligned. If you need to fine-tune the alignment, use the knob on your printer to manually adjust the alignment.

11. Make any horizontal adjustments that may be necessary by moving the paper clamps.

    Once you have aligned your checks properly, you should examine the location of the checks in your printer; notice where your position numbers line up with a part of your printer, such as the edge of the sprocket cover.

Writing Checks and Maintaining Records

12. Press [Enter] in the Position Number field when your sample check is properly aligned.

You are now ready to print your checks.

Printing Samples with Inkjet or Laser Printers

QuickBooks' laser-printer checks come either one or three to a page and, as mentioned, are the easiest of the checks to print. When using these forms, all you need to do is insert the forms into your printer the same way you insert regular paper (face up, with the top of the paper positioned toward the printer). If you tear the tractor-feed strips off the sample checks that come with QuickBooks, you can use them with your laser printer. You can also use regular printer paper. You can purchase Laser Form Leaders from Intuit, which allow you to use check stock that is less than a full sheet in length.

The key point to remember with laser printers is to check the printer settings before printing your checks. This can be accomplished from QuickBooks' Write/Print Checks menu:

1. Press [F2] to activate the File/Print menu and select 2 Print Checks to display the Print Checks window shown in Figure 3-9.
2. Press [Tab] twice to move to the Print to field and press [Ctrl]-[L].

   This accepts the defaults of printing all checks through the current date and printing all checks rather than the ones that you select.
3. Press [F9] for Printer Setup and select the number of the printer that you want to use.
4. Press [Ctrl]-[L] to display the Choose Printer Brand window, then use [↑] or [↓] to place the arrow next to your type of printer, and press [Enter] three times.
5. Press [Ctrl]-[L] to select a style and press [Enter].
6. Press [Ctrl]-[Enter] to close the Set Up Printer window.
7. Press [Esc] to return to the Print Checks window.

   Place a sheet of plain paper in your printer.
8. Press [F9] to select Print Sample.

Hold the sample up to the light with a sheet of check stock to check alignment. If the check is not properly aligned follow these steps:

1. Press [Shift]-[Tab] to return to the Print to field.
2. Press [Ctrl]-[L], then press [F9] to select Printer Setup.
3. Select the number of the printer that you need to adjust.
4. If the check was misaligned vertically, that is, too high or too low, you have the wrong printer selected for the Printer name field. Press [Ctrl]-[L] and use the [↑] and [↓] keys to select the desired printer, then press [Enter].
5. If the check is misaligned horizontally, that is, side to side, press [Tab] to move to the Check Style field. Then press [F8] to select Customize style to open the Customize Style window and press [Ctrl]-[D] to return the settings to the default.
6. Press [Ctrl]-[Enter], then press [Enter].
7. Print another sample check to verify the correctness of output by pressing [F9] to select Print Sample again.

Selecting Checks to Print

When you are ready to print checks, you need to tell QuickBooks the printer you want to use, the check style you have selected, the checks to print, and the first check number. You can choose to print a check you need right away, a selection of check numbers, all the checks dated prior to a specified date, or all the checks that have not as yet been printed. The instructions that follow assume that you have already checked the alignment for your check stock and that you are beginning from the Main Menu.

1. Press [F2] to activate the File/Print menu.
2. Select 2 Print Checks.

   Another option is to press [Ctrl]-[P] rather than opening the File/Print menu. The Print Checks window appears.
3. Press [Enter] or [Tab], then type **S** to print selected checks. Typing **A** causes QuickBooks to print all the checks.
4. Press [Enter] or [Tab] and then press [Ctrl]-[L] to select another printer if desired. Highlight it and press [Enter].

5. Press [Ctrl]-[L] again and select the type of check that you want to use, then press [Tab] or [Enter].
6. If you want extra copies for your records enter a number for this field.
7. Press [Ctrl]-[Enter] and the Select Checks to Print window appears. Checks that will be printed show "Print" in the far-right column. You can change the selection status to the opposite of its current setting by highlighting the entry and pressing [Spacebar]. This allows you to select specific checks.

   If you do not want to print checks that are marked for printing, you can press [Spacebar] with the cursor pointing at the check to turn off the print command for that check. [Spacebar] toggles the print designation on and off.
8. Press [Ctrl]-[Enter] and type the beginning check number in the Set Check Number window, shown here:

   ```
                    Set Check Number
        Enter the check number of the check
        that QuickBooks is about to print.
        Next check number: 113

                 F9-Print on Partial Page
        Esc-Cancel      F1-Help      ↵ Continue
   ```

   You must always make this check number agree with the number of the first check you place in the printer. You should double-check this entry since QuickBooks will use it to complete the register entry for the check transaction. As it prints a check, it replaces the asterisks in the register with the actual check number. You can use [+] and [-] to change the check number. You can also select [F9] Partial Page to tell QuickBooks that you have less than a full page of laser checks and specify the checks remaining in the Partial Page Printing window shown in Figure 3-10.
9. Press [Enter] to print your checks.

   QuickBooks responds with a Did Checks Print OK? window.

Partial Page
Printing
window
Figure 3-10.

```
                    Partial Page Printing
 If your first page of checks has already been partially used,
 enter the number of checks remaining on the page, and indicate
 whether you want to print in Portrait (normal) mode using the
 Intuit Ink Jet Forms Leader, or in Landscape (sideways) mode.

 Number of checks remaining on page:

 Print in Portrait or Landscape mode (P/L):

 Esc-Cancel              F1-Help                    ←┘ Continue
```

> **NOTE:** There is also an option to change the number of copies printed if you want a duplicate for your records.

Review the checks printed and check for errors in printing. If you used preprinted check forms, your checks might look something like the ones shown in Figures 3-1 and 3-2, earlier in the chapter.

10. If there are errors in your checks follow the instructions in the next section. If there are no errors, select 1 Yes to close the check printing windows and to return to the Write Checks screen. Press Ctrl-R to look at the register entries with the check numbers inserted. If there are problems with the checks, follow the directions in the next section.

Correcting Mistakes in Checks

QuickBooks allows you to reprint checks that have been printed incorrectly. Since you are using prenumbered checks, new numbers will have to be assigned to the reprinted checks as QuickBooks prints them. First, make sure before starting again that you correct any feed problems with the printer.

Writing Checks and Maintaining Records

If you find yourself frequently correcting printer jams and having to reprint checks, you may want to print checks in smaller batches or set your printer to wait after each page.

Complete the following steps to restart and finish your printing batch:

1. Select 2 No.
2. The Print Checks window appears. Press `Ctrl`-`Enter` to open the Select Checks to Print window.
3. Select the checks to be reprinted by highlighting the check and using `Spacebar` to change the selection status to Print. Then press `Enter`.
4. Check the Next Check Number field against the number of the next check in your printer. Type a new number if appropriate. Press `Enter` to confirm the beginning check number for this batch and begin printing.
5. Select Yes to indicate that all the checks have printed correctly when they stop printing; otherwise repeat the steps described in this section.

TIP: If you use the payables register to record your payments to vendors, as discussed in Chapter 9, you will be able to print labels as well as checks. This way you can save the work of addressing envelopes if you do not use window envelopes.

TIP: To save even more time, order Intuit's window envelopes for mailing. You will save the time normally spent addressing the envelopes and not waste a second.

Reconciling Your Account

Reconciling a checking account is the process of comparing your entries with the ones that the bank has recorded. You can determine whether any differences are due to timing or errors in the recording process on your part or the bank's. Timing differences occur because your balance is accurate up to the present date but the bank records were compiled at an earlier date before transactions that you recorded cleared the bank. These timing differences must be reconciled to ensure that discrepancies were not caused by an error. A monthly reconciliation of your business checking accounts is a necessary step in financial record keeping.

CAUTION: Overdraft charges can be substantial. If your checking account balances are typically low, do not delay reconciling your statement when it comes. You could incur unnecessary charges from both the bank and your suppliers. Bad checks will also keep you from qualifying for your supplier's best credit terms in the future.

In addition to timing differences, there may be transactions not recorded in your register or errors in the amounts. With manual check registers, there can also be addition and subtraction errors when checks and deposits are recorded. This is one type of error you do not need to worry about with QuickBooks, since its calculations are always perfect if you record the amount correctly.

Another cause of differences is transactions the bank has recorded on your bank statement that you haven't entered in your register. For example, you may have automatic monthly withdrawals for a business loan or transfers to another bank account. In addition, you may have a bank service charge for maintaining your checking account or printing checks, or you may have earned interest. These differences are addressed in more detail throughout this chapter.

First, you will look at how reconciliation works and the procedure that you will follow each month to reconcile each checking account. Next, you will look at problems that can occur and the methods for getting your account to agree with your bank's records.

QuickBooks' Reconciliation Process

QuickBooks reduces the frustration of the monthly reconciliation process by providing a systematic approach to reconciling your checking accounts. There are a number of steps in this process, but if you use this book to follow them the first few times you will find that it is quite easy.

A Few Key Points

There are three points to remember when using the QuickBooks reconciliation system. First, QuickBooks reconciles only one checking account at a time, so you have to reconcile each of your accounts separately.

Second, you should make it a habit to reconcile your checking accounts on a monthly basis. You can easily monitor your checking balances once you begin a monthly routine of reconciling your accounts, but attempting to reconcile six months of statements at one sitting is a frustrating experience, even with QuickBooks.

Third, before beginning the formal QuickBooks reconciliation process, visually examine your bank statement and look for any unusual entries, such as check numbers that are out of the range of numbers you expected to find on the statement. (If checks 501 and 502 have cleared, for example, while all the rest of the checks are numbered in the 900s, you might find the bank has charged another customer's checks against your account.) This examination provides an indication of what to look for during the reconciliation process.

An Overview of the Process

When you begin reconciliation, QuickBooks asks for information from your current bank statement, such as the opening and ending dollar balances, service charges, and any interest earned on your account. (QuickBooks also records these transactions in the check register and marks them as cleared, since the bank has already processed these items.)

Once you have entered this information, QuickBooks presents a summary screen for marking cleared items. All the transactions recorded in the account, as well as the service charge and interest-earned transactions, are shown on this screen.

QuickBooks maintains a running total of your balance as you proceed through the reconciliation process. Each payment or deposit is applied to the opening balance total as it is marked cleared. You can determine the difference between the cleared balance amount and the bank statement balance at any time. Your end objective is a difference of zero.

The first step is to check the amounts of your QuickBooks entries against the bank statement. Where there are discrepancies, you can switch to your QuickBooks register and check the entries. You may find incorrect amounts recorded in the QuickBooks register or by your bank. You may also find that you forgot to record a check or a deposit. You can create or change register entries from the Register window.

Once you have finished with the entry, you put an asterisk (*) in the C column to mark the transaction as cleared. After resolving any differences between your balance and the bank's, you can print the reconciliation reports. The asterisks are used in the cleared column until QuickBooks confirms an entry. Then QuickBooks automatically replaces them with an X, which you will see as this lesson proceeds.

You can correct check register errors quickly if you reconcile your checking account regularly.

Preparing the Printer for Reconciliation

Before you begin reconciliation, you should check your printer settings. This is important because at the end of the reconciliation process you are given an opportunity to print reconciliation reports. You can't change printer settings after QuickBooks presents you with the Print Reconciliation Report window; it's too late. If you attempt to make a change by pressing [Esc], you are returned to the Main Menu and have to start over. However, you will not need to complete the detailed reconciliation procedure again.

Use 7 Set Up/Customize to check your printer settings now. When you return to the Main Menu, you will be ready to start the reconciliation example.

Steps to Follow for a Successful Reconciliation

To ensure that you spend as little time as possible reconciling your accounts it is important to keep accurate records. You will also find that the step-by-step approach presented here provides the road map to success that you are looking for.

1. Press [Ctrl]-[A] and select the account that you want to reconcile.

Writing Checks and Maintaining Records

2. Press [F6] to activate the Activities menu and choose 2 Reconcile, or use the [Ctrl]-[Y] shortcut.

   QuickBooks displays the Reconcile Register with Bank Statement window shown in Figure 3-11.

3. If the opening statement balance is not the same as the one on your bank statement, type the one on the bank statement over the amount displayed and press [Enter].

   (You will learn more about opening balance adjustments later in this chapter.)

4. Type the ending balance amount from your statement in the correct location and press [Enter].

5. Type the service charge from your bank statement if one exists and press [Enter]. Use [Ctrl]-[L] to select an account to allocate this expense to.

6. If your account statement shows interest earned, enter the amount in the Interest Earned field and press [Enter]. Press [Ctrl]-[L] and select an account to allocate the interest to.

   Your window might look something like Figure 3-12, depending on the service charge and interest earned, and the accounts you have allocated these to.

7. Press [F10] or [Ctrl]-[Enter] to finalize your entries.

   A window showing the detail checks and a reconciliation summary is displayed, as shown in Figure 3-13. An asterisk is displayed in the C column for any entries that have cleared on an earlier statement.

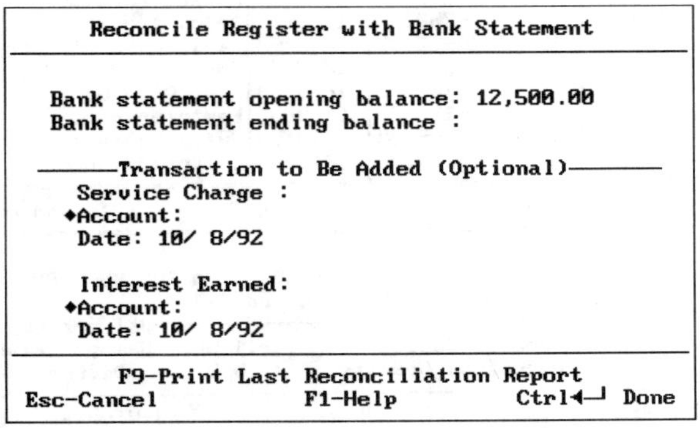

```
           Reconcile Register with Bank Statement

    Bank statement opening balance: 12,500.00
    Bank statement ending balance :

          ──────Transaction to Be Added (Optional)──────
       Service Charge :
       ♦Account:
       Date: 10/ 8/92

       Interest Earned:
       ♦Account:
       Date: 10/ 8/92

            F9-Print Last Reconciliation Report
    Esc-Cancel           F1-Help         Ctrl↵ Done
```

Reconcile Register with Bank Statement window
Figure 3-11.

QuickBooks for Profit: Making the Numbers Work

```
           Reconcile Register with Bank Statement

     Bank statement opening balance: 12,500.00
     Bank statement ending balance : 9,719.32

     ─────────Transaction to Be Added (Optional)─────────
        Service Charge : 11.50
       ◆Account: Bank Chrg
        Date:   2/ 1/93

        Interest Earned: 9.27
       ◆Account: Int Inc
        Date:   2/1 /93

               F9-Print Last Reconciliation Report
     Esc-Cancel              F1-Help           Ctrl⏎ Done
```

Ending balance, service charge, and interest entered
Figure 3-12.

8. With a transaction highlighted, press [Enter] or [Spacebar] to mark it as cleared, or use [F8] Mark Range and specify the range of transactions to be cleared.

> **NOTE:** If you notice an error in your transaction entry in QuickBooks you can switch to the register by pressing [F9]. Correct the entry and press [F9] to return to the list of uncleared transactions.

```
 F1-Help      File/Print      Find/Edit      Lists      Reports      Activities
┌─────┬───┬───────────┬─────────┬───────────────────────┬───────────────────────┐
│ NUM │ C │  AMOUNT   │  DATE   │        PAYEE          │         MEMO          │
├─────┼───┼───────────┼─────────┼───────────────────────┼───────────────────────┤
│▶    │ * │    -11.50 │ 2/ 1/93 │ Service charge        │                       │
│     │ * │      9.27 │ 2/ 1/93 │ Interest earned       │                       │
│     │   │ -1,200.00 │ 2/ 5/93 │ Manaco Leasing        │ March Rent            │
│ 101 │   │   -250.00 │ 1/ 2/93 │ Arlo, Inc.            │ Credenza              │
│ 102 │   │    -52.97 │ 1/ 2/93 │ Carlings Office Supply│ Folders               │
│ 103 │   │   -324.56 │ 1/ 2/93 │ Consumer Power        │ December 92 Electric  │
│ 104 │   │   -121.98 │ 1/ 9/93 │ East Ohio Gas         │ December 92 Gas Bill  │
│ 105 │   │   -102.00 │ 1/ 9/93 │ Postmaster            │ Stamps                │
│ 106 │   │    -45.00 │ 1/10/93 │ Quick Delivery        │ Overnight delivery fo │
│ 107 │   │   -156.94 │ 1/15/93 │ Computers, Etc.       │ 486 System            │
└─────┴───┴───────────┴─────────┴───────────────────────┴───────────────────────┘
 ■ To mark cleared items, press ⏎        ■ To add or change items, press F9.

                          RECONCILIATION SUMMARY
          Items You Have Marked Cleared (*)
         ──────────────────────────────────────  Bal per register (X,*)  12,497.77
          1   Checks, Debits          -11.50     Bal per bank statement   9,719.32
          1   Deposits, Credits         9.27     Difference               2,778.45

 F1-Help         F8-Mark range        F9-View as register        Ctrl-F10 Done
```

List of uncleared transactions
Figure 3-13.

Writing Checks and Maintaining Records

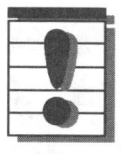

TIP: Check the amount of each transaction carefully as you check it off the bank statement. This way you will catch any errors in the transaction amounts before completing the reconciliation. If you wait you will have to go back through all the transactions again to find the error.

9. Press `Ctrl`-`F10` when you are finished.

If your account balances, you will see the congratulatory message shown in Figure 3-14. If your account does not balance consult the section, "Additional Reconciliation Issues and Features," later in this chapter.

10. If you want to print the reconciliation reports described in the next section type a **Y** and press `Enter`. Select either a full or a summary report before pressing `Ctrl`-`Enter` to print them; otherwise, just press `Enter`.

QuickBooks' Reconciliation Reports

If you choose to print the full set of reconciliation reports, four reconciliation reports will print:

+ A reconciliation summary
+ A cleared transaction detail
+ An uncleared transaction detail before the reconciliation date
+ An uncleared transaction detail after the reconciliation date

Figure 3-15 shows a reconciliation summary report.

The first page of the reconciliation summary report shows the beginning balance and summarizes the activity the bank reported for your account during the reconciliation period. The report also summarizes the difference between your register balance at the date of the reconciliation and the bank's balance. The report shows any checks and deposits recorded since the reconciliation date.

The cleared transaction detail report provides a detailed list with sections called "Cleared Checks and Payments" and "Cleared Deposits and Other Credits"—the items they contain were part of the

QuickBooks for Profit: Making the Numbers Work

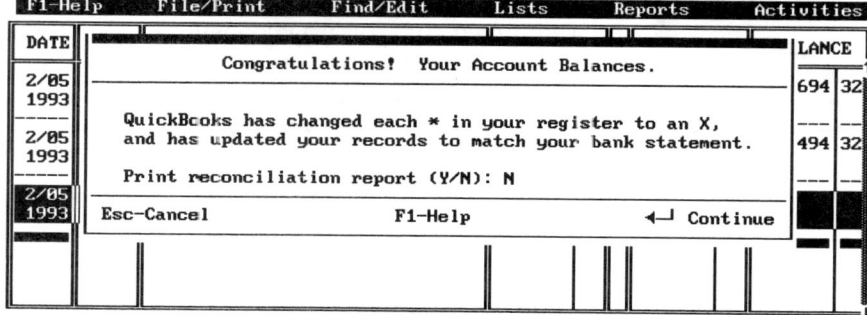

```
F1-Help      File/Print      Find/Edit       Lists        Reports      Activities
DATE                                                                    LANCE
2/05              Congratulations!  Your Account Balances.              694 32
1993
           QuickBooks has changed each * in your register to an X,
2/05       and has updated your records to match your bank statement.   494 32
1993
           Print reconciliation report (Y/N): N
2/05
1993       Esc-Cancel              F1-Help              ←┘ Continue


                           RECONCILIATION SUMMARY
           Items You Have Marked Cleared (*)
                                              Bal per register (X,*)    9,719.32
              0   Checks, Debits      0.00    Bal per bank statement    9,719.32
              0   Deposits, Credits   0.00    Difference                    0.00
```

Congratulatory window that appears when account is balanced
Figure 3-14.

```
                              Reconciliation Report
First Federal                                                          Page 1
2/21/93                         RECONCILIATION SUMMARY

    BANK STATEMENT -- CLEARED TRANSACTIONS:
         Previous Balance:                                                0.00
                                                                  --------------
              Checks and Payments:         1 Item                    -4,700.00
              Deposits and Other Credits:  1 Item                    12,500.00
                                                                  --------------
         Ending Balance of Bank Statement:                            7,800.00

    YOUR RECORDS -- UNCLEARED TRANSACTIONS:
         Cleared Balance:                                             7,800.00
                                                                  --------------
              Checks and Payments:        14 Items                   -4,601.42
              Deposits and Other Credits:  0 Items                        0.00
                                                                  --------------
         Register Balance as of  2/21/93:                             3,198.58
                                                                  --------------
              Checks and Payments:         1 Item                      -434.00
              Deposits and Other Credits:  0 Items                        0.00
                                                                  --------------
         Register Ending Balance:                                     2,764.58
```

Reconciliation Summary report
Figure 3-15.

Writing Checks and Maintaining Records

reconciliation process. This report provides detail for the "Cleared Transactions" section of the reconciliation summary report.

The uncleared transaction detail report up to the reconciliation date has sections headed "Uncleared Checks and Payments" and "Uncleared Deposits and Other Credits," to provide the details of uncleared transactions included in your register up to the date of reconciliation. This report provides detail for the "Uncleared Transactions" section of the reconciliation summary report.

The uncleared transaction detail report after the reconciliation date provides detail for those transactions that are recorded in the check register after the date of the reconciliation report. This information is shown in the final section of the reconciliation summary report.

These four reports are all printed automatically when you select QuickBooks' Full Report option. If you selected QuickBooks' Summary option, which is the default option, you would have received only the reconciliation summary report and the uncleared transaction detail up to the reconciliation date.

Additional Reconciliation Issues and Features

The reconciliation procedures discussed earlier provide a foundation for using QuickBooks to reconcile your accounts. Some additional issues covered in this section may prove useful in balancing your accounts in the future.

Updating Your Opening Balance

The importance of maintaining a regular reconciliation schedule has already been noted, and you should balance your checking account before you begin to use QuickBooks to record your transactions. However, there may be times when the opening balance QuickBooks enters in the Reconcile Register with Bank Statement window differs from the opening balance shown in the check register.

This can happen in three different situations. First, when you reconcile in QuickBooks the first time, there may be a discrepancy due to timing differences. Second, there may be a difference if you start QuickBooks at a point other than the beginning of the year and then try to add transactions from earlier in the year. Third, balances may differ if you use the reconciliation feature *after* recording QuickBooks transactions for several periods.

First-Time Reconciliations

If you open a new account and begin to use QuickBooks immediately, there will not be a discrepancy, but a discrepancy will occur if you do not enter the first transaction or two in QuickBooks. For example, suppose you opened an account on 12/31/92 for $1300.00 and immediately wrote a check for a 1992 expenditure of $100.00. Then you decided to start your QuickBooks register on 1/1/93, when the balance in your manual register was $1200.00. The bank statement would show the opening balance at $1300.00. After you exit the Reconcile Register with Bank Statement window in which you changed the Bank Statement opening balance field, and attempt to reconcile the account, QuickBooks displays the Opening Balance Does Not Match Bank window shown in Figure 3-16. In order to reconcile the difference between the bank statement and the QuickBooks register balance on 1/1/93, you can do one of two things.

The first alternative is to open the check register by pressing F9 while in the reconciliation procedures. Enter the $100.00 check, correct the

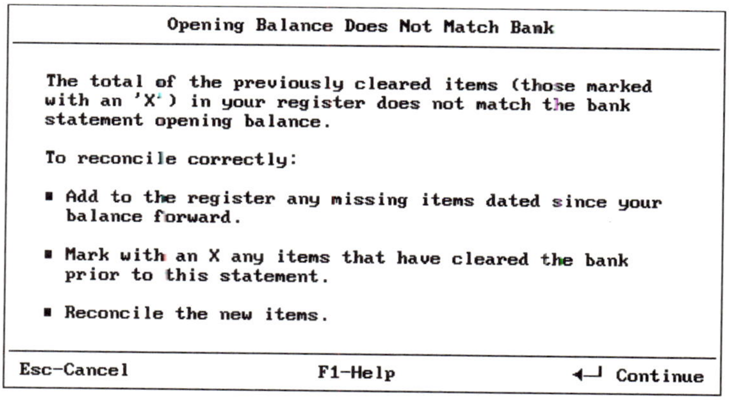

Opening Balance Does Not Match Bank window
Figure 3-16.

Writing Checks and Maintaining Records

opening balance to reflect the beginning bank balance of $1300.00, and proceed with the reconciliation process.

A second option is to have QuickBooks enter an adjustment in the reconciliation to correct for the difference between the check register and bank statement beginning balances. After you press `Ctrl`-`F10` to finalize cleared transactions while still having an opening balance difference, QuickBooks displays a Create Opening Balance Adjustment window, as shown in Figure 3-17. The example is offering to make a huge adjustment in the opening balance, which would not be a good idea to accept due to the size of the adjustment. If you do not want to accept it, press `Esc` to continue with reconciliation. If the difference were smaller, and you understood the reason for it as in the earlier example, you could accept the offer to make an adjustment.

Instead of pressing `Esc`, you can have QuickBooks make a correction by following these steps:

1. Type **Y** and press `Enter`, press `Ctrl`-`L` and select an account to use, then press `Enter` again.

   QuickBooks then reconciles the balances by making an adjustment to the check register for the $100.00 transaction. If there are other differences between the bank statement ending balance and the

Create Opening Balance Adjustment window
Figure 3-17.

```
                Create Opening Balance Adjustment

    The total of the items marked 'X' (those that have cleared
    in previous statements), does not match the opening bank
    statement balance.

    If you have already marked all the items in the Register
    that have cleared the bank in previous statements with an
    'X', type 'Y' to have QuickBooks create an adjustment.

    If you would like to reconcile the current statement
    without correcting the opening balance, type 'N'; QuickBooks
    will reconcile the transactions only, not the balance.

    To continue reconciling, press Escape.

    Add adjustment for $12,410.00 (Y/N) ? N

    ◆Account for adjustment:


    Esc-Cancel             F1-Help              Ctrl⏎ Done
```

register, QuickBooks will display the Problem: Check Register Does Not Balance with Bank Statement window.

2. If you want to search for the problem on your own, press `Esc` followed by `F9` to return to the list of transactions and the reconciliation summary.

   If you want QuickBooks to make an adjustment for you, press `Enter` instead, and the Adding Balance Adjustment Entry window appears. Then type **Y** and press `Enter` twice. The Register Adjusted to Agree with Statement window appears after QuickBooks makes an adjustment for the difference. Type **Y** and press `Enter`.

QuickBooks brings the Print Reconciliation Report window to the screen. You can now complete the reconciliation report printing process. Note that if you select N in any of these windows, you will be returned to the reconciliation process.

Adding Previous Transactions to QuickBooks

You most likely purchased QuickBooks sometime other than the beginning of your personal or business financial reporting year. In this case, you probably started recording your transactions when you purchased QuickBooks and entered your checking account balance at that time as your opening balance. This discussion assumes that you have been preparing reconciliations using QuickBooks and now want to go back and record all your previous transactions for the current year in QuickBooks. Obviously, your bank balance and QuickBooks balance will not agree after the transactions have been added.

Follow these steps:

1. Since you are going to be adding to your QuickBooks register, be sure to have the latest printout. If you do not, print your check register now, before you enter any additional transactions. This gives you a record of your transactions to date, which is important should you later need to reconstruct them.

2. Go to your QuickBooks Register window and change the date and balance columns to correspond to the bank statement that you used at the beginning of the year.

Writing Checks and Maintaining Records

> **NOTE:** The importance of saving your earlier bank statements is apparent. Old statements are not only important for the reconstruction of your QuickBooks system, but also in the event you are audited by the Internal Revenue Service. It only takes one IRS audit to realize the importance of maintaining a complete and accurate history of your financial transactions.

3. Using your manual records and past bank statements, enter the previous transactions in your QuickBooks register. Remember to enter bank service charges and automatic payment deductions if you have not been doing so prior to using QuickBooks.

4. When you have completed the updating process, compare your ending check register balance with the printed copy you made in step 1. This is important because if they do not balance, you have made an error in entering your transactions. If this is the case, determine whether the difference is an opening account balance difference or an error. (Your options for fixing any discrepancies between opening balances were described earlier in this chapter in the section "First-Time Reconciliations.")

5. The next time you reconcile your QuickBooks account (assuming you have reconciled the account before), type the opening balance on the latest bank statement over that provided by QuickBooks in the Reconcile Register with Bank Statement window.

6. Before completing the new reconciliation, go to the check register and type **X** to indicate the cleared transactions in the C column for all transactions that have cleared in previous months.

7. Reconcile the current month's transaction. (Go back to the section, "Steps to Follow for a Successful Reconciliation," if you need help.)

First-Time Reconciliation for Existing Users

Although you may have been using QuickBooks for some time, you may not have used the Reconciliation feature before. The recommended process is as follows:

1. Begin with the first bank statement, and start reconciling each of the past bank statements as if you were reconciling your account upon receipt of each of the statements.

2. Follow this process for each subsequent statement until you have caught up to the current bank statement.

Correcting Errors in Reconciliation

Let's hope there will not be many times when you need QuickBooks to correct errors during the reconciliation process. However, when you can't find the amount displayed in the Difference field on your reconciliation screen, and you'd rather not search further for your error, you want QuickBooks to make an adjustment to balance your register with your bank statement.

This situation could occur in any reconciling process. You might need to make an adjustment of $90.00 to a check number in order to correct for your recording error. But if you had been careless in the reconciliation process, you might have missed the error when comparing your bank statement with your check register. In this case, your Uncleared Transaction List window would show a $90.00 difference after clearing all items. If you search for the difference and still can't find the amount, you can follow the next steps to have QuickBooks make the adjustment.

CAUTION: This process could have a serious impact on your future reports and check register; don't take this approach to adjusting the reconciliation difference lightly.

1. Press (Ctrl)-(F10), and the Problem: Check Register Does Not Balance With Bank Statement window appears, as shown in Figure 3-18. This time QuickBooks informs you that there's a $90.00 difference.

   At this point you can still return to the register and check for the difference by pressing the (Esc) key.

2. Press (Enter), and the Adding Balance Adjustment Entry window appears.

3. Type **Y** and press (Enter).

   You have told QuickBooks that you do not want to search any longer for the difference and you want an adjustment to be made.

Writing Checks and Maintaining Records

Check Register Does Not Balance With Bank Statement window
Figure 3-18.

```
Problem:   Check Register Does Not Balance With Bank Statement
There is a difference of $90.00.  Your register may have:
                 ■ too few payments marked cleared
                 ■ too many deposits marked cleared
                 ■ incorrect dollar amounts on some items

To find the difference compare the Summary below with your bank statement.
To return to the register to find and fix the problem, press Esc.
To have QuickBooks adjust for the difference, press ↵.
TIP: press F9 at the register to view the list of Uncleared items.

Esc-Cancel                       F1-Help                      ↵ Continue
```

The adjustment will be dated the current date and will be recorded as "Balance Adjustment." If you typed **N** QuickBooks would return you to the reconciliation screen and you would continue to search for the difference.

4. Press [Ctrl]-[L], select an account, then press [Enter] again. The Register Adjusted to Agree with Statement window appears telling you that *'s have been changed to X's.

   This indicates that QuickBooks has made a check register entry for the difference and that you are going to accept the Balance Adjustment description in the Payee row of the register. (You can always make a correction later if you find the error.) Otherwise, you could have used another description, such as "misc." or "expense/income."

5. Type **Y** and press [Enter].

CHAPTER

4

MAKING REGISTER ENTRIES

The register is the backbone of the QuickBooks system. You have already seen how it is used whenever you write a check with QuickBooks. Register entries allow you to maintain information on checking accounts, cash accounts, fixed assets, credit cards, and other liability accounts. With the register, you maintain current information for an account so you know the precise balance. You also keep a history of all the transactions affecting the balance. Since QuickBooks entries allow you to easily categorize information as you enter it, the capabilities of the QuickBooks register extend beyond the entries normally made in a checkbook register. These extra capabilities enhance the usefulness of the recorded information and facilitate report creation.

In this chapter you will learn to create and maintain a single account. This account will represent a checking account balance. You would use the techniques in this chapter anytime an event occurs which increases or decreases your checking account balance. The following are some of the events that might require a QuickBooks register entry:

- Writing a check manually
- Recording a deposit to an account
- Deducting an overdraft charge
- Deducting the cost of printing checks

Notice that writing a check with QuickBooks is not part of this list—QuickBooks makes this register entry for you automatically.

You will use the techniques you learn here repeatedly as you work with the other QuickBooks registers throughout this book. You will find that similar register entries are used whether you are recording depreciation expense or writing a check against your checking account.

Maintaining a Register

A QuickBooks register provides an organized record of all financial activity.

QuickBooks' register works much like the manual checking account register shown in Figure 4-1. Starting with the account balance at the beginning of the period, each check written is recorded as a separate entry, including the date, amount, payee, and check number. Additional information can be added to document the reason for the check. This information can be useful in the preparation of taxes or to verify that an invoice has been paid. As each check is entered, a new balance is computed. You have seen how QuickBooks records all this information for you if you record your checks on the Write Checks screen, but you will need to do it yourself for the checks that you write manually or your records will not be complete. Also, other bank charges, such as check printing, overdraft charges, and service fees, must be subtracted from the account balance. Deposits are recorded in

Making Register Entries

NUMBER	DATE	DESCRIPTION OF TRANSACTION	PAYMENT/DEBIT (-)	√T	FEE (IF ANY) (-)	DEPOSIT/CREDIT (+)	BALANCE
	1/1/93	Deposit for opening account	$		$	$ 5000 00	5000 00 5000 00
1001	1/5/93	Abbot Supply Pharmacuticals	1200 00				1200 00 3800 00
1002	1/6/93	McCarvey Insurance	500 00				500 00 3300 00
1003	1/6/93	Sally Clark	259 00				259 00 3041 00
	1/8/93	Deposit Office receipts				2200 00	2200 00 5241 00
1004	1/10/93	Standard Office Envelopes	80 00				80 00 5161 00

Manual checking account register Figure 4-1.

Using QuickBooks eliminates many of the computation mistakes possible in manual registers.

a similar fashion. Since interest earned on the account is often automatically credited to the account, it should be entered as it appears on the monthly bank statement. (QuickBooks cannot compute the interest earned on your account since there is no way for the package to know the dates checks clear at your bank, and this information is needed to compute the interest earned.)

Although it is easy to record entries in a manual check register, most people occasionally make mistakes in computing the new balance. Recording transactions in QuickBooks' register eliminates this problem. It also provides many other advantages, such as accounts for classifying each entry, reports that are easy to create, and a Search feature for quickly locating specific entries.

To display a QuickBooks check register you can select 1 Checkbook from the Main Menu. Next, choose 2 Check Register. QuickBooks displays the current account, if it is a checking account, or the register for the checking account used most recently, if you have another type of account open. Before entering any transactions in this register, check the bottom-left corner of the window where the account name is displayed to see if you have the correct checking account. If you do not have the correct account displayed, press Ctrl-A and select the account you want to work with.

Figure 4-2 shows the top of the register window with some transactions entered. QuickBooks has also automatically entered X in the C (cleared) field of the register, indicating the transactions that have cleared during the reconciliation process. If you switch to the register while you are still in the reconciliation process you will see an asterisk (*) rather than an X. The *'s are converted to X's when you complete the reconciliation.

QuickBooks marks cleared transactions with an X after you reconcile your checking account.

The area at the far right of the register window is the *scroll bar*. It has an arrow at the top and bottom and a scroll box inside it. As you enter more transactions, you can use a mouse with these screen elements to scroll through the register.

If you press Ctrl-End to move to the bottom of the register, the highlighted area below the last transaction is where the next transaction will be entered. Remember, a transaction is just a record of financial activity, such as a deposit or withdrawal (credit or debit). The

QuickBooks register with some entries
Figure 4-2.

DATE	NUM	♦PAYEE · MEMO · ♦ACCOUNT	PAYMENT	C	DEPOSIT	BALANCE
		BEGINNING				
1/01 1993		Opening Balance [Open Bal Equi→]		X	5,000 00	5,000 00
1/05 1993	1001	Abbott Supply Pharmaceuticals Supp:Medical	1,200 00	X		3,800 00
1/06 1993	1002	McCarvey Insurance Monthly premium Insur:Malpract	500 00	X		3,300 00
1/06 1993	1003	Sally Clark Paycheck for th→Payroll	259 00	X		3,041 00
1/08 1993		Deposit Memo: Office receipts ♦Acct Fees:Patients		X	2,200 00	5,241 00

1st City
Esc-Leave   Ctrl↵ Record   Ending Balance: $5,161.00

Making Register Entries

fields used are the same for all transactions, as seen in Figure 4-2. Table 4-1 provides a detailed description of each of these fields.

If a Project field does not appear in the register, you can turn project tracking on to display a Project field, as shown in Figure 4-3. To make the change, follow these steps:

1. Select 7 Set Up/Customize from the Main Menu.
2. Choose 4 Customize Current Company.
3. Choose 2 Options and set the Project tracking on option to Y.

Field	Description
Date	Transaction date. You can accept the current entry or type a new date.
Num	Check number for check transactions. Leave blank by pressing [Enter] for noncheck transactions.
Payee	Payee's name for check transactions. For ATM transactions, deposits, service fees, and so on; a description is entered here.
Payment	Payment or withdrawal amount. For deposits this field is left blank. It can be as large as $9,999,999.99.
C	Used in reconciliation for noting checks that have cleared.
Deposit	Deposit amount. For payments this field is left blank.
Balance	A running total or sum of all prior transactions.
Memo	Optional description for the transaction.
Account	Used to organize similar transactions. Depending on your settings, this may or may not be required.
Project	Optional category that only appears when project tracking is on. Lets you monitor costs by job or project.

Fields Used in Check Register Entries
Table 4-1.

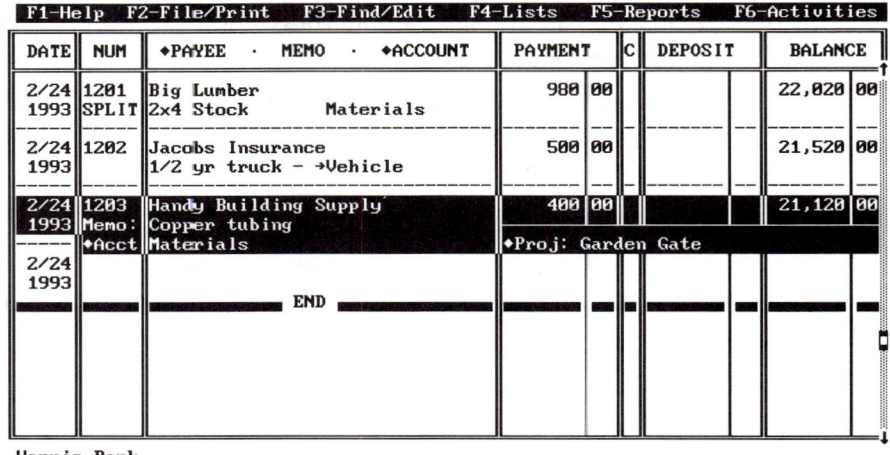

```
F1-Help   F2-File/Print   F3-Find/Edit   F4-Lists   F5-Reports   F6-Activities
```

DATE	NUM	♦PAYEE · MEMO · ♦ACCOUNT	PAYMENT	C	DEPOSIT	BALANCE
2/24 1993	1201 SPLIT	Big Lumber 2x4 Stock Materials	980 00			22,020 00
2/24 1993	1202	Jacobs Insurance 1/2 yr truck – →Vehicle	500 00			21,520 00
2/24 1993	1203 Memo: ♦Acct	Handy Building Supply Copper tubing Materials ♦Proj: Garden Gate	400 00			21,120 00
2/24 1993		END				

Harris Bank
Esc-Leave   Ctrl↵ Record   Ending Balance: $21,120.00

QuickBooks Register with project tracking on
Figure 4-3.

> **TIP:** If you are in construction, consulting, or any other business with many projects you will want to be certain to turn project tracking on.

As you make the entries for your transaction, notice that QuickBooks moves through the fields in a specific order. After entering data in a field, press [Enter] or [Tab], and the cursor automatically moves to the next field in which you can enter data. Some fields, such as Date and Payee, must have an entry in all transactions, and either the Payment or Deposit field requires an entry. Other fields are optional. If you do not need an entry in an optional field, just press [Enter] and the cursor moves to the next field. For example, you need a number in the check number (Num) field only when writing checks.

Recording Your Transactions in the Register

The highlighting is already positioned for your next transaction entry when you open the register window. If you have used the [↑] key to

Making Register Entries

move to another entry, press [Ctrl]-[End] to reposition the highlight properly. Don't worry if you make a mistake in recording your first transaction. You can always correct it by retyping the entry for the field.

> **NOTE:** When you type a day, followed by a slash, and a month, they are displayed on the first line of the Date field, and the cursor automatically moves to the second line of the column the second time you press the [/] key. Also note that even though you only enter **93**, QuickBooks displays the full year, 1993.

Using the [+] and [-] keys to change the date is the fastest approach when only a minor adjustment is necessary.

QuickBooks automatically records the date from the previous transaction unless it is the first transaction, in which case it records the current date. You can change the dates by moving the cursor to the Date field using [←], and pressing [+] or [-] to increase or decrease the current date. A light touch to the key alters the date by one day. Holding down these keys causes a rapid date change. If you use the [+] or [-] option to change the date, [Enter] or [Tab] is still required to move to the next field.

To place the check number in the Num field, type a number and press [Enter]. Type the payee, and press [Enter] to complete the entry for Payee for this check. There is a limit of 31 characters on the Payee line for each transaction. Notice that the cursor moves to the Payment field, where QuickBooks expects the next entry.

To record a check that you have written manually, or any other transaction that reduces the balance in your account, type an amount and press [Enter]. Since this is a check transaction, the amount should be placed in the Payment field. Notice that when you type the decimal, QuickBooks automatically moves to the cents column of the Payment field. Type a description on the Memo line and press [Enter]. You are limited to 31 characters on the Memo line. Press [Ctrl]-[L] to display a list of accounts, highlight the one you want, and press [Enter].

If the Require account on all transactions company option is set to Y, QuickBooks requires an account for every transaction before it will record the transaction. This option is set by selecting 7 Set Up/Customize, 4 Customize Current Company, and 2 Options. You can type the account yourself, but you must enter a valid chart of accounts entry or add your new entry to the chart of accounts. If you want to use an account that is not part of the chart of accounts, follow the steps in the next section to add an account as you record the transaction. Press `Ctrl`-`L` with the cursor in the Account field to display the chart of accounts.

If you have chosen to display a Project field, you can display a list of the projects currently defined. Just press `Ctrl`-`L` with the cursor in the Project field, and highlight the desired selection before pressing `Enter`.

Your transaction will look just like one of the check transactions that were already in the register, except it will not be marked as cleared.

Press `Enter` to complete the transaction data entry. QuickBooks displays the OK to Record Transaction? window. To confirm the recording of the transaction, select 1 Record Transaction. Your screen displays a new balance after the payment is recorded. If the entry has a date after the current date it is a postdated transaction. If there is even one postdated transaction, QuickBooks displays both Current Balance and Ending Balance at the bottom of the register window.

NOTE: You can also press `Ctrl`-`Enter` to record a transaction. You will not see the prompt message if you take this approach.

Adding Accounts as You Record a Transaction

Although you should try to do your chart of accounts maintenance before recording a transaction, sometimes you need to add an account while you are entering a transaction. It is easy to add an account that QuickBooks does not recognize. Follow these steps:

1. While in the transaction, type the new account name in the Account field and press `Tab` or `Enter`.

    QuickBooks displays an Account Not Found window, as shown in the following:

Making Register Entries

```
           Account Not Found
  1. Add to Chart Of Accounts List
▶ 2. Select from Chart Of Accounts List
  Esc-Cancel                    ⏎ Select
```

2. Select 1 Add to Chart Of Accounts List.
3. Select the account type by highlighting it in the Select Type of Account to Add window and pressing [Enter].
4. Type an optional description in the next window, if you want one, and press [Ctrl]-[Enter].
5. If project tracking is on, you can complete the project entry before completing the transaction. If it is off, the new account will be the last field in the transaction, and you need to choose 1 Record transaction from the OK to Record Transaction? window to proceed to the next blank transaction form.

Catching Up with Entries

When entering historical data, it is important to record accounts payable and accounts receivable in the appropriate register to minimize the required work.

If you start recording your transactions in QuickBooks at the beginning of the year, you do not have to worry about entering historical data from past accounting periods. If you start entering data in June, however, you will not be able to produce accurate reports unless you enter the data from the beginning of the year. You may consider entering summary transactions to save time if you are not concerned with all the detail. For example, if your debt payment is $600 per month, and you have not recorded this for the first five months of the year, you can make one $3,000 entry. What you will miss is the detail by month.

If you use accounts payable to pay bills and accounts receivable to record payments, get these registers up to date before working with the check register, since entries in these registers will generate some of the transactions in the check register.

Reviewing Register Entries

Reviewing transaction entries in the QuickBooks register is as easy as (and more versatile than) flipping through the pages of a manual register. You can scroll through the register to see all the recorded transactions or use the Find feature to search for a specific transaction. You can also focus on transactions for a specific time period with the Go to Date feature.

Scrolling Through the Register

When you have only a few transactions, the ↑ and ↓ keys are all you need to scroll through the register. Once you get all your data into QuickBooks, you need to learn some other keys and key combinations to move quickly through a register.

You can put some of the keys introduced in Chapter 2 to work in the QuickBooks register. You can probably guess the effects some of the keys will have from their names. The ↑ and ↓ keys move the highlighting up or down one transaction. QuickBooks scrolls information off the screen to show additional transactions not formerly in view on the screen. Once a transaction is highlighted, the → and ← keys move across it. The [Pg Up] and [Pg Dn] keys move up and down one screen of transactions at a time.

The [Home] key moves the cursor to the beginning of the current field in a transaction. When [Home] is pressed twice, the cursor moves to the beginning of the current transaction. If you press [Home] three times or press [Ctrl]-[Home], QuickBooks moves the cursor to the top of the register.

The [End] key moves the cursor to the end of the current field. If you press [End] twice, QuickBooks moves the cursor to the last field in the current transaction. If you press [End] three times or press [Ctrl]-[End], QuickBooks moves the cursor to the bottom of the register.

Pressing [Ctrl]-[Pg Up] moves the highlight to the beginning of the current month. Pressing it a second time moves the highlight to the beginning of the previous month. Pressing [Ctrl]-[Pg Dn] moves the highlight to the first transaction in the next month.

You can use the mouse rather than the keyboard to scroll in the register. The following mouse actions will help you quickly locate the place you want to be:

- ◆ Click the vertical scroll arrows to move to the first or last transaction
- ◆ Hold the mouse button down on the scroll bar to move quickly through the transactions
- ◆ Drag the scroll box up or down in the scroll bar to move to a different location

Making Register Entries

As you enter more transactions, the value of knowing quick ways to move between transactions will become apparent.

Using the Find Feature

QuickBooks' Find feature allows you to locate a specific transaction easily. You can find a transaction by entering a minimal amount of information from the transaction on a special Find window. Activate the Find window with the Quick Key, Ctrl-F, or press F3 to activate the Find/Edit menu and then select 1 Find. The Find window that displays is tailored to the type of register you are working in. Figure 4-4 shows the Find window for a checking account. The receivables, payables, and help Find windows look a little different, but work the same way.

QuickBooks can look for an entry in any specific field that contains the text you have entered with a forward or backward search. You can also use wildcards to locate a transaction when you want more flexible matching capabilities.

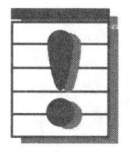

TIP: Payee, Memo, and Account all appear at the top of the Find window. The Payee is entered in the first line, with Memo and Account information entered on the lines that follow.

Transaction to Find window
Figure 4-4.

Finding Matching Entries

To look for a transaction that contains an entry for a specific field, all you need to do is fill in some data in the window. QuickBooks finds the first transaction that contains the entry you have typed. With the exception of the Date and Amount fields, the match does not have to be exact, as data before or after the matching text is automatically ignored. For example, if you enter **Jacobs** in the Payee field on the Find window,

```
                    Transaction to Find

     ┌────────┬──────────────────────────────────┬─────────┐
     │ NUMBER │ ◆PAYEE  ·  MEMO  ·  ◆ACCOUNT     │ AMOUNT  │
     ├────────┼──────────────────────────────────┼─────────┤
     │        │ Jacobs                           │▒▒▒▒▒▒▒▒▒│
     │  Memo: │                                  │▒▒▒▒▒▒▒▒▒│
     │ ◆Acct: │                                  │▒▒▒▒▒▒▒▒▒│
     │ ◆Proj: │                                  │▒▒▒▒▒▒▒▒▒│
     └────────┴──────────────────────────────────┴─────────┘
           Ctrl-↑ Find backward    Ctrl-↓ Find next
     Esc-Cancel              Ctrl-D Clear         Ctrl⏎ Done
```

QuickBooks locates entries for Harris & Jacobs, Ltd., Jacobs Company, or Paul Jacobs in the Payee field. A transaction with Jacobs Company in the Memo field would not be a match.

You can have QuickBooks search for entries in the Num, Payee, Memo, Category, Payment, Project, or Deposit field. You do not need to worry about capitalization of your data entry since QuickBooks is not case sensitive. When you enter the data for your first Find operation, the fields will be blank. For subsequent Find operations you can edit the data in the window, type over what's there, or clear the entire window by pressing `Ctrl`-`D` and begin again with blank fields.

You can conduct a complete forward search through the data by pressing `Ctrl`-`↓` after completing the entries in the Find window. QuickBooks also supports a backward search, with `Ctrl`-`↑`, to allow you to locate entries above the currently highlighted transaction. You can press these key combinations repeatedly to look for additional matches.

The more transactions in the register, the more useful QuickBooks' Find capability becomes. For instance, you might want to find all the transactions involving a specific payee or all the transactions on a certain date. Visually scanning through hundreds of transactions could take a long time, and you could still miss a matching transaction. QuickBooks makes no mistakes and finds the matching transactions quickly.

Using Wildcard Search Characters

QuickBooks allows you to type some special characters, referred to as *wildcard* characters, within the Find window. These characters affect the way that QuickBooks looks for a match. They either require an exact match, look for anything but the entry, or act like the blank tiles in a Scrabble game—they will accept any entry within a transaction at the position of the wildcard. The wildcard characters are as follows:

=	Requires an exact match with your entry
~	Matches with anything but your entry
?	Matches any character in a transaction at this location within the field
..	Allows characters other than what you have entered only in the position where this is typed. For example, **..Jacobs** allows something to precede Jacobs but not follow it; whereas **Jacobs..** allows text to follow Jacobs but not precede it.

To look for an exact match, you must precede your entry with an = (equal sign). To look for any account other than Rent you would type **~Rent** in the Account field on the Find window.

Searching for Multiple Entries

You can enter data in multiple fields in the Find window if you want to specify multiple criteria for locating transactions. You might make entries for the Date, Payee, and Memo fields all in one Find window. QuickBooks finds only transactions that match *all* of your entries. The Find window below shows multiple conditions:

```
                    Transaction to Find

   ┌────────┬──────────────────────────────────┬────────┐
   │ NUMBER │ ♦PAYEE  ·  MEMO  ·  ♦ACCOUNT     │ AMOUNT │
   ├────────┼──────────────────────────────────┼────────┤
   │        │ Smith                            │        │
   │  Memo: │ Construction..                   │        │
   │ ♦Acct: │ Mat                              │        │
   │ ♦Proj: │                                  │        │
   └────────┴──────────────────────────────────┴────────┘
          Ctrl-↑ Find backward   Ctrl-↓ Find next
    Esc-Cancel              Ctrl-D Clear         Ctrl-⏎ Done
```

Before a record can match with this, the following conditions must be met:

- The Payee name must contain "Smith"
- The Memo field must start with "Construction"
- The Account name must contain "Mat"

REMEMBER: You could also type **smith**, **construction**, or **mat**. QuickBooks is not case sensitive.

Using the Go to Date Feature

There are times when you may want to find one or more transactions for a given date. The Go to Date feature allows you to locate the first transaction entry for a specified date. You can use F3 to open the Find/Edit menu, then select 3 Go to Date.

When the Go to Date window opens, as shown here, fill in the date that you are searching for and press Enter:

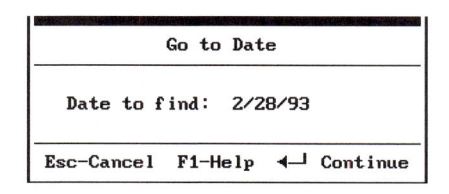

```
              Go to Date

    Date to find:  2/28/93

    Esc-Cancel  F1-Help  ←┘ Continue
```

A date search works a little differently than Find, since you do not have to be concerned with whether the date is before or after the current transaction. QuickBooks searches both forward and backward for the required date.

Revising Transactions

You can make revisions to transactions in the check register as you are recording a transaction, as well as to previously recorded transactions. It

Making Register Entries

To maintain a full and accurate history, void a transaction instead of deleting it.

is important to note that although QuickBooks allows you to modify previously recorded transactions, you cannot change the balance amount directly. This protects you from unauthorized changes in the register account balances. By forcing you to enter another transaction or change the amount of an existing transaction, QuickBooks is able to maintain a log of any changes to an account balance.

You may also find it necessary to void a previously written check, deposit, or any other adjustment to an account. Voiding removes the effect of the original transaction from the account balance, although it maintains the history of the original transaction and shows it as voided. To remove all trace of the original transaction, you must use QuickBooks' Delete Transaction command from the Find/Edit menu. You can use either Quick Keys or selections from QuickBooks' Find/Edit menu to void and delete transactions. To reinstate voided transactions, you delete the word "VOID" and the X in the C column (which was entered automatically) and press [Ctrl]-[Enter] to finalize the change.

Changing a Transaction

QuickBooks lets you change the current transaction whether or not you have already saved it. If it has been recorded, press [Ctrl]-[Enter] after making your changes to record the updated transaction.

You can move to a field that you want to change and type over an existing character to replace it, since QuickBooks' default mode is typeover. If you want to insert characters, press [Ins] before typing. You can use the [Backspace] or [Del] keys to remove characters that are not needed anymore.

QuickBooks does not allow you to change the balance amount directly. You need to enter another transaction to make an adjustment or alter the Amount field in an existing transaction. Another option is to void the original transaction and enter a new transaction.

REMEMBER: You must resave a transaction in order to replace the old copy with the new copy.

Voiding a Transaction

To quickly identify a voided transaction, look for an X in the C field of your register.

When you void a transaction, you undo the financial effect of the transaction. Using the Void feature creates an automatic audit trail (or record) of all transactions against an account, including those that are voided. Press Ctrl-V and select Void Transaction to void the current transaction. Another option is pressing F3 to open the Find/Edit menu. Select 6 Void Transaction from the menu. With either approach, the word "VOID" is now entered in front of the payee name, as shown in Figure 4-5. You must press Ctrl-End to record this change for the transaction.

Deleting a Transaction

You can delete a transaction with Ctrl-Del, or open the Find/Edit menu with F3 and select 5 Delete Transaction. QuickBooks displays the OK to Delete Transaction? window. Press Enter to confirm the deletion.

Reinstating a Transaction

There is no "undo" key to eliminate the effect of a delete; you must reenter the transaction. Avoid unnecessary work by confirming the

**Voided transaction
Figure 4-5.**

Making Register Entries

void or deletion before you complete it. For a voided transaction you can delete the word "VOID" in the Payee field and eliminate the X in the C field, then press `Ctrl`-`Enter` to reinstate it.

Reversing Transactions

Reversing a transaction requires another transaction entry that has the opposite effect of the first transaction.

There are times when you want to enter a transaction that reverses the effect of a transaction rather than voiding or deleting it. If a customer's check did not clear, you want a record of the initial deposit, but you also want to show a reduction in your balance for the amount of the check plus the bank's fee for depositing a check that did not clear. In this way the complete history of the transaction is recorded in your register.

If a customer's $1200 check was part of a recent deposit and you are notified that it did not clear the bank, record a payment to the bank for the amount of this check plus any charge the bank has added for processing this check. Your memo entry should indicate the reason for this problem. Later in this chapter you will learn about split transactions, which allow you to split the payment between the two accounts.

Using Projects

Projects are another way of organizing transactions. They allow you to define the who, when, or why of a transaction. It is important to understand that although they, too, allow you to group data, projects are distinct from accounts. You will continue to use accounts to provide specific information about the transactions to which they are assigned.

Accounts tell you what kind of income or expense a specific transaction represents. You can tell at a glance which costs are for utilities and which are for entertainment, for example. In summary reports, you might show transactions totaled by account. Projects allow you to slice the transaction pie in a different way, providing a different view or perspective of your data. For example, you can continue to organize data in accounts such as "Utilities" or "Paving," yet also classify it by the property, job, or department requiring the service.

Defining Projects

QuickBooks provides a completed chart of accounts but does not provide a standard list of projects. As with other company lists, you can set up what you need before you start making entries, or you can add the projects you need as you enter transactions. To assign a project while entering a transaction, type the project name in the Project field. QuickBooks will display a Project Not Found window. Choose 1 Add to Project List to display the Add New Project window, shown here:

```
                    Add New Project
    Name: Saunders
    Description (optional):

    Esc-Cancel                              Ctrl⏎ Done
```

Type an optional description for the project and press Ctrl-Enter. Select 1 Record transaction, and the transaction is finalized as the new project is added to the project list.

Entering Transactions with Subprojects

QuickBooks allows you to break down a project entry into subprojects. When you add to the project list using the 6 Company Lists feature from the Main Menu, QuickBooks will add a project at either the project or subproject level. You can use Move Left or Right commands to change the level of a project or subproject. If you have a project that has subprojects and want to assign a subproject to a transaction, you can pick it from the list that displays when you press Ctrl-L, or type the name of the project followed by a colon (:), followed by the name of the subproject.

Splitting Transactions

Splitting a transaction allows you to allocate the amount of a transaction among as many as 31 different accounts.

Split transactions are transactions that affect more than one account. You decide how a transaction affects each of the accounts or account/project combinations involved. If you split an expense transaction, you are saying that portions of the transaction should be considered as expenses in two different accounts or projects. For example, a purchase at a building supply store might include materials for two different client jobs. You need to know exactly how much was spent for each job in this transaction since you will be billing these materials to your clients. QuickBooks allows you to allocate the amount of any transaction among different accounts or projects with a special

Making Register Entries

Split Transaction window. Before using the Split Transaction feature, you can define accounts more precisely with the Subaccount feature, explained in the next section.

QuickBooks displays a Split Transaction window for entries in the Account field if you press Ctrl-S. You can enter different accounts or projects for each part of the transaction with this method, as shown in Figure 4-6. Even though the largest portion of the expense was for one client, part of the amount was for another customer and must be reflected in the transaction. QuickBooks displays the entire amount of the transaction in the Amount field but adjusts it as you make a new entry. Alternatively, you can leave the Amount field blank and QuickBooks will add all of the split amounts to get the total.

Using Subaccounts

Since you are quickly becoming proficient at basic transaction entry, you will want to see some other options for recording transactions. One new option is to create subaccounts of an existing account. These subaccounts further define an account. Unlike projects or subprojects, which use a different perspective for organizing transactions, subaccounts provide a more detailed breakdown of the existing

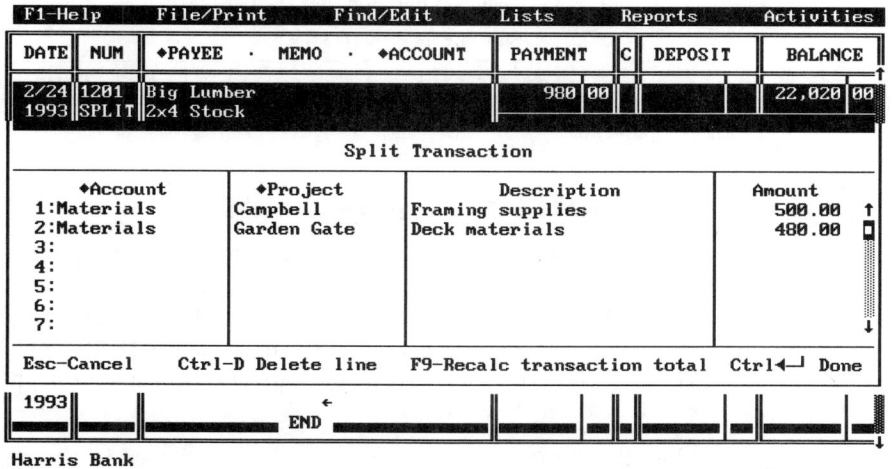

Split Transaction window
Figure 4-6.

account. For instance, the Utilities account could contain subaccounts that allow you to allocate expenses to electricity, water, or gas. You can then use project or subproject entries to classify these transactions by department or rental unit.

You can add the subaccounts by modifying the chart of accounts, as you do when you add new accounts, or you can create them as you enter transactions if you realize the existing account entries do not provide the breakdown you want.

Entering a New Subaccount

When you enter a subaccount for a transaction, type the account name, followed by a colon (:), and then the subaccount name. It is important that the account be specified first and the subaccount second. The transaction can still have a project assigned, if project tracking is on and you make an entry in the Project field.

If the subaccount does not currently exist, QuickBooks will display the Add New Expense Subaccount window for defining the subaccount, as shown here:

```
          Add New Expense Subaccount
   Name: Cable
   Description (optional): Cable TV
   Subacct of: Utilities
  Esc-Cancel                       Ctrl⏎ Done
```

Memorized Transactions

Many of your financial transactions are likely to repeat; you pay your utility bills each month, for instance. Likewise, courier charges, phone bills, payroll, and other bills are paid at about the same time each month. Cash inflows for some businesses are daily, weekly, or monthly. Other payments, such as supply purchases, also repeat, but perhaps not on the same dates each month.

QuickBooks can memorize transactions entered in the register or check writing screen. Once memorized, these transactions can be used to

Making Register Entries

generate identical transactions. Although amounts and dates may change, you can edit these fields and not have to reenter payee, memo, and account information.

Memorizing a Register Entry

Memorized transactions can be edited once they are recalled.

Any transaction in the account register can be memorized. Memorized transactions can be recalled for later use, printed, changed, and even deleted. You can elect to memorize as many transactions as you feel will repeat in the same relative time frame. QuickBooks memorizes split transactions in the same way as any other transaction. Carefully review the Split Transaction screen for amounts that change each month to reduce errors. To memorize a transaction follow these steps:

1. Highlight the transaction that you want to memorize.
2. Press Ctrl-M to request that QuickBooks memorize the transaction.
3. Press Enter to memorize the transaction.
4. Press Ctrl-Enter if the transaction is not as yet recorded in the register.
5. Press Ctrl-T to display the memorized transactions like the ones shown in Figure 4-7; your list should include the transaction that you just memorized.
6. Press Esc to return to the register.

QuickBooks maintains only one list of memorized transactions for each company. In Figure 4-7, each of the memorized transactions has the type, Pmt, since it was memorized from the register. Transactions memorized from the check writing window will have the type, Chk.

Using Memorized Transactions

To recall a memorized transaction and place it in the register, move to the next blank transaction record. If you recall a memorized transaction while a previously recorded transaction is highlighted, the existing transaction will be replaced by the memorized transaction. Press Ctrl-T to recall the Memorized Transaction List window. The next step is to select the transaction you want to add to the register and then press Enter. If you type the first letter of the payee name before pressing Ctrl-T, QuickBooks will take you to the correct area of the transaction list, since it is in alphabetical

```
           Standard Memorized Transaction List
         Name             Memo           Account      Type:Amt
    ▶ Jacobs Insurance   1/2 yr truck - Po  Vehicle       Pmt:    500
      Jacobs Insurance   Property and Casu  Insur:Prope   Pmt:    400

    Esc-Cancel              F7-Actions              Ctrl↵ Done
```

Standard Memorized Transaction List window
Figure 4-7.

order by payee. When it is added, the selected transaction appears with the date of the preceding transaction in the register, not the date on which it was last recorded. You can edit the transaction in the register and press [Ctrl]-[Enter] when you are ready to record the entry.

> **NOTE:** You can press [F4] to activate the Lists menu and then memorize or recall transactions, but the Quick Key approach saves time.

Changing and Deleting Memorized Transactions

To change a memorized transaction, you must first recall it from the memorized transaction list and place it into a blank transaction form in the register. Then make your changes and memorize it again. When you press [Ctrl]-[M] to memorize it again, QuickBooks asks if you want to replace the transaction memorized earlier or add a new transaction. If you confirm the replacement, QuickBooks makes the change.

To delete a memorized transaction, first open the transaction list by pressing [Ctrl]-[T]. Select the transaction you want to delete and press [Ctrl]-[Del]. A warning message appears asking you to confirm the deletion. When you press [Enter], the transaction is no longer memorized.

Making Register Entries

Memorizing a Check

The procedure for memorizing transactions while writing checks is identical to the one used to memorize register transactions. You must be in the check writing window when you begin, but otherwise it is the same. Check and register transactions for the same company will appear in the same memorized transaction list and can be edited, deleted, or recalled from either the check writing or account register window.

Working with Transaction Groups

A transaction group allows you to enter a group of transactions without having to type them in.

Although you can recall memorized transactions individually as a way to reenter similar transactions, a better method is to define several memorized transactions that occur at the same time as a *transaction group*. When you are ready to pay these transactions, you can have QuickBooks record the entire group for you automatically after you make any changes in amounts or other parts of the transaction entries. You can even have QuickBooks remind you when it is time to record these transactions again.

Defining a Transaction Group

QuickBooks allows you to set up many transaction groups. Defining a group is easy, but it requires several steps after memorizing all the transactions that will be placed in the group. You will need to describe the group, how often you want to schedule the group, the next scheduled date, and optionally, the account to be opened before the group is recalled. Finally, you will need to assign specific memorized transactions to the group. Although expense transactions are frequently used to create groups, you could include an entry for depositing retainers received at the same time each month.

When you press [Ctrl]-[J], QuickBooks displays a window, shown in Figure 4-8, that allows you to define the group. You can press [F7] to display the Actions menu, then choose 1 Add/New to display the Add New Standard Transaction Group window shown in Figure 4-9.

After you complete the window describing the new transaction group, press [Ctrl]-[Enter] to tell QuickBooks you are finished. QuickBooks displays a list of the memorized transactions. Use the [Spacebar] to mark the ones in the transaction group as "Include" before pressing `Ctrl`-`Enter`. Figure 4-10 shows two memorized transactions with both marked for inclusion.

You may want to define other transaction groups to include payroll, loan payments, and anything else that you pay at the beginning of the month.

You can also create transaction groups that generate checks for you. These groups contain transactions that are memorized from the check writing window. Remember that "Pmt" in the Type field indicates an account register transaction.

Changing a Transaction Group

You can add to a transaction group at any time after pressing `F4` to open the Lists menu, then choosing 4 Transaction Group. You can also press `Ctrl`-`J`. Highlight the group to be changed and press `Ctrl`-`E` to edit the group. As you proceed through the normal group definition procedure, you can select additional transactions for inclusion in the group.

To delete a transaction group, press `Ctrl`-`J` to display the list of transaction groups. Select the group you want to delete and press `Ctrl`-`Del`. QuickBooks eliminates the group but does not delete the memorized transactions that are part of it. It also does not affect any transactions recorded in the register by earlier executions of the transaction group.

Standard Transaction Group List window
Figure 4-8.

Making Register Entries

Add New Standard Transaction Group window
Figure 4-9.

```
┌─────────────────────────────────────────────────────────────┐
│            Add New Standard Transaction Group               │
│  Group name: Insurance                                      │
│  ◆Account to load before executing (optional): [Harris Bank]│
│  ◆Frequency: Twice a year                                   │
│  Next scheduled date: 8/28/93                               │
│                                                             │
│  Esc-Cancel                                    Ctrl⏎ Done   │
└─────────────────────────────────────────────────────────────┘
```

If you want to alter a transaction that is part of the transaction group, you will need to alter the memorized transaction. This means you have to recall the transaction on the check writing screen or in the account register, depending on the type of transaction you have. Next, you need to make your changes and memorize the transaction again. Follow the procedures in the "Changing and Deleting Memorized Transactions" section earlier in this chapter.

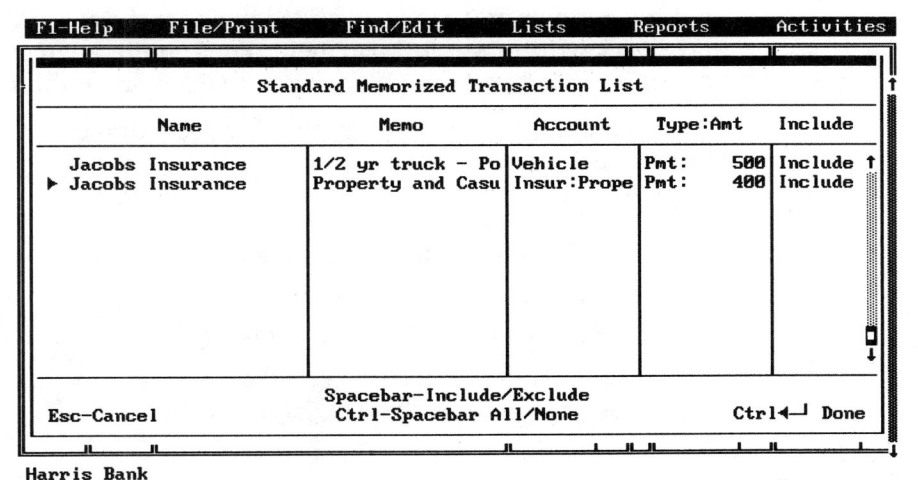

Memorized transactions marked for inclusion
Figure 4-10.

```
┌─ F1-Help    File/Print    Find/Edit    Lists    Reports    Activities ─┐
│              Standard Memorized Transaction List                        │
│   Name              Memo              Account       Type:Amt   Include  │
│                                                                         │
│  Jacobs Insurance   1/2 yr truck - Po Vehicle       Pmt:  500  Include  │
│► Jacobs Insurance   Property and Casu Insur:Prope   Pmt:  400  Include  │
│                                                                         │
│                                                                         │
│                     Spacebar-Include/Exclude                            │
│  Esc-Cancel         Ctrl-Spacebar All/None              Ctrl⏎ Done      │
└─────────────────────────────────────────────────────────────────────────┘
  Harris Bank
                                              Ending Balance:  $20,695.00
```

Having QuickBooks Remind You to Record Transactions

Bizminder, the utility that ships with QuickBooks, provides necessary reminders.

QuickBooks will remind you to enter upcoming transaction groups. The reminder will occur at the DOS prompt when you boot your system. If the default setting for Bizminder is still set at Yes, you will see a message at the DOS prompt reminding you to pay postdated checks or to record transaction groups. If you have turned Bizminder off, you can turn it on again by choosing 7 Set Up/Customize. Next, choose 5 Customize QuickBooks. Choose 1 Options, then change the Bizminder active option to Y. The prompt will not appear until you start QuickBooks again.

To change the frequency of the reminder press [F4] to open the Lists menu, then choose 4 Transaction Group. Make the changes you want in the Frequency field.

Recording a Transaction Group

Once you have defined a transaction group, you do not need to wait for the reminder to record the group in your register or check writing window. Since you can memorize entries for either the register or the check writing window, make sure you have the group correctly defined for your current needs. A group type of Chk is created in the check writing window and can be recorded in either the account register or the check writing window. Payment (Pmt) groups are recorded in the account register and can only be used to record account register entries.

To execute a transaction group from the account register, complete the following steps:

1. Press [F4] to activate the Lists menu.
2. Highlight the group you want to execute.
3. Change the date if desired and press [Enter].
4. Make any transaction changes that you want to make, pressing [Ctrl]-[Enter] to save each changed transaction.

CHAPTER

5

PREPARING BUDGET REPORTS

Operating a successful business involves more than having a good product or service to sell to customers or clients; you also need to develop a financial management program that will allow your business to grow and develop. Financial management is more than just being able to prepare the basic reports your banker or other creditors request; it includes a plan of action that will show your creditors you are prepared to manage your business in a changing environment. This means you should develop a program to manage the finances of your business. Your program could consist of the following:

- A business plan
- The development of strong business relations with your banker or other creditors
- The use of budgets and cash flow statements to help manage your financial resources

In order to develop a financial management program, you need a sound accounting system that provides the financial information you need to make better management decisions. QuickBooks can help you generate this type of information for your business. In this chapter you will learn how to put together a business plan and budget. In Chapter 11, you will learn how to project your cash flow.

Developing a Financial Management Program

If you look closely at the parts of the financial management program just listed, you will notice that two of the three parts do not directly involve the accounting system. Let's take a more in-depth look at the program components.

A business plan is a well-developed concept of where your business has been and where it is going. The special section entitled "Preparing a Business Plan" highlights the key points that should be covered in a business plan. You can see that nonfinancial considerations play a major role in your business plan—that is, you need to know your product and potential market before you can begin to budget sales and cost for your business. The budget process you learn in this chapter demonstrates how budgeting is done and how budget reports are prepared. More importantly, you will see that the decisions you make in estimating budget income and expenses often come from nonfinancial considerations. In short, developing a business plan forces you to think through your business, both financially and operationally, which, in the long run, will make it easier for you to estimate the expected sales and related costs.

Preparing Budget Reports

> ## Preparing a Business Plan
>
> If you have never prepared a business plan before, you might not know what to include. Your goal should be to create a concise document that presents a realistic picture of your company, including its needs, assets, and products. Outside lenders will be especially interested in the financial history and resources of the firm and your sales projections. Be sure to include the following as you prepare your plan:
>
> - A brief overview of your firm, its products, and its financing requirements. It is important to keep this short and simple.
>
> - A brief history of the firm, including product successes and copyrights or patents held. Include résumés of the firm's owners or partners.
>
> - A short description of your product(s). Include information on the competition, production plans, and prices.
>
> - A description of the market for the product(s) and your distribution plans.
>
> - Sales and cost projections showing current capital and financing requirements.

Don't underestimate the importance of developing strong relations with your banker and creditors. However, a word of caution: don't expect a bank to finance a new business for you. A good banker expects you to provide a significant part of the necessary capital. You might think that you wouldn't need the banker if you had the money to finance your ideas. But from the banker's perspective, it isn't good business to risk the bank's money if you aren't willing to invest your own capital. The special section entitled "Sources of Funding" shows some alternative ways of obtaining financing for your business if a bank is not a realistic source of cash. An important point to remember is that you need to maintain a strong relationship with your banker over the long term. Although you may not need a loan now, you could in the future. To help strengthen the relationship with your bank, you might obtain a modest bank loan when your business is prospering. Then when you really need a loan, your banker will already be familiar with you and your business activities. This could make the difference between loan approval or rejection.

The final part of the financial management program is the use of budgets and the regular monitoring of your cash flow. A budget is a plan in which you estimate the income and expenses of your business for a period of time: a week, month, quarter, year, or longer. Creating a budget report requires some advance work since you enter projected

Sources of Funding

It can be difficult to secure financing for a new business even if you have a good product. Banks are often wary of lending money for a new venture unless you are willing to take the high-risk position of offering your home or other assets as collateral. Some other financing options to consider are

- ◆ A commercial bank loan under the Small Business Administration Loan Guarantee Program
- ◆ Borrowing against your life insurance policy
- ◆ Short-term borrowing through supplier credit extensions
- ◆ Finance companies
- ◆ Venture capitalists (you must normally give up a part of the ownership of your business with this option)
- ◆ Small business investment enterprises
- ◆ Government sources, such as local small business advocacy offices and special programs for economically disadvantaged and minority groups

Budget Planning

Begin the budgeting process before you start making budget entries in QuickBooks. Start with an analysis of expected income. If your income flow is irregular, estimate on the low side. Remember to use only the net amount received from each income source. Do not include projected revenue increases until they are confirmed. You can look at "Analyzing Cash Flows" in Chapter 11 to see how QuickBooks can help you project your cash flows.

The next step is analyzing projected expenses. Consider debt repayment and other essentials such as medical insurance premiums and utilities first. In addition to monthly items, such as mortgage or equipment loan payments, consider irregular expenses that are paid only once or twice a year. Property tax, insurance premiums, and charitable donations are examples. Project these expenses for one year, then save toward these major expenses so that the entire amount does not need to come from a single month's revenue.

The next type of expense to plan into your budget is savings. By saving to make large purchases, you avoid the cost of credit. If you wait until you cover day-to-day expenses, it is too easy to find there is nothing left to save, and your business expansion must be delayed.

Finally, you must budget for the day-to-day expenses such as supplies, automobile costs (if your car is used for business), and other essential items.

Naturally, if your totals for expenses exceed income projection, you must reassess before entering projected amounts in QuickBooks.

During the first few months of budgeting, keep plenty of detailed notes. At the end of the month you will need to know exactly how your money was spent. You can make realistic adjustments between expense accounts to ensure that your budget stays in balance.

amounts for each category in the budget. QuickBooks guides you through the budget development process to minimize the work required. Then, you can enter your income and expenses and check the status of your actual and budgeted amounts whenever you wish. You can also use your budget figures to project the future cash flow of your business. This type of information is valuable in forecasting loans you may need, and demonstrates to your banker that you are anticipating your financial needs. It is a sign of sound business and financial planning.

In this chapter, you learn how to use QuickBooks in the preparation of a business budget. Remember the concepts discussed here; you are learning more than just the procedures involved. Budgeting analysis can give you and your creditors important information. QuickBooks provides the necessary ingredients to help you prepare a financial management program that will make you a better business manager.

QuickBooks' Budgeting Process

In popular opinion, a budget is a constraint on spending. But that is not what budgets are designed to be. Instead, a budget is a financial plan that shows the business's projected income and expenses to allow you to plan expenses within the limits of income. Although a budget may sometimes necessitate a temporary denial, this denial will supply the funds for business expenses that have a higher priority.

A budget is nothing more than a plan. It should allow you to chart a financial course for your business, given expected revenues and expenses.

QuickBooks allows you to enter projected income and expense levels for any category or subcategory. You can enter the same projection for each month of the year or choose to change the amount allocated by month. Royalties and dividends, for example, are two kinds of income received at the end of each quarter, so some months show a zero income in the account. Other income-generating activities are seasonal, and vary widely between months.

Once you have entered the budget amounts, QuickBooks matches your planned expenses with the actual expense entries and displays the results in a budget report. Although there is only one entry point for budget information, QuickBooks can collect the actual entries from all of the accounts in the current company.

QuickBooks can take much of the work out of entering and managing your budget, but it cannot prepare a budget without your projections. Once you have put together a plan, it is time to record your decisions

Preparing Budget Reports

in QuickBooks. You can enter the QuickBooks budgeting process through the Main Menu by selecting 5 Reports, or through the Reports menu from the Account Register or Write Checks window. This chapter presents QuickBooks' budgeting process in two stages: specifying budget amounts and entering the monthly detail, if required.

Specifying Budget Amounts

The Create Budget Report window is the starting place for the entry of budget amounts. It may seem a little strange to request a report when you have not yet specified your plan, but you must make this selection to enter QuickBooks' budgeting process. In fact, QuickBooks will not allow you to create a budget report until you have made your budget entries. From the Main Menu, select 5 Reports and then 7 Budget Report to access the Create Budget Report window, shown in the following illustration.

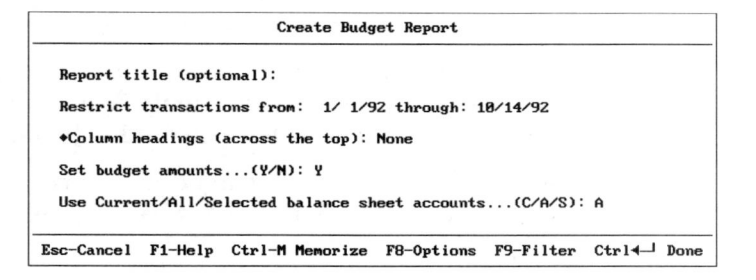

```
                    Create Budget Report

 Report title (optional):

 Restrict transactions from:   1/ 1/92 through: 10/14/92

 *Column headings (across the top): None

 Set budget amounts...(Y/N): Y

 Use Current/All/Selected balance sheet accounts...(C/A/S): A

 Esc-Cancel  F1-Help  Ctrl-M Memorize  F8-Options  F9-Filter  Ctrl⏎ Done
```

To proceed to the Specify Monthly Budget Amounts window, enter **Y** in the Set Budget Amounts field in this window, then press [Ctrl]-[Enter]. Figure 5-1 shows the Specify Monthly Budget Amounts window.

Consider these points before completing the budget entries:

✦ Enter a budget amount for each account you want included in your budget report.

✦ All the accounts in your company are accessible in the Specify Monthly Budget Amounts window. However, if you leave the budget amount blank for any account when completing this window, the account will not be shown on the budget report. If you want an account to be included because you will be using it later in

Set budget amounts in the Specify Monthly Budget Amounts window Figure 5-1.

```
                    Specify Monthly Budget Amounts
  Income/Expense                                      Budget      Varies
     Accounts          Type         Description       Amount     by Month

     Int Inc         Income     Interest Income
     Other Inc       Income     Other Income          200.00
     Prof Fees       Income     Professional Fees     150.00
     Reimb Exp       Income     Reimbursed Expenses
     Advert          Expense    Advertising         2,100.00
     Auto            Expense    Automobile Expenses    40.00
     Cash Disc       Expense    Cash Discounts
     Charges         Expense    Charges
       Bank          Expense    Bank Service Charge     7.00
       Fin           Expense    Finance Charge
     Contrib         Expense    Contributions          20.00
     Deprec Exp      Expense    Depreciation Expense

                           ↑,↓ Select
  Esc-Cancel     F1-Help   Ctrl-E Set/Edit Monthly Budgets    Ctrl⏎ Done

Kirk Enterprises (Checking)
```

the year, or in future years, type **0** (zero) in the Budget Amount field and it will be included in the current report.

◆ You only set monthly budget amounts once. QuickBooks assumes that the amounts established should be used as the budget amounts for all future months, unless you modify them.

◆ You can only assign budget amounts to income and expense accounts and subaccounts, not to balance sheet accounts.

To set the budget amounts in the Specify Monthly Budget Amounts window, highlight the account and type an amount. The accounts are listed in order, just as they are in the chart of accounts, with the income accounts coming first and then the expense accounts. Subaccounts are indented, but are marked as the same type of account as the parent, rather than as subaccounts.

TIP: When you find you are consistently over budget in a specific expense area, consider adding subaccounts to help you pinpoint the problem.

Preparing Budget Reports

When you are finished in the Specify Monthly Budget Amounts window, press Ctrl-Enter to create a budget report using those budget amounts and the settings you specified in the Create Budget Report window. If all you wanted to do was to establish your budget and not to create a budget report, you can press Esc until you are at the Main Menu again.

If you want to modify any of the amounts assigned in the Specify Monthly Budget Amounts window, simply highlight the correct account and type a new amount in place of the old. If you want to delete the amount completely, so that the account does not appear in the budget report, use the Del key to completely delete the amount in the Specify Monthly Budget Amounts window.

Entering Monthly Detail for Budget Categories

QuickBooks generates the same entry for each month in the budget year, using the amount you enter in the Specify Monthly Budget Amounts window. You can edit an entry to vary the amount each month. To do so, highlight the account you want to edit and press Ctrl-E to open the Monthly Budget For Account window, shown here:

```
        Monthly Budget For Account:   Int Inc
   Jan:
   Feb:
   Mar: 3,000.00
   Apr:
   May:
   Jun: 3,000.00
   Jul:
   Aug:
   Sep: 4,000.00
   Oct:
   Nov:
   Dec: 5,000.00

   Esc-Cancel    F9-Fill w/Amt      ←┘ Continue
```

Notice that the months appear down the left side of this window. Use the arrow keys to highlight the months you want to edit and then enter the new amounts. If you want the new amount used from the month where it was changed to the end of the budget year, press F9 Fill w/Amt. For example, if you change the amount in June to 275 and press F9, QuickBooks enters 275 in the remaining months of the year, as shown in Figure 5-2.

When you are finished in this window, press Ctrl-Enter to return to the Specify Monthly Budget Amounts window.

```
                    Specify Monthly Budget Amounts
        ┌─────────┬───────────────────────────────────────┬────────┐
        │Income/E │ Monthly Budget For Account: Other Inc │ Varies │
        │Accounts │                                       │by Month│
        │         │ Jan: 200.00                           │        │
        │ Int Inc │ Feb: 200.00                           │  Yes   │
        │Other Inc│ Mar: 200.00                           │   00   │
        │Prof Fees│ Apr: 200.00                           │   00   │
        │Reimb Exp│ May: 200.00                           │        │
        │ Advert  │ Jun: 275.00                           │   00   │
        │  Auto   │ Jul: 275.00                           │   00   │
        │Cash Disc│ Aug: 275.00                           │        │
        │ Charges │ Sep: 275.00                           │        │
        │  Bank   │ Oct: 275.00                           │   00   │
        │   Fin   │ Nov: 275.00                           │        │
        │ Contrib │ Dec: 275.00                           │   00   │
        │Deprec Exp│                                      │        │
        │         │ Esc-Cancel    F9-Fill w/Amt   ⏎ Continue│     │
        └─────────┴───────────────────────────────────────┴────────┘
        Kirk Enterprises (Checking)
```

Use F9 Fill w/Amt to repeat an amount through the end of the year
Figure 5-2.

> **TIP:** If you have a seasonal business, such as landscaping or construction, be sure to take the time to enter individually varying budget amounts. Otherwise, you, and everyone else that reviews budget reports, will become accustomed to ignoring variances, and you will not spot problems until too late.

Creating and Printing a Budget Report

Creating a standard budget report merely requires that you have created a budget at some point. Then you can open the Create Budget Report window by opening the Reports menu—either from the Main Menu or the Write Checks or Account Register window—and then selecting 7 Budget Report. Press Ctrl-Enter and the budget report is created. Many options are also available to modify the report to suit your particular needs.

> **TIP:** Distribute copies of the budget report to employees who can help you get expenses under control and monitor your progress.

Modifying a Budget Report

In the Create Budget Report window shown in Figure 5-3, several changes have been made. A new report title has been specified in order to customize the report and make its contents clearer to the reader.

The transactions to be used in the report are limited to those entered during the month of October. Monthly budget reports help you view ongoing compliance with your budget. However, at the end of fiscal quarters or years, you may want to print a quarterly or yearly budget in order to view the budget compliance for that time period. You can also specify transactions from a shorter time period than one month. By specifying the dates in these fields, you can tailor the length of time the budget report covers, even though all budget amounts are entered as monthly amounts. QuickBooks calculates the correct budget amount for the period specified and uses that amount to create the budget report.

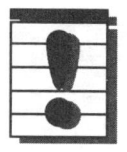

TIP: Change the column headings period to weekly if you think excess expenses might all be occurring at the same time in the month. This will help you analyze the situation.

```
                    Create Budget Report

   Report title (optional): Kirk Enterprise - October Budget Report

   Restrict transactions from: 10/ 1/93 through: 10/31/93

   *Column headings (across the top): None

   Set budget amounts...(Y/N): N

   Use Current/All/Selected balance sheet accounts...(C/A/S): A

   Esc-Cancel  F1-Help  Ctrl-M Memorize  F8-Options  F9-Filter  Ctrl⏎ Done
                              9. Memorized Reports

   Kirk Enterprises (Checking)
```

Changes made to the Create Budget Report window
Figure 5-3.

In the Column headings field you can specify the periods of time that appear across the top of the report by pressing `Ctrl-L` and selecting an item from the list. All budget amounts are subtotaled by these time periods. For example, you could create a quarterly budget with monthly column heads, so that the subtotals for each month appear, as well as totals for the quarter.

Typing **Y** in the Set budget amounts field causes the Specify Monthly Budget Amounts window to be opened after you have completed the Create Budget Report window. This allows you to specify the amounts budgeted, as discussed in the earlier section, "Specifying Budget Amounts." Enter C, A, or S in the Use Current/All/Selected balance sheet accounts field in order to use the current balance sheet account only (C), transactions from all balance sheet accounts (A), or selected balance sheet accounts (S), in the creation of the budget report.

If you want the values that appear in the budget report to be rounded to the nearest dollar (so that cents do not appear), press `F8`, which opens the Report Options window.

```
                        Report Options
      Round amounts to nearest dollar            (Y/N): N
      Esc-Cancel            Ctrl-D Reset         Ctrl-↵ Done
```

Enter **Y** in the Round amounts to nearest dollar field, then press `Ctrl-Enter`.

When you are finished with the Create Budget Report window, press `Ctrl-Enter` to create the budget report. Alternatively, you can first open the Filter Report Transactions window to further modify your budget report.

Filtering Transactions for Budget Reports

You can *filter* transactions—that is, choose which transactions are acknowledged in the report—by pressing `F9` Filter in the Create Budget Report window. You can filter transactions based on contents of the Payee, Memo, Project, Num, or Account fields in your company

Preparing Budget Reports

lists, by entering text from those fields in the appropriate field in the Filter Report Transactions window, shown in the following illustration:

```
                   Filter Report Transactions
    Restrict report to transactions meeting these criteria
        ◆Payee contains   :
         Memo contains    :
        ◆Account contains :
        ◆Project contains :
         Number contains  :

    Select Inc/Exp accounts to include... (Y/N): N
    Select projects to include... (Y/N): N

    Include only Below/Equal/Above (B/E/A):    the amount:

    Esc-Cancel              Ctrl-D Reset              Ctrl←⎦ Done
```

Enter text to be used as criteria in any of these fields, for all the transactions you want used. You can use the special characters shown in Table 5-1 to control the transactions used. As an example, if you use projects in QuickBooks, you might type "consult" on the Project contains line so the budget report only includes consulting project budget items.

If you want to select which accounts to include, type **Y** in the Select Inc/Exp accounts to include field. If you set this field to Y, when you press [Ctrl]-[Enter] to leave the Filter Report Transactions window, you see

Special Characters Used to Filter Transactions
Table 5-1.

Entry	QuickBooks Finds
electric	electric, Electric, ELECTRIC, Electric Company, Consumer Electric
=Electric	electric, Electric, ELECTRIC
~electric	Advert, Dues, Utilities (anything other than electric)
e..c	electric, eccentric
s?n	sun, sin, son (any single letter between an *s* and an *n*)
..	Advert, electric, and anything else except blanks
~..	All transactions in this field that are blank

the Income/Expense Account List window. Highlight an account and press the [Spacebar] to include or exclude the account.

```
                    Income/Expense Account
                    Company: Kirk Enterprises

      Account           Type          Description         Include

    Unspecified
  ► Int Inc            Income      Interest Income        Include
    Other Inc          Income      Other Income           Include
    Prof Fees          Income      Professional Fees      Include
    Reimb Exp          Income      Reimbursed Expenses    Include
    Advert             Expense     Advertising            Include
    Auto               Expense     Automobile Expenses    Include
    Cash Disc          Expense     Cash Discounts         Include
    Charges            Expense     Charges                Include
    Bank               Expense     Bank Service Charge    Include

                    Spacebar-Include/Exclude
    Esc-Cancel      Ctrl-Spacebar All/None              Ctrl↵ Done
```

If you wish to select the projects to include, type a **Y** in the Select projects to include field in the Filter Report Transactions window. Again, once you press [Ctrl]-[Enter] to exit this window, the Project List window will open, and you can use the [Spacebar] to select the projects to include. This is more effective, if you are choosing multiple projects, than entering text in the Project contains field since all of the projects selected will not need to include the same text.

You can also choose to include only those transactions that are below, equal to, or above a specified amount. Type **B**, **E**, or **A** in the Include only Below/Equal/Above field and then specify the amount in the next field. When you do this, only the transactions that fit the criteria are included in the budget report.

Settings are retained after the creation of a budget report. By pressing [Ctrl]-[D] you can reset all the fields in the window to their defaults. When you are finished with the Filter Report Transactions window, press [Ctrl]-[Enter]. If you so specified, the Income/Expense Account List or Project List windows may appear. If they do, select which accounts or projects to include in the budget report. If these windows do not appear, or after you exit these windows, you are returned to the Create Budget Report window. The last step in creating the budget report is to press [Ctrl]-[Enter].

Preparing Budget Reports

Report Discussion

Take a look at the report shown in Figure 5-4. It compares the actual expenditures made during the quarter with those budgeted. An analysis of the income section shows more income was received than was budgeted for the period. This was due to receiving more in consulting income than anticipated, although no income from articles was received. These differences could be examined to determine whether they were caused by failing to project all the consulting activities during the quarter or perhaps by a client paying earlier than expected.

The expense portion of the report shows the actual and budgeted expenses for the period. You can see that the report compares budgeted with actual expenses and shows the differences in the "Diff" column. In general, you should be concerned with all the differences in this report, but you would probably only want to spend time checking the large differences between budgeted and actual amounts. For example, you might decide to investigate only those budget differences that exceed $300. For these categories, you might want to examine the underlying transactions in more detail.

The essence of budgeting is to determine where potential problems exist in your business and detect them early. QuickBooks' budget reporting capabilities helps you make sound business decisions.

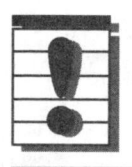

TIP: Consider implementing an incentive system for employees who develop cost-saving ideas or plans.

Wide-Screen Reports

The monthly budget report spreads across more than one QuickBooks screen, since it is wider than the screen width of 80 columns. It may be difficult to comprehend until you realize how it is structured. In this section, you explore the wide-screen report and become more familiar with QuickBooks results.

```
                    Kirk Enterprises - Budget Report
                        1/ 1/93 Through 3/31/93
Kirk Enterprises-All Accounts                                         Page 1
10/30/93
                                          1/ 1/93      -         3/31/93
              Inc/Exp Description         Actual      Budget        Diff
------------------------------------     -----------------------------------

INCOME/EXPENSE
  INCOME
     Inc Art-Article Income                   0.00      150.00      -150.00
     Inc Cons-Consulting Income           37,500.00   30,000.00    7,500.00
     Inc Roy-Royalty Income               10,000.00   10,000.00        0.00
                                          ----------  ----------  ----------
     TOTAL INCOME                         47,500.00   40,150.00    7,350.00

  EXPENSES
     Advert-Advertising                      120.00        0.00      120.00
     Del Overngt-Overnight Delivery          270.00      600.00     -330.00
     Equip Mnt-Equipment Maintenance       1,100.00      300.00      800.00
     Misc-Miscellaneous                        6.24       75.00      -68.76
     Payroll-Payroll Expense:
        Comp FICA-Payroll Taxes-FICA         930.00      930.00        0.00
        Comp MCARE-Payroll Taxes-MCARE       217.50      219.00       -1.50
        Gross-Gross Earnings              15,000.00   15,000.00        0.00
                                          ----------  ----------  ----------
        Total Payroll-Payroll Expense     16,147.50   16,149.00       -1.50
     Postage-Postage Expense                  28.25       30.00       -1.75
     Supp Comp-Computer Supplies             375.76      630.00     -254.24
     Supplies-Supplies                        65.00      150.00      -85.00
     Telephone-Telephone Expense             305.00      360.00      -55.00
     Travel-Travel Expenses                  905.00      900.00        5.00
     Utilities-Water, Gas, Electric:
        Electric-Electric Utilities          152.00       90.00       62.00
        Gas-Gas Utilities                     85.00       90.00       -5.00
                                          ----------  ----------  ----------
        Total Utilities-Water, Gas, Electric 237.00      180.00       57.00
                                          ----------  ----------  ----------
     TOTAL EXPENSES                       19,559.75   19,374.00      185.75
                                          ----------  ----------  ----------
TOTAL INCOME/EXPENSE                      27,940.25   20,776.00    7,164.25
                                          ==========  ==========  ==========
```

A QuickBooks budget report for Kirk Enterprises
Figure 5-4.

Use Tab to move one time period to the right and Shift-Tab to move one time period to the left in the report. Each time period has three columns, one for the actual amount, one for the budgeted amount, and

Preparing Budget Reports

one for the difference. The `→` and `←` move you one column to the right or left in the report. `Pg Up` and `Pg Dn` move one window up or down in the report. `Home` moves to the upper-left corner of the report, and `End` to the lower-right corner. You may want to generate a wide-screen report to accustom yourself to the appearance and practice navigating in it. Note that to open the Print Report window, you only have to press `Ctrl`-`P`. You can memorize this report for later use by pressing `Ctrl`-`M`.

If you have a compressed print option on your printer, that setting is recommended for printing wide reports. This option significantly increases the amount of material you can print on a page. When you print wide-screen reports, QuickBooks numbers the pages of the report so you can more easily follow on hard copy.

PART 2

MANAGING ACCOUNTS RECEIVABLE

CHAPTER

6 INVOICING CUSTOMERS

When your business sells its goods or services, you need to tell customers how much they owe. An invoice is the document for communicating this information. Besides telling your customers what they owe, the invoice also describes what they are paying for. An invoice can include additional information such as payment terms, reminders, or personalized notes. You will want to use QuickBooks for printing invoices rather than doing them by hand or typing them with a typewriter, since

QuickBooks provides so many shortcuts. These shortcuts are provided through the lists that you learned about in Chapter 2. In an invoice, you can use the customer list to automatically supply the customer's address. You can use the item list to correctly provide the spelling and price or rate. Also, the shipping methods and payment terms lists let you quickly enter the appropriate descriptions. Besides having all of these shortcuts available to you, creating your invoices in QuickBooks lets QuickBooks handle all of the arithmetic. You do not have to consult a tax table to calculate the correct sales tax; QuickBooks calculates it for you. QuickBooks also handles totaling the items and updating any account totals that affect the invoice by automatically adding to sales, sales tax, and accounts receivable totals when appropriate.

Printing the invoices you create with QuickBooks is just as easy. Using QuickBooks to print your invoices means that as soon as you create the invoice on the screen, you are ready to create a printed copy. You can print your invoices on blank paper, your own personalized letterhead, or one of the invoice forms you can order through Intuit. You can also use QuickBooks to print mailing labels that you can use for mailing the invoices you have printed or for mailing flyers to all of your customers.

Types of Invoices

Use the customize option to select the invoice style and format that best suits your needs.

QuickBooks has three types of invoices: service, professional, and product. The first time you try to create an invoice, the program prompts you for the type of invoice you want to create. You are not locked into a particular design, so if you later decide that you want to use a different invoice type, you can change the type and reprint your data with the new invoice style. Look at each type of invoice and decide which one fits your application.

✦ *Service* This invoice assumes you are selling services that are measured by time. You can also use this invoice type for retail applications. Figure 6-1 shows an example of a service invoice.

✦ *Professional* This invoice is for billing professional services. You might use this when you are billing for a flat rate service, such as a filling or a checkup by a dentist. Figure 6-2 shows an example of a professional invoice.

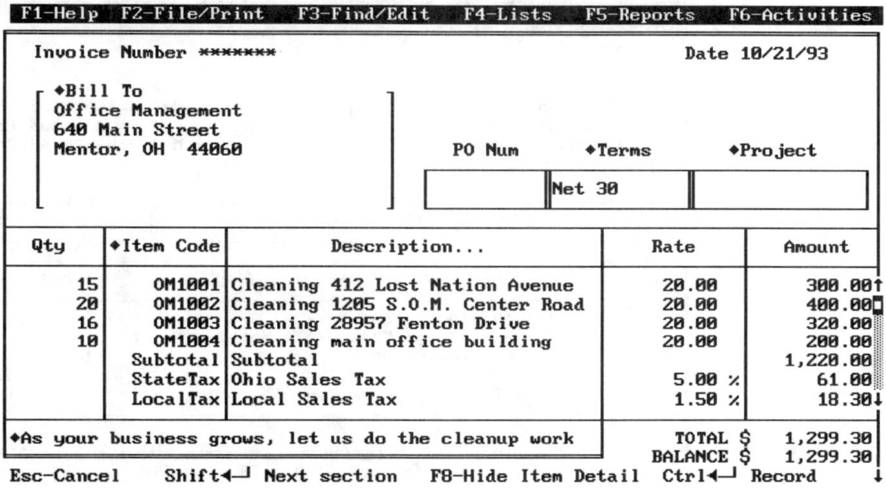

Invoicing Customers

```
F1-Help   F2-File/Print   F3-Find/Edit   F4-Lists   F5-Reports   F6-Activities
Invoice Number *******                                  Date 10/21/93
 ◆Bill To
 Office Management
 640 Main Street
 Mentor, OH  44060              PO Num      ◆Terms        ◆Project
                                            Net 30

 Qty    ◆Item Code      Description...         Rate         Amount
   15      OM1001   Cleaning 412 Lost Nation Avenue   20.00     300.00↑
   20      OM1002   Cleaning 1205 S.O.M. Center Road  20.00     400.00
   16      OM1003   Cleaning 28957 Fenton Drive       20.00     320.00
   10      OM1004   Cleaning main office building     20.00     200.00
           Subtotal Subtotal                                   1,220.00
           StateTax Ohio Sales Tax                5.00 %         61.00
           LocalTax Local Sales Tax               1.50 %         18.30↓
◆As your business grows, let us do the cleanup work    TOTAL $  1,299.30
                                                     BALANCE $  1,299.30
Esc-Cancel     Shift←⏎ Next section   F8-Hide Item Detail   Ctrl←⏎ Record   ↓
```

Service invoice
Figure 6-1.

✦ *Product* This invoice assumes that you are selling products. This invoice type has areas for shipping information. Figure 6-3 shows an example of a product invoice.

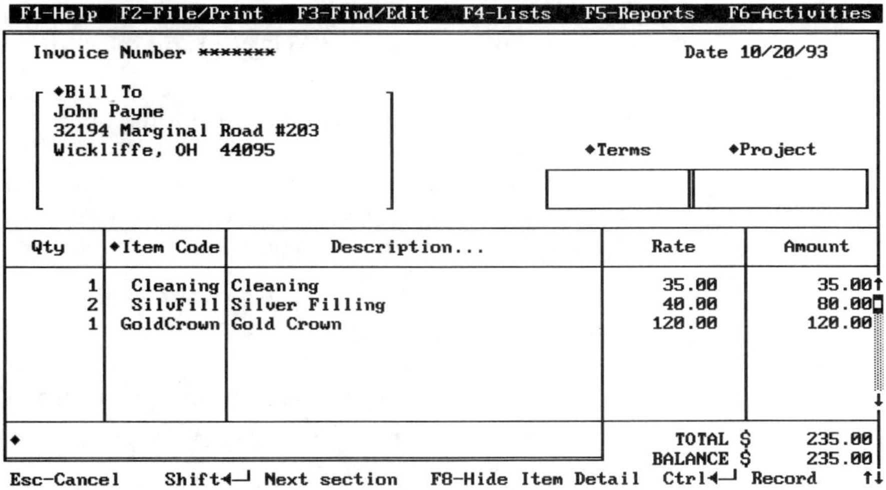

```
F1-Help   F2-File/Print   F3-Find/Edit   F4-Lists   F5-Reports   F6-Activities
Invoice Number *******                                  Date 10/20/93
 ◆Bill To
 John Payne
 32194 Marginal Road #203
 Wickliffe, OH  44095                       ◆Terms        ◆Project


 Qty    ◆Item Code      Description...         Rate         Amount
    1      Cleaning  Cleaning                     35.00       35.00↑
    2      SilvFill  Silver Filling               40.00       80.00
    1      GoldCrown Gold Crown                  120.00      120.00




 ◆                                                    TOTAL $   235.00
                                                    BALANCE $   235.00
Esc-Cancel     Shift←⏎ Next section   F8-Hide Item Detail   Ctrl←⏎ Record   ↑↓
```

Professional
invoice
Figure 6-2.

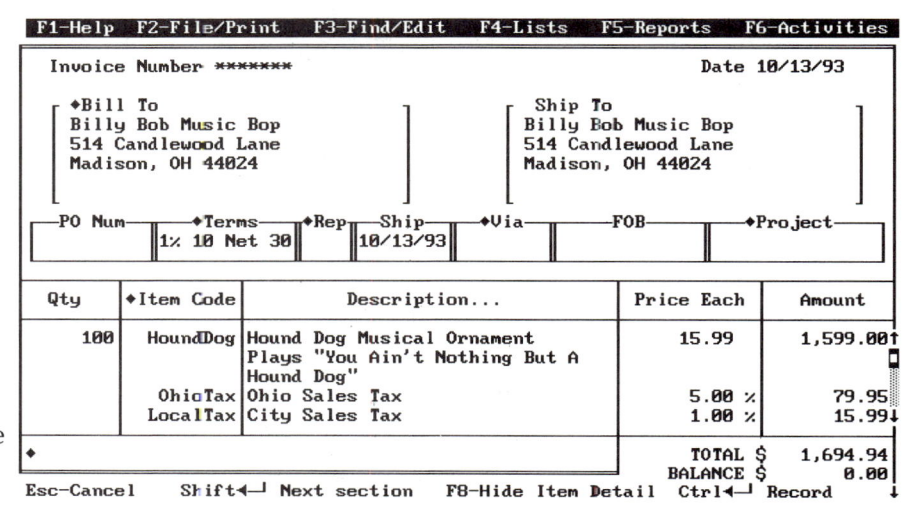

QuickBooks for Profit: Making the Numbers Work

```
F1-Help  F2-File/Print  F3-Find/Edit  F4-Lists  F5-Reports  F6-Activities
 Invoice Number *******                                  Date 10/13/93
 ┌─◆Bill To─────────────────┐ ┌─Ship To──────────────────┐
 │ Billy Bob Music Bop      │ │ Billy Bob Music Bop      │
 │ 514 Candlewood Lane      │ │ 514 Candlewood Lane      │
 │ Madison, OH 44024        │ │ Madison, OH 44024        │
 └──────────────────────────┘ └──────────────────────────┘

 ─PO Num──  ─◆Terms──── ◆Rep─ ─Ship──── ◆Via──  ─FOB──  ◆Project─
            1% 10 Net 30      10/13/93

   Qty     ◆Item Code      Description...        Price Each    Amount
    100    HoundDog    Hound Dog Musical Ornament    15.99     1,599.00↑
                       Plays "You Ain't Nothing But A
                       Hound Dog"
           OhioTax     Ohio Sales Tax                 5.00 %      79.95
           LocalTax    City Sales Tax                 1.00 %      15.99↓
 ◆                                                 TOTAL $    1,694.94
                                                   BALANCE $       0.00
 Esc-Cancel    Shift◄┘ Next section   F8-Hide Item Detail  Ctrl◄┘ Record
```

Product invoice
Figure 6-3.

The invoice type is set as one of the company's options. You can set the type of invoice your customer uses by following these steps:

1. Select 7 Set Up/Customize from the Main Menu.
2. Select 4 Customize Current Company.
3. Select 2 Options.
4. Type **Service**, **Professional**, or **Product** in response to the Invoice type option, or press Ctrl-L and select one of the invoice types.
5. Press Ctrl-Enter to finish choosing options.

If you try to create an invoice without selecting the invoice type, as soon as you try to display the screen to enter an invoice, QuickBooks prompts for the type of invoice you want.

Creating an Invoice

Creating an invoice is as simple as entering the information to appear in the invoice in the areas QuickBooks provides.

1. From the Main Menu, select 2 Invoicing/Receivables.

Invoicing Customers

Using the diamond fields speeds up invoice entries because you select entries from a list rather than typing them.

2. Select 1 Write/Print Invoices.

   QuickBooks displays an empty invoice screen. If you haven't selected an invoice type, you are prompted for one now. The cursor is in the Bill To section and all you have to do is fill it in. (The cursor starts in the Bill To section because the QuickBooks option, On new checks/invoices, start with the Payee/customer or Date field, is set to P for Payee/customer. You will see how to change this option later.)

   Notice how many of the fields in the invoice have a diamond. These are all fields that you can fill in by pressing `Ctrl`-`L` and selecting one of the listed items. Of course, you can always overwrite the information.

3. Enter the necessary invoice information.

4. Press `Ctrl`-`Enter` to finish recording the invoice and display the next empty invoice screen.

   Pressing `Ctrl`-`Enter` records the invoice and removes it from the screen for the next invoice. Pressing `Shift`-`Enter`, on the other hand, moves you to the next section of the invoice.

To see how easy it is to create an invoice, suppose you need to bill Billy Bob's Music Bop for 50 Big Bopper music boxes at $19.99 each. Assuming Billy Bob's Music Bop is already on your customer list, press `Ctrl`-`L` and select Billy Bob's Music Bop from the customer list. You don't need to supply the rest of the customer address, the shipping address, or the payment terms. QuickBooks enters this information for you. You also do not need to supply the date or invoice number. The date on the invoice is the current date. The invoice number now contains asterisks, but when you print the invoice, QuickBooks replaces the asterisks with the next unused number.

Next, enter the line item for the invoice. In the Qty column, type **50** (since it is more than the default of 1). Press `Ctrl`-`L` and select BigBop from the item list. QuickBooks fills the Item Code, Description, and Amount columns using the information already supplied for the BigBop item. QuickBooks also multiplies the quantity by the price per item and calculates the total. The completed invoice looks like Figure 6-4. At this point, you are ready to press `Ctrl`-`Enter` to finish the invoice and continue with the next one.

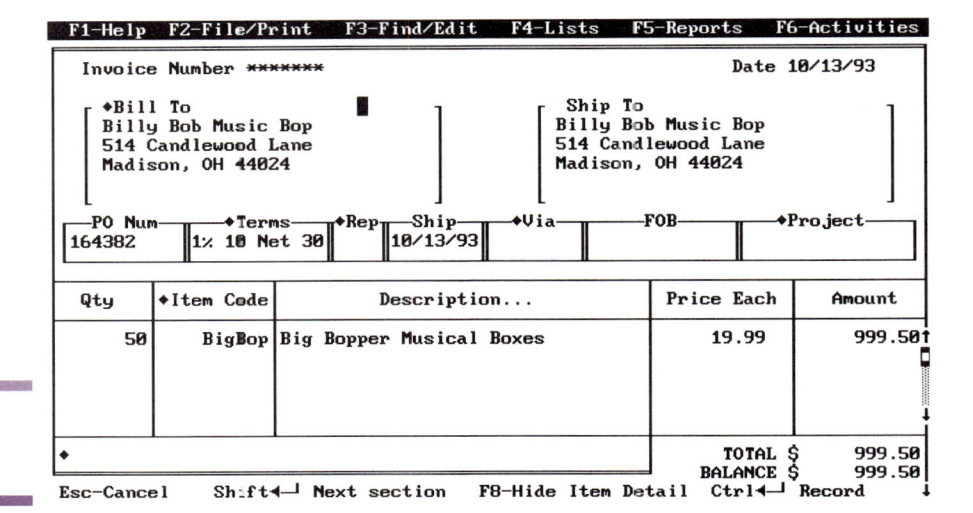

```
F1-Help  F2-File/Print   F3-Find/Edit    F4-Lists    F5-Reports   F6-Activities
```
```
 Invoice Number *******                                    Date 10/13/93
 ┌ ◆Bill To ─────────────────┐   ┌ Ship To ──────────────────┐
 │  Billy Bob Music Bop      │   │  Billy Bob Music Bop      │
 │  514 Candlewood Lane      │   │  514 Candlewood Lane      │
 │  Madison, OH 44024        │   │  Madison, OH 44024        │
 └───────────────────────────┘   └───────────────────────────┘

 ┌PO Num──┬─◆Terms─────┬◆Rep┬─Ship────┬◆Via──┬─FOB───┬◆Project─┐
 │164382  │1% 10 Net 30│    │10/13/93 │      │       │         │
 └────────┴────────────┴────┴─────────┴──────┴───────┴─────────┘

  Qty    ◆Item Code        Description...        Price Each    Amount

   50     BigBop    Big Bopper Musical Boxes        19.99        999.50


                                                    TOTAL  $    999.50
                                                    BALANCE $   999.50
  Esc-Cancel    Shift⏎ Next section   F8-Hide Item Detail   Ctrl⏎ Record
```

Completed invoice
Figure 6-4.

> **TIP:** If you do not see the Item Code column, press `F8`. Pressing `F8` switches the view of the invoice on the screen between the detail and printing views.

The Invoice Window

You can overwrite any of the information that appears in the different sections of the invoice. Simply move to the data you want to replace and type the new entry. You can move from one field to another by pressing `Tab` or `Enter`. You can move to the different sections by pressing `Shift`-`Enter`.

When you enter the Bill To information, if the customer is not already part of your customer list, you are prompted as follows:

Invoicing Customers

```
        Customer Not Found
 ▶ 1. Add to Customer List
   2. Select from Customer List
   3. One-Time Customer

 Esc-Cancel              ⏎ Select
```

You can select 1 Add to Customer List and then supply the customer's information just as if you are adding to the customer list any other way. Selecting 2 Select from Customer List lets you replace the entry you have made with another in the customer list. (Select this when QuickBooks does not recognize the customer name because you have made a typing error.) The third choice, 3 One-Time Customer, is for customers who are paying as they order the items. When you add this type of customer, the invoice must have a final total of 0 since QuickBooks is not setting up an account for this customer.

When you have a customer with the same shipping and billing information for a product invoice, you can type " in the Ship To section and QuickBooks repeats the Bill To information in the Ship To section. You can type the " to repeat the name and address when you are entering a customer or when you are entering an invoice.

Enter the customer's purchase order number in the PO Num field as a reminder for the customer of the order they sent. Payment terms are set by the customer's record. The shipping date is today's date. The Via field (shipping method) and the FOB field (the customer assumes responsibility for the goods) are initially set as part of the company information. Project can be filled in by selecting an applicable project.

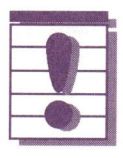

TIP: If you receive an order without a purchase order number, you might want to enter the order date in the PO Num field. This way you can use the Find command to search for the company name and a purchase order number of a specific date.

> **TIP:** Consider changing payment terms during slow periods to stimulate sales. But be sure that customers understand that this is a special promotion for sales during a specific period of time and not a permanent loosening of credit policies.

The bottom half of the invoice is where you enter the line items. You can add up to 30 line items on an invoice. Press the arrow keys or click the line to move to a line item you want to change or to a new line to add an item. Since you can add more line items to an invoice than can fit on the screen, the line item contents may partially scroll off the invoice to show the line items you are working with. The line item you are currently working on will be highlighted.

Press `Ctrl`-`L` to display the item list. The last column of the Item List window is Rate for service and professional invoices and Price for product invoices. When you select an item from this window, QuickBooks adds the rate or price to the invoice as well as the item code and description. You can quickly move to the first line item for a specific type by pressing `Tab`. These items are arranged alphabetically by type so you can quickly find the one you want. You can add and remove lines by pressing `F3` for the Find/Edit menu and choosing 9 Insert Line Item or A Delete Line Item. (As shortcuts, you can press `Ctrl`-`I` or `Ctrl`-`D`.) When you want to replace one line item with another, press `Ctrl`-`L` and select another line item to replace the one in the current line.

Most of the entries that appear in an invoice are not required. As the music box example shows, you only need to enter the fields you want the invoice to contain.

To finish recording an invoice, you press `Ctrl`-`Enter`, or, after entering text in the memo field (discussed next), you can press `Enter` and then select 1 Record. If you select 2 Do not Record, the invoice will not be recorded and you will remain on the invoice screen.

> **TIP:** Put all of your items in the item list. This way you consistently present the same items, and your invoice has a more professional appearance because of reduced typing errors. You can enter a line item on an invoice that is not on the list by typing the information directly.

Invoicing Customers

However, it is best to save adding an item this way for rare purchases of items you normally do not sell.

Invoice Memos

There is a memo field in the lower-left corner of the invoice where you can provide informative text that will appear at the bottom of the invoice. You can use this area to let the customer know who and where to call if they have a question about the invoice, for example. Select any item from the invoice memo list or type your own entry. This area is often used for payment reminders, thanking your customers for their patronage, or other small reminders. The area can contain up to 2 lines of 50 characters each, even though you only see a small section of the entry. When you print the invoice, the entire text will appear.

Invoice Date

The quickest way to change the date by a day or two is to use the [+] or [-] keys.

The date that appears at the top of the invoice initially contains today's date because QuickBooks assumes you are sending out your invoices as you create them. You can replace the date with another date by moving to the part of the date you want to replace and typing the new entry. A shortcut is to press the [+] and [-] keys, which increases or decreases the date by one. (Pressing [=] has the same effect as [+] since they are on the same key.)

If you want to start the invoice screen with the cursor on the invoice's Date field instead of the Bill To field, follow these steps:

1. Select 7 Set Up/Customize from the Main Menu.
2. Select 5 Customize QuickBooks.
3. Select 1 Options.
4. Type **D** for the option, On new checks/invoices, start with the Payee/customer field or Date field.
5. Press [Ctrl]-[Enter] to finish choosing options.

You can return to having QuickBooks start invoices with the Bill To field by repeating the preceding steps and typing **P** in step 4.

Transactions Created By an Invoice

When you enter an invoice, QuickBooks creates transactions that represent the information you have entered in the invoice. The transactions made depend on the information entered in the invoice.

You can focus on the invoice you need—all the accounting entries you need are automatically generated by QuickBooks.

In most cases, recording an invoice creates a transaction to set up an accounts receivable for this customer for the total of the invoice. For the Billy Bob Music Bop invoice in Figure 6-4, for example, QuickBooks sets up an account for Billy Bob Music Bop which tells you that he owes your company $999.50. Also, most of the items are connected to another account. For the Billy Bob Music Bop invoice, you also have sales of $999.50. Other items in the item list will create their own transactions. When an invoice includes sales tax, recording the invoice adds a payable to the governmental agency for the amount of sales tax collected.

When you create an item in the item list, you select the account to be affected. This account is the one that is increased or decreased every time you use that item in an invoice.

Line Items in the Item List

You have already learned the basics about lists in Chapter 2, but you will want to learn more about the items/parts/services list to use QuickBooks effectively in creating invoices. In Figure 6-4, the invoice has only one line item. Most invoices have other types of line items that are not necessarily the products you sell and the services you render. For example, you may want a subtotal or calculation of sales tax. These are line items that appear in the item list, although you may not think of them as items because they do not appear as part of your inventory. Think of every line you want to see in the invoice as a separate line item. Each entry in the item section is a separate item you will want in the list. This includes taxes, discounts, markups, refunds, markdowns, and subtotals. Certain line items *must* be part of the item list; these include subtotals, refunds, payments, and sales tax.

Besides pressing [F7] for the Actions menu and selecting 1 Add New or pressing [Ctrl]-[Ins], you can also add line items by typing the item code. When you try moving to the Description field, after typing an undefined item code, QuickBooks prompts whether you want to add

Invoicing Customers

the item to the item list. You can subsequently select 1 Add to Item List and the line item type, to add the line item. When you finish creating the line item, it is added to the invoice as well as to the item list. The item codes are required as a default so every line item has an item code. This requirement does not prevent a line item from using more than one line for the description, since the subsequent lines for the item contain the continued description but do not have amounts or quantities. You can change the default of requiring codes if you do not want to be able to separately list the sales by items. To change the default, follow these steps:

1. Select 7 Set Up/Customize from the Main Menu.
2. Select 4 Customize Current Company.
3. Select 2 Options.
4. Type **N** for 3 Require item codes on invoice line items.
5. Press Ctrl-Enter to finish choosing options.

You can return to the default of requiring item codes by changing the N you have typed to Y in step 4.

Several of the line item types use percentages. For example, a discount or sales tax may be applied as five percent of the item's cost. When you enter these items, instead of entering a price, you type the percentage amount. So, for the discount percentage, you would type **5%** as the discount's price. An example of a percentage line item looks like this:

Qty	♦Item Code	Description...	Price Each	Amount
5,000	BigBop	Big Bopper Musical Boxes	19.99	99,950.00↑
	Volume	Volume Discount	-5.00 %	-4,997.50
	Subtotal	Taxable Subtotal		94,952.50
	OhioTax	Ohio Sales Tax	5.00 %	4,747.63
	LocalTax	City Sales Tax	1.00 %	949.53↓
♦			TOTAL $	100,649.66
			BALANCE $	100,649.66

"Volume Discount" is five percent of the amount above it (percentage-priced line items are calculated on the prior line item). You may need to use a subtotal line item, as shown in the preceding illustration, to sum the items when you want the percentage to apply to a group of items. The line items in the illustration have a subtotal, so the sales tax is calculated as the percentage of the difference between the product's cost and the discount. When one percentage line item follows another, the subsequent line item uses the line item amount of the last item that is not calculated as a percentage. This means that both the state sales tax and the local sales tax line items in the example calculate their percentages based on the subtotal. The local sales tax will not use the $4747.63 sales tax because this is a percentage calculation.

Tip: When you start using QuickBooks to create invoices, you will want to add most of the items in the invoice as new items for the items/parts/services list. Initially this list is empty, but as you add more items, the invoices you subsequently enter will be completed faster as you build the list of the items you want in the list.

Other Charges Line Items

Some of the items you include on your invoice are for billings that are indirectly related to the products or services you are providing. Use an "other charges" line item for these purposes. This item type can be for fees for bounced checks or shipping charges, for example. QuickBooks has a charge item already created for you—the "Bal Forwd" line item. This is for entering the balance the customer owes from previous invoices. Use this line item when you start using QuickBooks to add the amounts your customers still owe you, without entering every invoice. Initially the amount is zero but when you replace the zero with the amount the customer currently owes, QuickBooks sets up an account for the customer.

Special line items let you create an invoice to meet almost every need, from offering discounts to showing a previous balance.

Discount Line Items

Your company may offer a variety of discounts that vary by occasion. You may have sale discount percentages, volume percentages, or special rebates. Adding a discount line item is like adding line items for parts and services. The only tricky part you will find is the account you want to record the discount. To decide which account to use, decide the purpose of the discount. If the discount is one to reduce the sales price, the discount belongs to the same sales account as the one for the part or service the discount applies to. You may also want to record a discount in an expense account.

Sales Tax Line Items

The items you sell may be subject to sales taxes. States and local municipalities determine the sales tax rates and which goods and services are taxed. QuickBooks would be incomplete if it did not let you add sales taxes as an item. Fortunately, if you add sales taxes as an item, QuickBooks calculates them for you. To add sales taxes, select 5 Sales Tax for the item type when you add a new item to the item list. From the Add New Sales Tax Item window, you can enter the tax rate, the tax district that collects the tax, the agency you must pay the sales tax to, and the description for the invoice.

When you add sales taxes to your invoices, QuickBooks keeps track of what you owe each of the governmental agencies. Since QuickBooks does this in the background, you can continue adding invoices, knowing that QuickBooks is calculating the sales tax and keeping a running total of the amount you owe. If you are charging sales tax, you may also want to add a subtotal item that totals the charges before taxes. When you have taxable and nontaxable items, you will want to subtotal them separately. An example of line items in an invoice for separating taxable and nontaxable items might look like Figure 6-5. The taxable items are listed as a group and the sales tax is calculated on the subtotal.

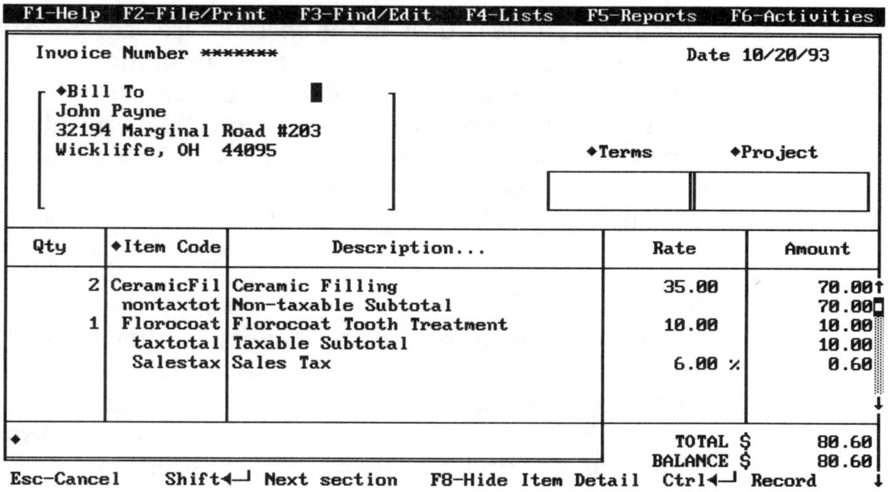

Invoice with subtotals and taxes
Figure 6-5.

TIP: Sales taxes are often charged by a combination of municipalities. For example, you might have a sales tax rate of 6.5 percent of which the state gets 5 percent, the county gets 1 percent, and the city gets .5 percent. You can use QuickBooks to break out the different sales taxes to keep track of what you owe each governmental agency.

Payment Line Items

Payment items are for deposits and prepayments for your goods or services. The amount of the prepayment item reduces the amount of the invoice. An example of a payment item is the payment line item shown here:

Qty	Item Code	Description...	Price Each	Amount
	BigBcp	Big Bopper Musical Boxes	19.99	19.99†
	Paymert	Payment received to date	-19.99	-19.99
			TOTAL $	19.99
			BALANCE $	0.00

This invoice is created when the check is received. Since this customer is not someone who will purchase again from the company and they have no outstanding balance, QuickBooks does not need to set up an account for this one-time customer. QuickBooks has also set up a deposit for you for the amount of payment. When you try to leave QuickBooks or switch to another company, QuickBooks displays a warning that you have a receivable to deposit.

Refund Line Items

While most of your invoice line items are for items you are charging a customer, your invoices may also have refunds—for returns or an overcharge, for example. When an invoice includes a refund item, the amount of the line item is negative. Also, including a refund in an invoice adds a check for the customer to the list of prepared checks

Invoicing Customers

QuickBooks creates for you. Refund line items always assume a check will be written, so reductions in the bill that are not refunded should be discount line items or negative amounts for part, service, or other charges line items.

Subtotal Line Items

Use a discount or negative amount to do the total bill and use a refund when you will write a refund check.

The line items can also total the other line items in an invoice. A subtotal line item adds all of the line items from the previous item to the beginning of the invoice or the previous subtotal. The only exception is when the subtotal item is below another subtotal. When two subtotals are right after one another, the second subtotal totals all other subtotal items. All subtotal line items provide the same function, but you can use different subtotal items to provide different text in the Description column of your item list.

Since line items that use percentages use the prior number, when you are calculating a discount, refund (percentage-based), or sales tax for more than one item, you will want to sum the values before you calculate the total. This means if you charge sales tax, you probably have a taxable total or subtotal line item just for this purpose. If your invoices have items that are taxable as well as nontaxable, separate the items into groups to calculate a subtotal for the taxable items and one for the nontaxable items. Figure 6-5 shows an invoice that uses several subtotals that separate the taxable and nontaxable amounts.

Special Checks Made While Entering an Invoice

QuickBooks does a lot of behind-the-scenes checking as you enter an invoice. You may have noticed some of it when you selected a customer and the customer's address was supplied. QuickBooks also checks whether the customer is beyond their credit limit, has other overdue invoices, and whether you have already used the invoice number.

When you record an invoice by pressing `Ctrl`-`Enter`, QuickBooks compares the customer's credit limit with the sum of the current invoice and any other unpaid balances the customer has. When the invoice you are recording would put the customer over their credit limit, QuickBooks displays a warning, like the following:

```
         W A R N I N G
 This customer's credit limit is $2,000.00.
 Recording this invoice will bring his
 outstanding balance to $2,714.43 which
 would exceed his credit limit by $714.43.

 Record this invoice anyway (Y/N)? N
Esc-Cancel                          ↵ Continue
```

From this point, you can type **Y** to continue recording the invoice or **N** to cancel recording the invoice. Then press [Enter]. When a customer is over the credit limit, the next time you try entering another invoice for the same customer, QuickBooks displays another message reminding you of their current credit limit and prompts for whether you want to cancel the invoice. You can type **Y** to cancel recording the invoice or **N** to continue recording the invoice, and then press [Enter].

When you are recording an invoice, QuickBooks also performs a check on whether the customer has overdue invoices. The due date of the invoice is set by the payment term. When you try entering an invoice for a customer that has overdue invoices, QuickBooks displays a message to tell you that the customer has an overdue invoice. At this point, you can type **Y** to continue recording the invoice or **N** to cancel recording the invoice, and then press [Enter].

TIP: It is easy to continue to extend credit with QuickBooks, but you need to watch customers that consistently exceed their credit. These customers may be slow in paying, which disrupts your own company's cash flow and ability to pay bills. Also, these customers may be having financial problems that you do not want resolved through a bankruptcy court.

QuickBooks handles numbering invoices that you print. While you can supply the invoice number yourself, using QuickBooks makes sure that you never duplicate an invoice number. Sometimes, you will want to supply the invoice number. Anytime you supply an invoice number, QuickBooks checks that the number is unique. If the invoice number

Invoicing Customers

you type has already been used, you are prompted to confirm that you want to reuse the same number. You can type **Y** to continue recording the invoice or **N** to cancel recording the invoice; then press `Enter`. Usually, you will not want to use the same number twice. QuickBooks provides other features that let you reprint an invoice you have already created.

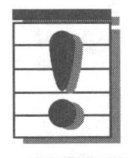

> **TIP:** Use consecutive numbers for invoices so you know that you are not missing any.

Entering an Invoice You Have Already Sent Out

When you first start using QuickBooks, you need to make a decision about historical data. You either compute a current customer balance and enter it or enter all open invoices.

Sometimes you will have invoices that you have not created through QuickBooks. Rather than keeping this invoice out of the system, enter this invoice so it is part of your company's records and can be printed if you ever need a copy. Entering the invoice ensures that the customer's balance is correct and that you have your sales entered. Enter an invoice you have already sent out as if you planned to send it. The only difference is in how the invoice number is treated: press the `Spacebar` to remove the * and leave it empty, or replace the * with the number of the invoice you have sent. This step tells QuickBooks that you do not want to print the invoice. Since you have provided an invoice number, QuickBooks knows not to repeat the number again when you print the invoices, and QuickBooks supplies the next unused invoice number.

If you are converting from another system to QuickBooks, you need to decide whether you want to enter only the amounts your customers currently owe or all of the invoices that you have written (although probably only for the current year). Entering this past data lets QuickBooks update its records for how much your customers currently owe your company. Now, when you look at your receivables, they include all of the customers' balances. When you want to include only their current balances, create an invoice that includes the Bal Forwd line item and change the amount from zero to the amount they currently owe. If you add all of the invoices for the customers with balances still due, such as when you want to be able to use QuickBooks to look at the detail of the invoices that they still owe, add the invoices as well as the payments they have made to date.

Reviewing Completed Invoices

After you record invoices, you can go back and review them. Select 2 Invoicing/Receivables from the Main Menu and 1 Write/Print Invoices, to return to the last invoice that appeared in the window. As you review your invoices, you may discover errors. How you fix them depends on whether you have sent the invoice to the customer. You can memorize parts of invoices when you want to repeat them in other invoices. You can also delete invoices that you have recorded. When you are reviewing past invoices, you may also need to create credit memos for incorrect sales.

Fixing Invoice Errors

When you discover a mistake in an invoice, the way you fix it depends on whether you have sent the customer the incorrect invoice. If you have not sent the invoice, you can go to the invoice and make the corrections. Like making entries in other locations, fixing an invoice means moving to where you want to make a change and typing the new entry. Press [Ins] to switch between *adding* the characters you type to the entry and *replacing* the characters already in the entry. When you make a change that affects the amounts in the invoice, the total for the line is not recalculated until you move to another column. The total of the invoice is not updated until you move to another line. Changing a line item in the invoice does not change the information for the line item in the item list. When the invoice is corrected, press [Ctrl]-[Enter]. If you leave the invoices window, you can select 1 Record changes to finish the invoice you have modified.

TIP: If you are making corrections to an invoice that you have printed but haven't sent to the customer, make sure you destroy the incorrect printed copy of the invoice.

Invoicing Customers

If you have sent an incorrect invoice to the customer, you have two choices. You can send the customer a corrected invoice. (Clearly mark the invoice as corrected, so the customer is not annoyed at receiving two bills for one set of goods or services.) The better choice is to send the customer a credit memo that corrects the error in the invoice they already have. Figure 6-6 shows an invoice correcting the previous one, which had the wrong quantity. When the customer receives this invoice, he or she will know that you are correcting the error from the first invoice. The second invoice is entered just like the other invoices you have entered.

Memorized Invoices

In Chapter 4, you learned about memorizing transactions. You can also memorize invoices to be recalled quickly. For example, if you have a customer who purchases the same items every time, use a memorized transaction to make invoices for that customer rapidly. Also, some items that are bought in groups can be stored as a unit, to add to other invoices that include that group of items. A third example is when you have only a few items to sell, you can memorize the invoice for each item. You can also use memorized transactions to create a reversing invoice quickly, for those times when a customer returns the goods you have sent them.

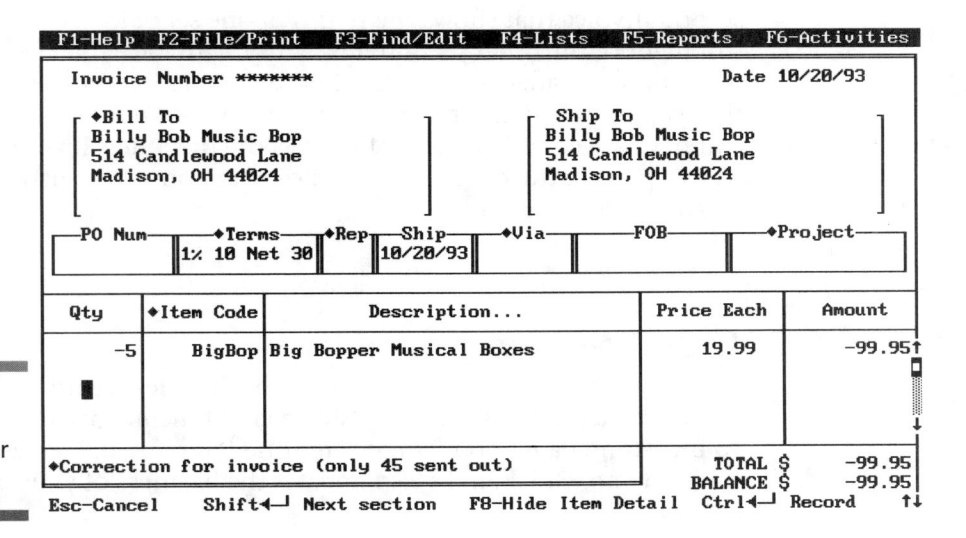

Invoice correcting a previous error
Figure 6-6.

To memorize a transaction, enter as much of the invoice as you want QuickBooks to memorize the same way you enter an invoice you would send to a customer. Then press `F4` for the Lists menu and choose 2 Memorize Invoice. (You can also use the shortcut key, `Ctrl`-`M`.) When QuickBooks prompts for a description, type the description and press `Enter`. When you want to use the memorized invoice in a new invoice, press `F4` for the Lists menu and choose 3 Recall Invoice. (This command is the same as pressing `Ctrl`-`T`.) Select the memorized invoice from the list. When QuickBooks memorizes an invoice, QuickBooks remembers all of the information supplied in the invoice except for the invoice number and date. Most of the information in the invoice that is displayed when you recall a memorized invoice is replaced.

Deleting an Invoice

You may have invoices that you want to delete; for example, you may have accidentally entered an invoice twice. To delete an invoice, switch to the invoice and press `Ctrl`-`Del`. This key combination is the same as pressing `F3` for the Find/Edit menu and then selecting 5 Delete Invoice. Next, select 1 Delete Invoice to remove the invoice.

Most of the time, you would not really want to delete the invoice. When customers change their orders, you are better off creating a second invoice that shows the return of one set of items and the shipment of the other set of items, with the invoice total being the net result of the change. By not deleting the invoice, you have a reminder that you must account for the goods the invoice bills for. Instead, you will have a second invoice that cancels the first one. However, the best way to remove the effect of an invoice when no sale is made is by creating a credit memo.

Credit Memos

A credit memo is an invoice that reverses the sales record you have made with a previous invoice. Using a credit memo gives both you and your customer a report of what is returned or refused. By creating a credit memo, QuickBooks also updates the balances of your sales and receivables.

Invoicing Customers

To create a credit memo, memorize the affected invoice. This prevents you from entering incorrect information, because the item codes, descriptions, and prices are supplied for you. Also, you will not forget to include items like sales tax. Next, go to a new invoice by pressing [Ctrl]-[End], and recall the memorized invoice. Once the items are listed, you probably only need to change the quantity for returned goods. You may also want to delete some of the items if the customer is returning part of the goods received. QuickBooks handles all of the calculations. When the customer has a balance due, you can provide a refund by adding a refund line item. Then let QuickBooks handle adding a check to the list of checks to be printed. You could also leave a balance due to the customer, if you want the amount of the refund to be applied to the next invoice. Don't forget to include "credit memo" as an item in the Description column or in the invoice memo.

QuickBooks also creates a credit memo for you when customers overpay their balance.

Printing an Invoice

When you are ready to print invoices, you can make a few selections to print the invoices you have prepared. QuickBooks keeps track of the invoices you have printed and the ones waiting to be printed. Intuit can supply you with preprinted invoices although you can use QuickBooks to print invoices on any paper your printer accepts.

Depending on the type of invoices you print, the fields that appear change. In the service invoice, the Item Code field disappears. In the professional invoice, the Qty, Item Code, and Rate fields do not appear. Product invoices include all of the same fields that you see on the screen except that item codes do not appear for subtotal or tax line item types.

To print the invoices, make sure you are at the invoice screen, or select 2 Invoicing/Receivables from the Main Menu and then select 1 Write/Print Invoices. Next, press [F2] for the File/Print menu and choose 2 Print Invoices. (You can also press [Ctrl]-[P].) You can change the fields in the Print Invoices window and press [Ctrl]-[Enter] when you are finished. Next, type the starting invoice number of the invoices QuickBooks will print. The default is the last unused number, starting with 1001, but you can enter another one. QuickBooks replaces the *'s you saw when you entered invoices with the next sequential number. After you press [Enter], QuickBooks prints the invoices. When QuickBooks cannot print the invoices, you will see the message "Waiting for printer" until QuickBooks can print the invoices. Press [Esc] if you need to cancel printing. Figure 6-7 shows a printed invoice.

After the invoices are printed, look at them. At the prompt for whether they printed correctly press [Enter] if they have. QuickBooks internally marks that it has printed all of them. If some or all of them did not print correctly, type the number of the first invoice of the group that did not print correctly and press [Enter]. QuickBooks internally marks that it has printed all the invoices up to that one. Next, QuickBooks returns to the Print Invoices window so you can repeat the printing process.

TIP: If you try printing and nothing happens, check three things. First, check that the printer is turned on. Second, check that the printer's "on line" button is pressed. Third, check that you have a cable connecting your printer to your computer. These very basic steps of printing are the cause of most printer problems.

Options for Printing Invoices

The Print Invoices window shown in Figure 6-8 has several fields that you can change to select which invoices print and how they appear. Enter a date in the field, Print invoices dated through, to print all invoices with that date or earlier. Since the default for this date is the current date, you are usually printing all invoices waiting to be printed. Postdated invoices, those with dates after today's date, are not printed unless you print a selection of invoices and include the postdated invoices in the selection. You can also print postdated invoices by changing the date in the Print invoices dated through field.

Use the remaining option on the Print Invoices window to select whether you are printing all of the invoices or just some of them. The default is to print all of them, so the Print All/Selected invoices field has an A. When you type **S** for this field, after pressing [Ctrl]-[Enter] to print, QuickBooks displays a window of all the invoices that are waiting to print, like the one shown in Figure 6-9. For each one in the list, you can highlight it and press the [Spacebar] (or click Spacebar-Select/Deselect at

Invoicing Customers

					Invoice	
				DATE	INVOICE #	
				31 Oct 93	1002	

BILL TO:
Billy Bob Music Bop
514 Candlewood Lane
Madison, OH 44024

SHIP TO:
Billy Bob Music Bop
514 Candlewood Lane
Madison, OH 44024

PO NUMBER	TERMS	REP	SHIP	VIA	F.O.B.	PROJECT
	1% 10 Net 30		13 Oct 93			

QUANTITY	ITEM CODE	DESCRIPTION	PRICE EACH	AMOUNT
100	HoundDog	Hound Dog Musical Ornament	15.99	1,599.00
		Plays "Ain't Nothing		
		But A Hound Dog"		
		Ohio Sales Tax	5.00 %	79.95
		City Sales Tax	1.00 %	15.99

TOTAL 1,694.94

Printed invoice
Figure 6-7.

```
                    Print Invoices
              There are 7 invoices to print.
        Print invoices dated through: 10/21/93
        Print All/Selected invoices (A/S): A
        ◆Type of paper: 11-inch form
        ◆Print to: HP LaserJet III/IIId, 10 cpi, Portrait, LP
        Additional copies (0-9): 0
        To print a sample invoice to help with alignment, press F9.
                         F9-Print Sample
        Esc-Cancel        F1-Help              Ctrl↵ Print
```

Print Invoices window
Figure 6-8.

the bottom of the window) to select whether the invoice is printed. You can switch between selecting all or none of them by pressing Ctrl-Spacebar. The list includes the date, customer, and amount of all of the invoices waiting to print with a "Print" or an empty space in the Print column. When you have finished selecting the invoices to print, press Ctrl-Enter to continue.

For the Type of paper and Print to fields, you can select one of the available paper sizes and printers you have installed. For Type of paper, you can also select whether you are printing on a letterhead and need more space at the top or whether you are printing on blank paper. You can select whether QuickBooks prints lines around the columns and

```
                    Select Invoices to Print
           Date          Customer              Amount      Print

         ▶ 10/13/93  Billy Bob Music Bop       1,694.94   Print
           10/13/93  Billy Bob Music Bop         999.50   Print
           10/13/93  Marianna Smith               19.99   Print
           10/13/93  Horsing Around, Inc.        164.85   Print
           10/20/93  Billy Bob Music Bop         -99.95   Print
           10/20/93  Big Bucks Department Stores 175,052.94 Print
           10/20/93  Big Bucks Department Stores 100,649.66 Print

         Spacebar-Select/Deselect    Ctrl-Spacebar All/None
         Esc-Cancel         F1-Help              Ctrl↵ Done
```

Select Invoices to Print window
Figure 6-9.

headings in the invoices or whether the invoice omits these lines. If you use preprinted forms, you do not need these lines, and on a dot matrix printer, these lines may take too long to print. For the Print to field, you can select .TXT File if you want the contents of the invoice placed in an ASCII text file. If you do select this output location, after you press `Ctrl`-`Enter` to start printing, you must enter the name for this file as well as how many lines fit on a page and how many columns across.

If you have an invoice style that requires you to print multiple copies, change the Additional copies field to a number one less than the total number of copies you need. Invoice forms that simultaneously print multiple copies do not need additional copies printed. When additional copies are printed, the invoices are marked as either the original or as one of the copies.

Dot matrix printers often have different settings for how much to the right or left you shift the page. Also, your paper may not be at the top of the page when you start printing. If you have one of these printers, it's a good idea to press `F9` to print a sample invoice, to check that the placement of the printed data matches the locations on the paper where you want the data printed. QuickBooks provides the data that appears on this sample invoice. Usually, adjusting the paper left or right is a one-time event, but you may need to adjust the paper up and down so the invoices start with the top of the page each time.

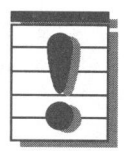

TIP: If you want your own personalized invoice form, print an invoice on a blank piece of paper with the Type of paper field set to Letterhead w/o lines. Bring this form to a print shop and they can design invoices with your company name on it that leaves blank space for the areas that QuickBooks will fill in. Also, you can add information on the back, such as your refund policy or what the customer should do if they disagree with the data on the invoice. The custom invoice form works well for printers that can use paper without the computer sprocket holes on the side. This includes laser printers and printers that have a single-sheet feeding mechanism.

Printing an Invoice Again

QuickBooks keeps track of the invoices you have already printed, but sometimes you may need another copy of an invoice you have already printed. For example, you may have spilled something on the customer's copy, or it may have become lost in the mail. To print an invoice again, find the invoice you want to reprint. Then, either replace the invoice number with an asterisk, to replace the invoice number with the next unused one, or type an **R** at the beginning of the invoice number, to use the same invoice number. "(REPRINT)" appears below the invoice number on the second printing. When you print invoices again, the invoice to which you have just added the R or the asterisk is included in the list of invoices to print.

Printing Mailing Labels

If you use invoices and envelopes supplied by Intuit, you do not have to address envelopes—the envelopes have windows for customers' and your addresses. Otherwise, you want QuickBooks to print the labels for mailing your invoices rather than writing them out yourself. QuickBooks can print on self-adhesive labels that are four inches wide, one inch high (measured from the top of one label to the top of the next), and two columns across. Intuit can provide these labels, or you can get them at office supply stores. You can use QuickBooks to quickly print mailing labels for a few customers or all of them. You will selectively print mailing labels when you are printing labels for mailing invoices, while you will want to print all of them when you are printing labels to mail a sales flyer.

To print mailing labels, make sure you are at the invoice screen, or select 2 Invoicing/Receivables from the Main Menu and then select 1 Write/Print Invoices. Next, press [F2] for the File/Print menu and choose 4 Print Mailing Labels. You can change the fields in the Print Customer Mailing Labels window and press [Ctrl]-[Enter] when you are finished. Next, in the Select Printer or File window, check that the printer in the Print to field is the one you want, or select another one from the list. You can press [F9] to print samples or press [Ctrl]-[Enter] to print the mailing labels. Figure 6-10 shows some printed mailing labels.

From the Select Printer or File window, you can select .TXT File to place the contents of the mailing labels into a file instead of printing the labels. If you do select this output location, after you press [Ctrl]-[Enter] to start printing, you must enter the name for this file as well as how many lines fit on a page and how many columns across.

Invoicing Customers

```
Billy Bob Music Bop           Horsing Around, Inc.
514 Candlewood Lane           16923 Center Road
Madison, OH 44024             Mentor, OH  44060

Big Bucks Department Stores
1 Commerce Drive
Beachwood, OH  44122
```

Printed mailing labels
Figure 6-10.

Options for Printing Mailing Labels

The Print Customer Mailing Labels window shown in Figure 6-11 has several fields that you can change to select the customer labels you print. In the Print sorted by Zip code or by Name field, type **Z** to print labels in the order of their ZIP code or **N** to print labels in order of the customer name. When you are printing labels to mail a sales flyer, print the labels in ZIP code order. When you are printing labels to mail invoices, print the labels in order of name so you can quickly match the invoices to the mailing labels.

The remaining option selects whether you are printing labels for all of the customers or just some of them. The default is to print all of them, so the Select specific customers to include field has an N. When you type **Y**, after pressing [Ctrl]-[Enter] to print, QuickBooks displays a window of all the customers. Just like selecting the invoices to print, you

```
                  Print Customer Mailing Labels

   Print sorted by Zip code or by Name   (Z/N): Z

   Select specific customers to include... (Y/N): N

   ─────────────── Restrict Labels As Follows ───────────────

   •Customer Type matches:

   Zip Code Matches:

   Include only customers whose average monthly purchases
         are greater than or equal to the amount: $


   Esc-Cancel            Ctrl-D Reset             Ctrl⏎ Done
```

Print Customer Mailing Labels window
Figure 6-11.

can highlight a customer and press the [Spacebar] (or you can click Spacebar-Select/Deselect at the bottom of the window) to select whether the label for the customer is printed. You can switch between selecting all or none of them by pressing [Ctrl]-[Spacebar]. The list includes the customer, their balance still due, and "Print" or an empty space in the final column, to indicate whether the label is printed. When you have finished selecting the labels to print, press [Ctrl]-[Enter] to continue to the Select Printer or File window to print the labels.

For the Customer Type matches and Zip Code Matches fields, you can select whether you are printing labels for customers with a specific customer type or ZIP code. For the Customer Type matches field, you can type one of the available customer types or press [Ctrl]-[L] and select one from the list. For the Zip Code Matches field, you can type the beginning or all of a specific ZIP code. When you only type the first few digits, type two periods for the remaining digits, as in **44..** (for ZIP codes that start with 44). In the Include only customers whose average monthly purchases are greater than or equal to the amount field, you can type a dollar value to compare with your customers' average monthly purchases. QuickBooks calculates which of your customers meet this requirement. Use this feature to mail sales flyers targeted to your better customers.

CHAPTER

7 RECORDING PAYMENTS AND MANAGING ACCOUNTS RECEIVABLE

Once you mail out invoices, your hope is that payments will be timely and complete. You will want to record these payments as soon as they are received in order to have an up-to-date picture of a customer's credit standing at all times. You will also want to deposit the payments in your bank account as soon as possible since it represents money that is available to you in the operation of your business.

QuickBooks provides a window for entering payments that makes recording this information simple. QuickBooks also adds the payments to your deposits and prepares deposit slips for you. Finally, QuickBooks creates statements that combine the summary information of a customer's invoices and payments.

You will learn how to match payments with invoices as they are received and how to manage your collectibles in this chapter. You will be able to record collection of your receivables and deposits using the instructions provided regardless of the invoice type you use.

Receiving Payments

The payments you receive from your customers need to be recorded so QuickBooks can mark the invoices you have sent out as paid. QuickBooks has a Receive Payments window that makes entering payments easy. QuickBooks can also handle special situations such as discounts or overpayments.

CAUTION: Falling behind in recording collections can cause you to make poor business decisions. You may deny credit to customers who have made payments you are not aware of, or continue to extend credit to customers whose accounts are delinquent.

When you receive a payment for an invoice, QuickBooks needs to be told how much you received and who you received it from. You can also provide the date when you received it and whether it is cash, check, or credit card. To enter a payment, follow these steps:

1. Select 2 Invoicing/Receivables from the Main Menu.
2. Select 2 Receive Payments.

    QuickBooks displays a Receive Payments window. The cursor is in the Customer field, ready for you to tell QuickBooks who has sent a payment.

Recording Payments and Managing Accounts Receivable

3. Select the customer you received payment from.

    This field has a diamond, so you can select a customer from the customer list. Just press `Ctrl`-`L` and select one of the listed customers. Of course, you can always type the customer name. As in other fields with a diamond, you can also display the list by clicking the field name.

4. Enter the amount received in the Amount rec'd field.

5. Enter the payment type, such as cash or check, in the Pmt method field.

    Entering the payment type makes preparing deposits easier because QuickBooks handles separating the check, cash, and credit information.

6. Press `Ctrl`-`Enter` to finish recording the payment and clear the window to enter the next payment.

To see an example of how easy it is to enter a payment, suppose you have just received a check from Billy Bob's Music Bop for $2,000. If Billy Bob's Music Bop is in your customer list, you can press `Ctrl`-`L` and select it from the list. The invoices for Billy Bob's Music Bop are now listed in the middle section of the Receive Payments window. Next, type **2000** in the Amount rec'd field. In the Pmt method field, press `Ctrl`-`L` to display a list of different payment types. Select Check. QuickBooks applies the payment to the invoice. You do not need to supply the date since QuickBooks enters the current date. If you wanted, you could enter Billy Bob's Music Bop's check number in the Pmt number field.

The completed payment looks like Figure 7-1. At this point, you are ready to press `Ctrl`-`Enter` to finish the payment and continue with the next one. When you are finished with the Receive Payments window, press `Esc` to return to the prior menu.

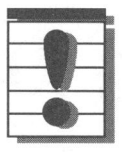

TIP: To prevent mishandling of your customers' payments, you can have them deposited directly to your bank account. The bank will provide confirmation that it has received your customers' checks.

```
                    R E C E I V E    P A Y M E N T S
    ◆Customer   : Billy Bob Music Bop     Amount rec'd:    2,000.00
    Date rec'd  : 10/22/93                Existing credits    99.95
    ◆Pmt method : Check
    Pmt number  : 10487                   Total to apply   2,099.95

         ┌─────────┬──────────┬──────────┬──────────┐
         │ Invoice │ Due Date │ Balance  │ Payment  │
         ├─────────┼──────────┼──────────┼──────────┤
         │ 0001001 │ 11/12/93 │   999.50 │   999.50 │
         │ 0001002 │ 11/12/93 │ 1,694.94 │ 1,100.45 │
         │         │          │          │          │
         │         │  TOTALS  │ 2,694.44 │ 2,099.95 │
         └─────────┴──────────┴──────────┴──────────┘

                           Unapplied (to credit memo)        0.00
    Esc-Cancel   F8-Apply Discount    F9-Paid in Full/Unpaid  Ctrl⏎ Done
    Musical Pony (Receivables)
```

Receive Payments window completed for a payment
Figure 7-1.

Receive Payments Window

You need to enter only a minimum of information in the Receive Payments window to record your payments—the customer and amount of the payment. You can also enter the date when it is not the current date, and if you enter the Pmt method and Pmt number, creating deposit slips is much easier.

The body of the Receive Payments window contains a listing of all the invoices, due dates, the balance, and payments to date for all of the unpaid invoices you have sent to a customer. The invoice numbers are the ones assigned when you printed the invoices. QuickBooks handles calculations when the invoices are due. QuickBooks also handles keeping track of the outstanding balance on the remaining invoices.

Several of the fields are calculations that QuickBooks performs for you. These are the Existing credits, Total to apply, Balance, Payment, and Unapplied (to credit memo) fields. You cannot enter new values for these fields, but as you change the other numbers in the window, QuickBooks automatically updates the amounts in these fields to reflect the amounts you have entered.

The Existing credits field shows the amounts of credit memo invoices that have not been applied to offset other invoices. When you create a

Recording Payments and Managing Accounts Receivable

credit memo, QuickBooks remembers the credit memo's amount for the customer. The Total to apply field contains the sum of the Amount rec'd and the Existing credits fields. This amount is the amount you can apply to the invoices. The Unapplied (to credit memo) field contains the value of the amount still owed to the customer. The Unapplied field will have a balance when the customer's credit exceeds the invoices due or when the customer has overpaid an invoice.

Applying a Discount

It is a good idea to use payment terms that encourage your customers to pay their bills promptly. When you use a payment term of 1% 10 Net 30, the customer is entitled to a 1 percent discount if they pay the invoice within 10 days. Of course, you must apply the discount specified in your payment terms when the customer pays within the time specified. QuickBooks handles calculating and applying this discount.

To apply a discount, open the invoice that receives the discount and move to the Payment column. Press F8 for the Apply Discount window, as shown in Figure 7-2. You can see that QuickBooks remembers how long the discount is valid and the percentage of the

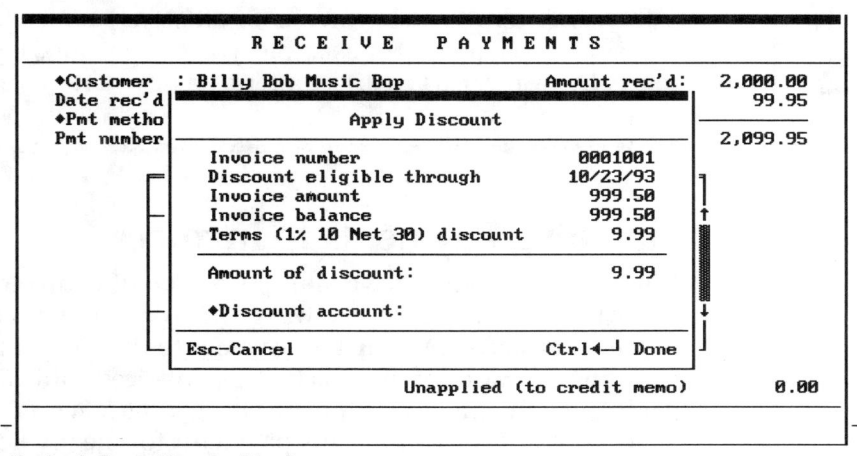

You have many factors to consider when deciding what payment terms to offer. Generous terms, for example, could possibly increase sales. QuickBooks can handle whatever you decide to do.

```
                    R E C E I V E    P A Y M E N T S
     ◆Customer  : Billy Bob Music Bop      Amount rec'd:    2,000.00
     Date rec'd                                                99.95
     ◆Pmt metho              Apply Discount
     Pmt number                                              2,099.95
                  Invoice number                  0001001
                  Discount eligible through      10/23/93
                  Invoice amount                   999.50
                  Invoice balance                  999.50
                  Terms (1% 10 Net 30) discount      9.99

                  Amount of discount:                9.99

                  ◆Discount account:

                  Esc-Cancel                  Ctrl↵ Done
                                   Unapplied (to credit memo)    0.00

     Musical Pony (Receivables)
```

Figure 7-2.
Apply Discount window

discount. QuickBooks will calculate the discount, although you can overwrite the amount of the discount for this invoice by entering a new number. You must also select the account that stores the discount. When you press `Ctrl`-`Enter` to finish, the invoice's Balance is reduced by the amount of the discount and has an asterisk after the new balance to indicate that the invoice has a discount applied.

As an example, to apply a discount for the first Billy Bob Music Bop invoice created in Chapter 6, move to the Payment field of the 0001001 invoice. Press `F8` to open the Apply Discount window and move to the Discount account field. Press `Ctrl`-`L`, select the Sales Disc account, and press `Ctrl`-`Enter` to apply the discount. Now the balance is 989.51. To update the Payment column, press `F9` to switch between paying all of the invoice and none of it, the `↑`, and `F9` again. The first time you press `F9` for the invoice, the payment changes to 0. The second time, all of the invoice is paid from the amount received. You may also need to press `F9` twice for the other invoices listed to update the amounts paid.

If you need to remove the discount (for example, the customer calls you and asks you not to cash the check for a few days), move to where you have applied the discount on the invoice and press `F8`. Type **0** for the Amount of discount field in the Apply Discount window and press `Ctrl`-`Enter`. When you return to the Receive Payments window, press `F9` to refresh the amounts entered in the Payment column.

TIP: Discounts can be offered for different payment methods as well as early payment. For example, you can encourage your customers to pay by cash versus credit by offering a discount for cash.

Matching Payments to Invoices

When your customers have multiple outstanding invoices, you can apply their remittance in two ways. One way is the *balance forward method* that starts applying the payment to the oldest invoice and then continues forward through each of the invoices until all of them are paid. The other method is the *open item method*. With this method, QuickBooks does not fill in any payments for the invoices and assumes that you will select the invoices that are being paid.

Recording Payments and Managing Accounts Receivable

As an example of the differences between the two methods, suppose you receive $30,000 from a customer. This customer has invoices of $15,000, $10,000, and $20,000. With the balance forward method, $15,000 is applied against the first invoice, $10,000 is applied against the second invoice, and $5,000 is applied against the third invoice. With the open item method, assuming that the customer indicated that the payment is for the second and third invoices, $10,000 is applied against the second invoice, and $20,000 is applied against the third invoice.

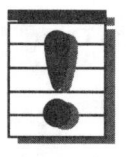

> **TIP:** Use the balance forward method of matching payments when you invoice a customer once a month for goods and services received during the month, as the payment you receive is likely to match the oldest invoice.

Your choice of a method for matching payments and invoices depends on the frequency with which you invoice customers.

You can override the balance forward method when you want a payment applied to a specific invoice. You may have a customer, a governmental agency for example, that matches its payments to specific invoices. To apply payments to specific invoices, move to each of the listed invoices in the Receive Payments window and press F9. The first time you press F9, the amount in the Payment column changes to 0. With all of the invoices marked as unpaid and the Unapplied (to credit memo) field equal to the Total to apply field, you can move to the first invoice you want paid. Press F9 again. The amount in the Payment column changes to the amount of the invoice or the amount of the payment, whichever is lower. The Unapplied (to credit memo) now contains the difference between the amount of the invoice's payment and the Total to apply field. You can continue to move to invoices and press F9 to apply part of the payment to pay the invoice until the Unapplied (to credit memo) field is 0.

When you are using the open item payment method, QuickBooks does not fill in the Payment column for any of the invoices. To tell QuickBooks to apply some or all of the payment received to a particular invoice, move to the invoice you want paid. Press F9 to change the amount in the Payment column to the amount of the invoice or the amount of the payment, whichever is lower. You can repeat moving to invoices and pressing F9 to apply part of the payment to pay the invoice until the Unapplied (to credit memo) field is 0.

Switching the Default Payment Method

The payment method is one of the company options you can set with QuickBooks. The default payment method is the balance forward method, but you can switch to the open item method by following these steps:

1. Select 7 Set Up/Customize from the Main Menu.
2. Select 4 Customize Current Company.
3. Select 2 Options.
4. Type **O** for the option, Receive payments from customers on Open item or Balance forward basis.
5. Press [Ctrl]-[Enter] to finish choosing options.

You can return to using the balance forward method of applying payments to invoices by repeating the preceding steps and typing **B** in step 4.

Overpayments

When a customer overpays the amount due, you will want to let them know that they have a credit balance. This way they will not feel that you attempted to overcharge them if they discover the overpayment on their own. QuickBooks will tell you when you enter a payment that is more than a customer owes. QuickBooks will even create the credit memo for you to send to the customer. When you press [Ctrl]-[Enter] and the Unapplied (to credit memo) field is more than zero, QuickBooks displays a message telling you how much money is left in the account.

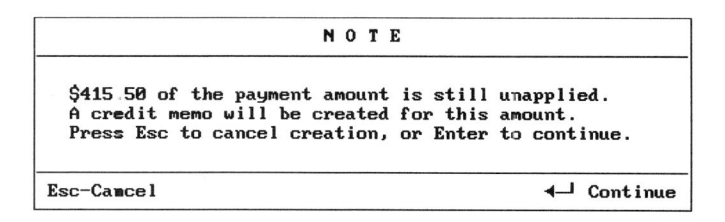

```
              N O T E

  $415.50 of the payment amount is still unapplied.
  A credit memo will be created for this amount.
  Press Esc to cancel creation, or Enter to continue.

 Esc-Cancel                              ←┘ Continue
```

You can press [Esc] to return to the Receive Payments window and mark other invoices from the customer as being paid. If you press [Enter],

Recording Payments and Managing Accounts Receivable

QuickBooks records the payment and creates a credit memo invoice for that customer. When you go to write another invoice, you will see the invoice for the credit memo QuickBooks has created.

Entries Created When You Enter a Payment

Behind the scenes, QuickBooks is making transaction entries that reflect the information you tell it through the Receive Payments window. If you want to see these entries, you can display the accounts receivable (A/R) register. To display this register, return to the menu that appears when you select 2 Invoicing/Receivables from the Main Menu. Next, select 3 View A/R Register. The screen looks like Figure 7-3.

In the accounts receivable register, every invoice is listed with its date, invoice number, customer name, due date, and amount. When you receive a payment, QuickBooks makes a new entry in the accounts receivable register. This new entry has the date of the payment, the number of the customer's check in the Number column, the customer name, and the amount of the payment in the Receipts column. Not only does QuickBooks make this entry, but it also changes the due date of the invoices to PAID. Partially paid invoices still have their same due date. When you move to any of these invoices in this screen, the entry

DATE	NUMBER	CUSTOMER	DUE	BILLINGS	RECEIPTS
10/20/93	1004	Big Bucks Department Stores	10/30	175,052 94	
10/20/93	1007	Big Bucks Department Stores	10/30	100,649 66	
10/22/93	1006	Billy Bob Music Bop	PAID	99 95-	
10/22/93	1008	Horsing Around, Inc.	10/22 Bal:	105 90 105 90	
10/22/93	2187	Horsing Around, Inc.			100 00
10/22/93	10487	Billy Bob Music Bop			2,000 00
10/22/93	10693	Billy Bob Music Bop			1,000 00
10/22/93		Billy Bob Music Bop	OPEN	0 00	

Ending Balance: $275,457.85

Accounts receivable register
Figure 7-3.

looks like the first one for Horsing Around, Inc., shown in Figure 7-3. This register entry tells you the amount of the invoice and any amount still remaining to be paid.

From the accounts receivable register, you can press (Enter) to look at the entry's detail more closely. Pressing (Enter) after highlighting an invoice entry displays the invoice window with the highlighted invoice. Pressing (Enter) after highlighting a deposit entry displays the Deposit Summary window that shows the deposit recorded by the entry.

When you press (Enter) to look at an invoice more closely, the bottom line items of the invoice might look like Figure 7-4. In the invoice in this figure, you can see that the bottom half of the line item section details the payments that have been applied to the invoice's balance. Also, the invoice shows any discounts applied. When you press (Esc) to leave the invoice, you return to the register. You can also look at the entries for the payments more closely by highlighting the payment entry in the register and pressing (Enter). This displays the Receive Payments window, although now you have a menu bar to select the same File/Print, Find/Edit, Lists, Reports, and Activities menus.

In the accounts receivable register, you may notice a double line followed by transactions that appear in a different color (or have some other distinguishing characteristic). These transactions are postdated or

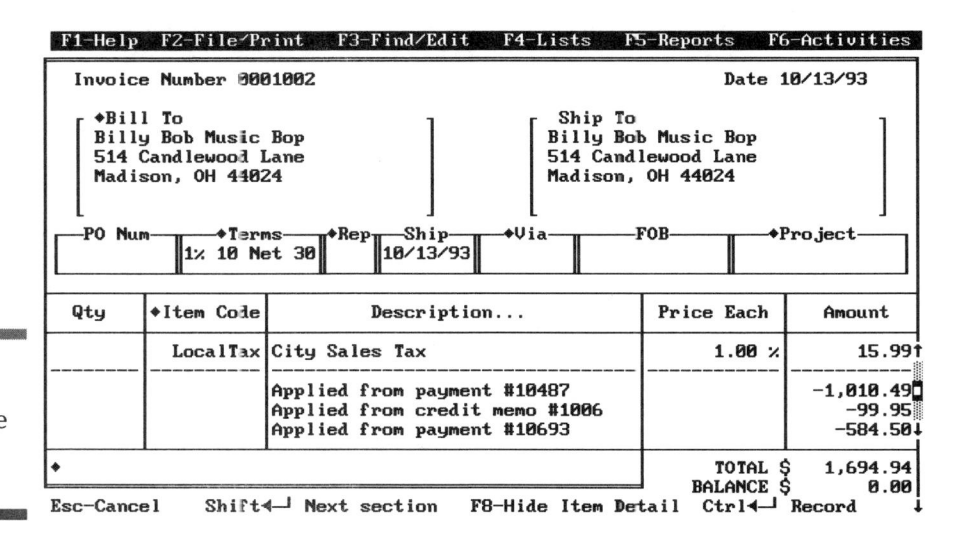

Invoice with payments applied to the balance
Figure 7-4.

Recording Payments and Managing Accounts Receivable

have a date later than the current one. You can also look at each part of the transaction listed separately by moving to an invoice or an entry in the accounts receivable register and displaying the *transaction history*. You can display the transaction history by pressing [F3] for the Find/Edit menu and selecting 8 Transaction History, or by pressing [Ctrl]-[H].

An example of a transaction history is shown in Figure 7-5. Notice that the lines in this transaction history have different entries in the Type field. In this example, the entry with INV shows the amount of the invoice, the XFER is for transfer of sales tax, the CM is for credit memo, and the PMT is for payments made on the account. You might also see DEP for deposits and DISC for discounts taken. From this point, you can highlight any part of the transaction and when you press [Enter], QuickBooks displays the register entry for that part of the transaction. The register that appears depends upon the account affected.

Fixing Errors in Payments

If you make an error in recording a payment, you can return to the Receive Payments window to review and amend the payment entry. To make this change, return to the menu that appears when you select 2 Invoicing/Receivables from the Main Menu. Next, select 3 View A/R Register to display your accounts receivable register. The entries are

Transaction History window
Figure 7-5.

```
 F1-Help      File/Print       Find/Edit      Lists       Reports      Activities
| DATE   | NUMBER |        CUSTOMER       |  DUE  | BILLINGS | RECEIPTS |
|10/13/93|  1002  | Billy Bob Music Bop   | PAID  | 1,694 94 |          |
|10/13/9 |                  Transaction History                        |
|10/13/9 |    Date      Type   Inv/Chk#      Amount        Balance      |
|        |  10/13/93    INV    1002         1,599.00      1,599.00      |
|10/20/9 |                                                              |
|        | ▶ 10/13/93   XFER   Sales Tax       79.95      1,678.95  ↑   |
|10/20/9 |   10/13/93   XFER   Sales Tax       15.99      1,694.94  ▯   |
|        |   10/22/93   CM     1006           -99.95      1,594.99      |
|10/22/9 |   10/22/93   PMT    10487       -1,010.49        584.50      |
|        |   10/22/93   PMT    10693         -584.50          0.00      |
|10/22/9 |                                                          ↓   |
|10/22/9 | Esc-Cancel              F1-Help            ↵  Goto | 100 00 |
|10/22/93|  10487 | Billy Bob Music Bop   |       |          | 2,000 00 |
 Receivables
                                              Ending Balance:  $275,457.85
```

7

listed in order by date, so look for the date of the payment you want to change. When you find this entry, press Enter. The same Receive Payments window appears with a menu bar at the top. You can change any of the entries in this payment except for the customer name. If you have entered the wrong customer for the payment, you need to delete the payment, then enter it again with the correct customer. When you are finished with changes, press Ctrl-Enter. If you need to delete a payment, press F3 for the Find/Edit menu and select 5 Delete Transaction. You can also do this by pressing Ctrl-Del. You will need to confirm by selecting 1 Delete Transaction.

TIP: If employees must handle cash payments, ensure that adequate controls are in place to help prevent theft. Having more than one employee handle cash is a good idea (they act as a control on one another). Also, the person receiving cash should not be the person making the bank deposit.

TIP: Another approach to preventing theft of cash in a retail establishment is to require that customers be given receipts. A prominently displayed sign announcing that the customer's purchase is free if they do not receive a receipt will have your customers helping to keep the clerks honest, since the sale must be rung up on the register to create a receipt.

Making Deposits

QuickBooks handles recording and applying the deposits you make, and it also prepares your deposit slip. When QuickBooks prepares your deposit slip, it separates the deposits according to their type—whether they are cash, credit card, or check. You can print a deposit summary. Also, you can tell QuickBooks the amount you are depositing for cash sales by creating an invoice for the sales.

TIP: If someone other than the business owner is handling the cash, you may want that person bonded. *Bonding* an employee is insurance against employee theft. Bonding, however, is not a substitute for checking an employee's references at prior jobs.

Recording Payments and Managing Accounts Receivable

Deposits Prepared by QuickBooks

As you enter payments, QuickBooks sets up the deposit for you. For example, suppose you need to deposit two checks for Billy Bob's Music Bop, one for Horsing Around, Inc., and a fourth one for a one-time customer. When you select 4 Make Deposits, the Deposit Summary window appears, as in Figure 7-6.

QuickBooks will also set up a deposit for you when you have a one-time customer that you have invoiced. For example, Figure 7-7 shows the Payment received to date line item that reduces the invoice total to zero. This line item is a payment type, so the amount is also recorded as an entry to be deposited.

From the Deposit Summary window, select the account you are depositing the money into from the Account for deposit field. Usually, the account is your checking account. All you need to do to tell QuickBooks which payments you are depositing is to move to the payment and press the [Spacebar]. Pressing the [Spacebar] changes the blank entry in the deposit (Dep) field to a Yes. QuickBooks assumes that all of the entries that have Yes in the last column are part of the deposit. When you have selected all of the payments you are depositing, press [Ctrl]-[Enter]. QuickBooks knows that you only want to make a deposit

Deposit Summary window
Figure 7-6.

```
                    D E P O S I T   S U M M A R Y

   Deposit date: 10/22/93         ◆Account for deposit:

   ┌─────────┬──────────┬──────────────────────┬──────────┬─────┐
   │  Type   │   Date   │      Customer        │  Amount  │ Dep │
   ├─────────┼──────────┼──────────────────────┼──────────┼─────┤
   │► Cash   │ 10/22/93 │ Cash Sales           │ 1,636.99 │     │
   │  Check  │ 10/13/93 │                      │    19.99 │     │
   │  Check  │ 10/22/93 │ Horsing Around, Inc. │   100.00 │     │
   │  Check  │ 10/22/93 │ Billy Bob Music Bop  │ 2,000.00 │     │
   │  Check  │ 10/22/93 │ Billy Bob Music Bop  │ 1,000.00 │     │
   ├─────────┴──────────┴──────────────────────┼──────────┼─────┤
   │                             TOTAL DEPOSIT │     0.00 │  0  │
   └───────────────────────────────────────────┴──────────┴─────┘
        Spacebar-Include/Exclude       Ctrl-Spacebar All/None of Type
        Esc-Cancel          Ctrl-P Print Deposit Summary    Ctrl↵ Done

   Musical Pony (Receivables)
```

QuickBooks for Profit: Making the Numbers Work

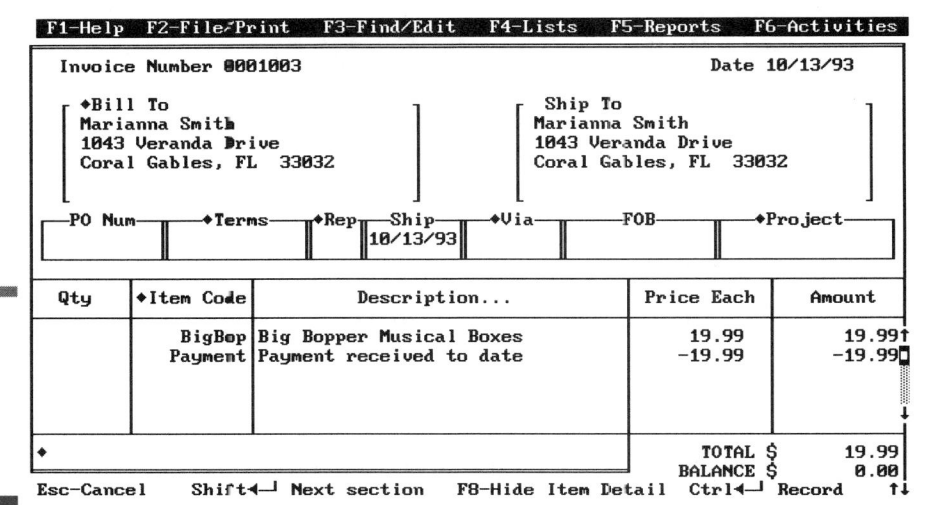

```
 F1-Help  F2-File/Print   F3-Find/Edit   F4-Lists   F5-Reports   F6-Activities
 Invoice Number 0001003                                       Date 10/13/93
 ┌─◆Bill To────────────────────────┐  ┌─Ship To─────────────────────────┐
 │ Marianna Smith                  │  │ Marianna Smith                  │
 │ 1043 Veranda Drive              │  │ 1043 Veranda Drive              │
 │ Coral Gables, FL   33032        │  │ Coral Gables, FL   33032        │
 └─────────────────────────────────┘  └─────────────────────────────────┘
 ┌─PO Num──┬─◆Terms──┬─◆Rep──┬─Ship────┬─◆Via──┬──FOB──┬──◆Project──┐
 │         │         │       │10/13/93 │       │       │            │
 └─────────┴─────────┴───────┴─────────┴───────┴───────┴────────────┘

 │ Qty  │ ◆Item Code │  Description...          │ Price Each │  Amount  │
              BigBop   Big Bopper Musical Boxes      19.99       19.99↑
              Payment  Payment received to date    -19.99      -19.99

                                                TOTAL   $     19.99
                                                BALANCE $      0.00
 Esc-Cancel    Shift⏎ Next section    F8-Hide Item Detail   Ctrl⏎ Record  ↑↓
```

Invoice with Payment line item that generates a deposit
Figure 7-7.

once, so after you complete the deposit, the next time you look at the Deposit Summary window, the window will not include the payments you included in the last deposit.

After you make a deposit, it is added to your accounts receivable register. You can look at the deposit summary information again by displaying the accounts receivable register, moving to the deposit entry, and pressing [Enter]. The register listing displays the date of the deposit, that it is a deposit (in the Number column), and the description of the deposit. From the register listing, you can edit or delete the deposit the same way you edit or delete payment receipts.

When you have entered payments that you have not yet deposited, every time you leave QuickBooks or change companies you will see a reminder that you have deposits to enter.

TIP: You may want to make separate deposits for the different types of payments (cash, check, credit card). If you do, your accounts receivable register and your check register will more closely match the bank statement and make reconciling your checkbook easier.

Printing the Deposit Summary

From the Deposit Summary window, you can print the summary you are making. Press [Ctrl]-[P]. Next, from the Select Printer or File window, leave the selected printer, select another printer, or select a .TXT file if you want the information printed to a file (you will be subsequently prompted for a filename). Press [Ctrl]-[Enter] to print the deposit summary. A sample deposit summary looks like this:

```
                         DEPOSIT SUMMARY
                   Deposited to Checking on 22 Oct 93

Num   Pmt Nbr    Pmt Type    Rec'd            Customer              Amount
---   -------    --------    --------   -----------------------   ---------
 1                   Cash    22 Oct 93  Cash Sales                 1,636.99
 2                  Check    13 Oct 93  Cash Sales                    19.99
 3      2187       Check    22 Oct 93  Horsing Around, Inc.          100.00
 4     10487       Check    22 Oct 93  Billy Bob Music Bop         2,000.00
 5     10693       Check    22 Oct 93  Billy Bob Music Bop         1,000.00
                                                                 ==========
                                         Total:  5 item(s) for $  4,756.98
```

Depositing Cash Sales

If your business has a lot of cash sales, you will want to record the deposits you make for these sales. Since the Receive Payments window does not let you add payments for unwritten invoices and you cannot add deposits that you have not recorded as payments you have received, you will need to create an invoice. An invoice for this purpose has the customer name of "Cash Sales" and a credit limit of zero so you cannot finalize the invoice without receiving a warning that the credit limit is expired. The line items for this invoice look like this:

Qty	♦Item Code	Description...	Price Each	Amount
1	CashSales	Cash Sales for the current day	1,539.32	1,539.32↑
	OhioTax	Ohio Sales Tax	5.00 %	76.97◻
	LocalTax	City Sales Tax	1.00 %	15.39▓
	Cash In	Cash Received on date	-1,636.99	-1,636.99▓
	Short/Over	Daily Shortage or Overage	5.31	5.31↓
♦			TOTAL $	1,636.99
			BALANCE $	0.00

This example combines the day's sales as a single item. The sales taxes are separated so that QuickBooks continues to keep track of the amount you must transfer to governmental agencies. The Cash In line is a payment item type, which also adds an entry for the cash you have received to the deposit summary. Since cash sales frequently have discrepancies between the cash on hand and the cash that the sales tally reports you should have, this invoice has a line item to record the amount—Short/Over. The final invoice balance is zero so QuickBooks will not display the credit limit warning when you save the invoice. The credit limit of zero makes sure you do not forget any line items.

Now when you display the Deposit Summary window, you have an entry for Cash (Type), today's date, Cash Sales (Customer), and $1636.99 (Amount).

Another option for creating an invoice to record daily sales is to separate line items for each of your products. When you do this, the invoice is filled with line items for the different products sold. The bottom of the invoice has the same sales tax line items, payment item for cash deposited, and other charges to record the amount you are over or short. Since an invoice is limited to 30 line items, you may need more than one invoice to record a day's sales this way. On the other hand, you can use QuickBooks reports to itemize the products you have sold, which you cannot do when you have a single line item, CashSales, that records all of the items sold.

When you record your daily cash sales by creating an invoice, you may have other line items. For example, if you pay some of your suppliers from the cash in the cash register, you will need to create line items that record the amount. The amount will appear as a negative value in the invoice's Amount column. The account to charge for the line item is the expense that you would select if you were writing a check to pay for that expense. Using this method of recording the expenses you have paid from available cash gives you a record of your expenses, and it records the amount of the reduction in cash you are depositing for sales.

TIP: With credit cards, you will often deposit the charged amounts using the amount of the sales, and then incur the expense of the usage fee later. American Express is not processed through your bank, so you may want to create a separate current asset account to store the balances owed.

Recording Payments and Managing Accounts Receivable

Transactions Created When You Make a Deposit

When you make a deposit, QuickBooks makes an entry for the amount of the deposit in the account you selected. For example, if you deposit all of the received payments listed in Figure 7-6 to the checking account, your checking account balance in QuickBooks' checking account increases by $4,756.98. When you look at the check register, you have an entry for the deposit you just made. When you look at the accounts receivable register, you will see this entry:

```
10/22/93  DEPOSIT  Checking: $4,756.98
```

From the accounts receivable register, you can highlight a deposit entry and press [Enter]. QuickBooks will display the deposit summary for that entry.

Customer Information

QuickBooks presents the customer invoice and payment information on statements. These *customer statements* list the invoices you have sent and payments you have received for a specific time period. The customer statements will not include invoices you have not printed. The statements do not list the individual items in the invoices, so if the customer wants an individual listing of the items in an invoice you will need to reprint the invoice. You can use customer statements Intuit provides or you can use your own paper.

To print customer statements, you must be looking at an invoice, the A/R register, or a payment receipt or deposit summary that is already finalized. Press [F2] for the File/Print menu and choose 5 Print Statements. You can change the fields in the Print Statements window; when you are finished, press [Ctrl]-[Enter]. QuickBooks prints the statements. When QuickBooks cannot print the invoices, you will see the message "Waiting for printer" until QuickBooks can print the invoices. Press [Esc] if you need to cancel printing. Figure 7-8 shows a printed statement for the Billy Bob Music Bop customer.

QuickBooks for Profit: Making the Numbers Work

Musical Pony

Statement

DATE
31 Oct 93

TO:
Billy Bob Music Bop
514 Candlewood Lane
Madison, OH 44024

Page 1 of 1

AMOUNT DUE	AMOUNT ENC.
(Cr Balance)	

DATE	TRANSACTION	AMOUNT	BALANCE
30 Sep 93	Balance Forward	0.00	0.00
13 Oct 93	Invoice #1001	999.50	999.50
13 Oct 93	Invoice #1002	1,694.94	2,694.44
22 Oct 93	Discount given on invoice #1001	-9.99	2,684.45
22 Oct 93	Credit Memo #1006	-99.95	2,584.50
	99.95 applied to Inv #1002		
22 Oct 93	Payment #10487	-2,000.00	584.50
	1,010.49 applied to Inv #1002		
	989.51 applied to Inv #1001		
22 Oct 93	Payment #10693	-1,000.00	-415.50
	584.50 applied to Inv #1002		
	415.50 credited to your account		

CURRENT	1-30 DAYS PAST DUE	31-60 DAYS PAST DUE	61-90 DAYS PAST DUE	OVER 90 DAYS PAST DUE	AMOUNT DUE
-415.50	0.00	0.00	0.00	0.00	(Cr Balance)

Statement for the Billy Bob Music Bop customer
Figure 7-8.

Recording Payments and Managing Accounts Receivable

Options for Printing Statements

The Print Statements window shown in Figure 7-9 has several fields that you can change to select the invoices and payments individually listed and the customers that you print statements for. In the Statement period from ... through field, you enter the beginning and ending dates for the items individually listed. (For the statement in Figure 7-9, the beginning date is 10/01/93 and the ending date is 10/22/93.) The first item shown in the statement is the balance still owed on the day before the beginning date. The default ending date is the current date.

The next field selects whether you are printing all of the invoices or just some of them. The default is to print all of them so the Select specific customers to include field has an N. When you type **Y** for this field, after pressing [Ctrl]-[Enter] to print, QuickBooks displays a window of all the customers. For each customer, you can highlight the customer and press the [Spacebar] to select whether their statement is printed. You can switch between selecting all or none of them by pressing [Ctrl]-[Spacebar]. The list includes the customer's name, their balance and "Print" or an empty space in the Print Stmt column. When you have finished selecting the invoices to print, press [Ctrl]-[Enter] to continue.

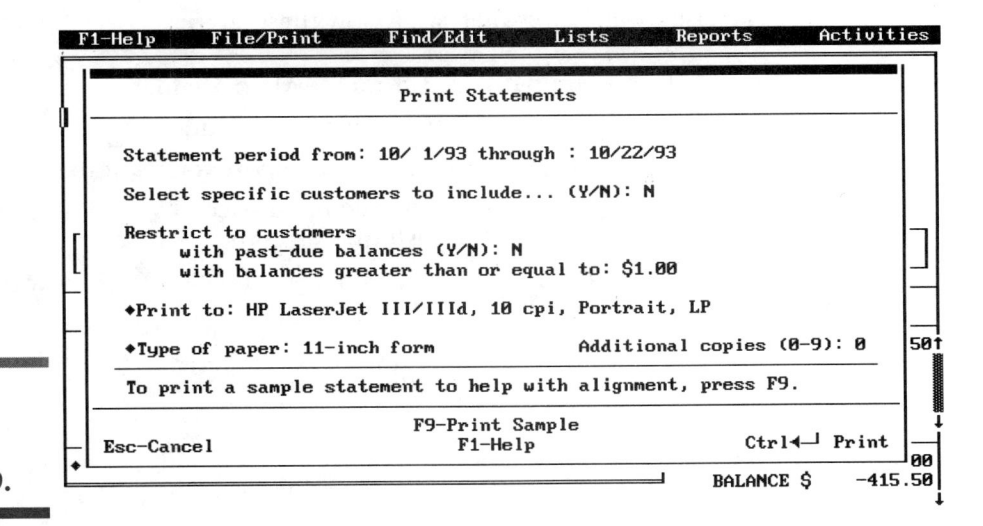

Print Statements window
Figure 7-9.

```
F1-Help     File/Print    Find/Edit    Lists    Reports    Activities

                          Print Statements

    Statement period from: 10/ 1/93 through : 10/22/93

    Select specific customers to include... (Y/N): N

    Restrict to customers
            with past-due balances (Y/N): N
            with balances greater than or equal to: $1.00

   •Print to: HP LaserJet III/IIId, 10 cpi, Portrait, LP

   •Type of paper: 11-inch form         Additional copies (0-9): 0

    To print a sample statement to help with alignment, press F9.
                          F9-Print Sample
    Esc-Cancel              F1-Help                    Ctrl⏎ Print

                                                     BALANCE $   -415.50
```

In the Restrict to customers with past-due balances field, you can type **Y** when you only want to print statements for customers that have an overdue invoice balance. You can also limit which customers you print statements for by typing an amount for the Restrict to customers with balances greater than or equal to field. Statements are printed only for the customers with balances over this amount.

The Type of paper, Print to, and Additional copies fields let you make the same selections for types of copies, location for printing, and number of copies to print that you learned about for invoices. As with invoices, you can press [F9] to print a sample statement to make sure your printer is lined up correctly with the paper. See "Options for Printing Invoices" in Chapter 6 for a more detailed discussion of these options.

Looking at Aging

The customer statements are one way to see how promptly customers pay their bills. When you are deciding on whether to extend customers additional credit, you may want a quick synopsis of their overdue amounts. In Chapter 11, you will learn how to create aging reports that list how much of your receivables is overdue by various numbers of days. For right now, you can quickly display a brief customer aging report for a single customer.

To display an aging analysis, follow these steps:

1. Select 6 Company Lists from the Main Menu.
2. Select Customers from the Select List window.
3. Select the customer whose aging report you want to see.
4. Press [F7] for the Actions menu and select 3 View/Edit or press [Ctrl]-[E] to display the customer's record.
5. Press [F8] to display the Customer Aging Status window like the one shown in Figure 7-10.

Recording Payments and Managing Accounts Receivable

```
┌─────────────────────────────────────────────────────────┐
│                    View/Edit Customer                    │
│    ┌Bill To┬──────────────────────────────────────┐      │
│    │Billy B│         Customer Aging Status        │      │
│    │514 Can│                                      │      │
│    │Madison│  Current          -415.50            │      │
│    │       │  1-30 Days           0.00            │      │
│    │       │  31-60 Days          0.00            │      │
│    │       │  61-90 Days          0.00            │      │
│    │       │  Over 90 Days        0.00            │      │
│    ◆Customer                                             │
│                   Balance Due    -415.50                 │
│    Contact:                                       1 ext  │
│    Contact:   Sales in last 12 months:  2,594.49    ext  │
│    ◆Represen                                             │
│               Esc-Cancel     F1-Help    ⏎ Continue       │
│    ◆Payment  └──────────────────────────────────────┘ 2,000.00│
└─────────────────────────────────────────────────────────┘
```

Customer Aging Status window
Figure 7-10.

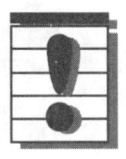

> **TIP:** Consider using a collection agency for accounts that are seriously delinquent. Although they will charge 30 percent to 50 percent of the amount, at least you will collect something.

If you notice a large number of delinquent accounts as you do this review, you might consider printing a Collections Report to provide the names and phone numbers for those delinquent accounts. You will learn more about this report in Chapter 11.

PART 3

MANAGING PAYABLES

CHAPTER

8 PAYROLL

For a small-business owner under the day-to-day pressure of running a business, preparing the payroll can be a time-consuming and frustrating task. Besides completing forms and tables for withholding taxes, you must be aware of annual earnings limits that affect the amount you withhold in social security taxes from employees. In addition to these weekly considerations, there are monthly, quarterly, and year-end reports that may need to be filed with the federal, state, or local government.

Your accountant can help provide more personalized guidance for all the regional and federal paperwork you must prepare as part of preparing your payroll.

In this chapter, you will see how QuickBooks can help to reduce the effort of preparing your payroll. You'll find that if you invest some time at first in setting up your system, it will substantially reduce your payroll activities once the system is running. You can record your payroll entries directly on a check, using the check voucher to show the various withholding amounts. If you do not have QuickBooks write your payroll checks, you can still record the entries in the check register using the Split Transaction screen. Regardless of the approach that you choose, you can easily prepare the payroll entry for each employee and maintain information for the Internal Revenue Service (IRS) about federal income tax withholding, Federal Insurance Contribution Act (FICA) withholding, and employer FICA payments.

You can also maintain accounts for any state and local withholding taxes or insurance payments that must be periodically deposited. In addition to this information, you can accumulate data to be used in the preparation of W-2 forms for your employees at the end of the year. See the special "Payroll Forms" section in this chapter for a list of some of the standard payroll-related payment and tax forms that QuickBooks can assist you with preparing.

Intuit offers a separate package, QuickPay, which has built-in payroll tables that provide additional help. QuickPay can be used with QuickBooks to assist you in payroll activities.

The QuickBooks Payroll System

Just as when you initially set up your company file, you have some preliminary work to do before you can process your first payroll. In brief, the required steps are as follows:

✦ Set up the payroll liability accounts for taxes and other withholdings.

✦ Compute each employee's net pay using tax tables and enter this information on a check or in the register.

✦ Print the payroll reports that you need and determine when you must pay taxes.

✦ Pay taxes at the specified time.

Payroll

You will take a closer look at the process as you proceed through this chapter.

Payroll entries are processed along with your other business-related payments in your QuickBooks checkbook. To set up your system to do this, you must establish some new accounts specifically related to payroll. Some of these accounts will already be set up if you selected one of QuickBooks' standard chart of accounts when setting up your company.

If you selected a standard chart of accounts, QuickBooks already has several payroll expense accounts to handle the gross wages, the employer's FICA contribution, and other payroll-related expenses such as workers' compensation that do not require employee withholding.

NOTE: If you set up your own chart of accounts, it is your responsibility to add all of the accounts that you need since the chart of accounts does not include these accounts. You can use the instructions in Chapter 2 for setting up a new account. The accounts that you need for payroll are liability accounts. They will be used to accumulate amounts needed for periodic payments to federal, state, and local tax authorities as well as insurance companies, if you offer payroll deductions for life, disability, or medical insurance.

The accounts that you set up for withholding are liability accounts, since once this money is withheld from the employee it represents an obligation that you have to a government agency or an insurance company.

With QuickBooks, you can monitor your liability for both withholding amounts and payroll expenses that are the company's responsibility. This is important since you will be assessed penalties and late fees for failing to file these payments on time. QuickBooks' ability to memorize payment formats and remind you of dates for periodic payments can be most helpful in this situation.

CAUTION: Penalties for late payment of your payroll liabilities are high. Monitor the due dates of these payments carefully to avoid unnecessary charges.

Payroll Forms

If you are thinking of hiring employees, be prepared for an increase in paper work. You must complete forms at the federal, state, and local levels regarding payroll information. To prevent problems with regulatory agencies these forms must be created accurately and on a timely basis.

Federal Payroll Forms

The following list provides an overview of the payroll-related tax forms that employers need to file with the IRS. You can obtain copies of the federal forms you need by calling the IRS toll-free number, 800-829-3676. If this number is not valid in your locale, check your telephone directory for the correct number. You will probably need to file these forms:

SS-4, Application for Federal Employer Identification Number The federal employer identification number is used to identify your business on all business-related tax forms.

Form 45-190, Federal Tax Deposit Receipt This is your record of deposits of withholding and payroll taxes made to a Federal Reserve bank or an authorized commercial bank.

Form 940, Employer's Annual Federal Unemployment (FUTA) Tax Return This is a return filed annually with the IRS summarizing your federal unemployment tax liability and deposits.

Form 941, Employer's Quarterly Federal Tax Return Summarizes your quarterly FICA taxes and federal income tax withholding liability and the amount of deposits your business has made during the quarter.

Form 943, Employer's Annual Tax Return for Agricultural Employees This is a special form completed annually for FICA taxes and federal income tax withholding liability for agricultural employees.

Form 1099-MISC, Statement for Recipients of Miscellaneous Income This must be filed for all nonemployees paid $600 or more in the current tax year.

Form W-2, Wage and Tax Statement This is a six-part form (one original and five duplicates) summarizing an employee's gross earnings and tax deductions for the year. The form must be prepared annually for each employee by January 31.

Form W-3, Transmittal of Income and Tax Statements This form summarizes your business's annual payroll-related FICA taxes and federal income tax withheld during the year. It must be sent with the Social Security Administration's copy of the employee's W-2 forms by February 28 of the following year.

Form W-4, Employee Withholding Allowance Certificate This form is completed annually by employees and is used to declare the number of withholding exemptions they claim.

State and Local Government Payroll Information

State and local government payroll forms vary by state. The following list provides an indication of some of the forms you will probably need to file.

Unemployment insurance tax payments

Workers' compensation tax payments

State income tax withholding payments

Local income tax withholding payments

Form W-2, Wage and Tax Statement (one copy of the federal form)

To monitor these liabilities, establish several current liability accounts to maintain records of taxes withheld and other employee-authorized payroll deductions for medical insurance, charitable contributions, and so on. These are called *current liability accounts* since you are holding the withheld funds for payment to a third party. Some examples of these are as follows:

Payroll-FICA	FICA liabilities owed by employer
Payroll-FWH	Federal income tax liabilities for employee withholdings
Payroll-MCARE	Medicare tax liabilities
Payroll-SDI	State disability insurance liabilities

Notice that all of these account names begin with "Payroll." This allows QuickBooks to prepare the payroll report by automatically finding all transactions with an account title beginning with "Payroll."

Writing a Payroll Check

Your employees' payroll checks can have all of the supporting detail showing the difference between their gross and net pay if you use voucher check stock. You record the check amount as the net amount, which you have precalculated using QuickBooks calculator (if you need it). You should familiarize yourself with federal and state withholding tables as well as any local regulations that may necessitate additional withholdings. Figure 8-1 shows the entries on a voucher check that represent the first part of the breakdown in the withholding amounts. Although you may use the check writing screen to record all of your payroll entries, the register is shown throughout the rest of the chapter, as it displays more of the detail than the voucher portion of a check.

TIP: Use memorized transactions and transaction groups to speed up payroll processing when checks are the same amount each pay period.

Payroll

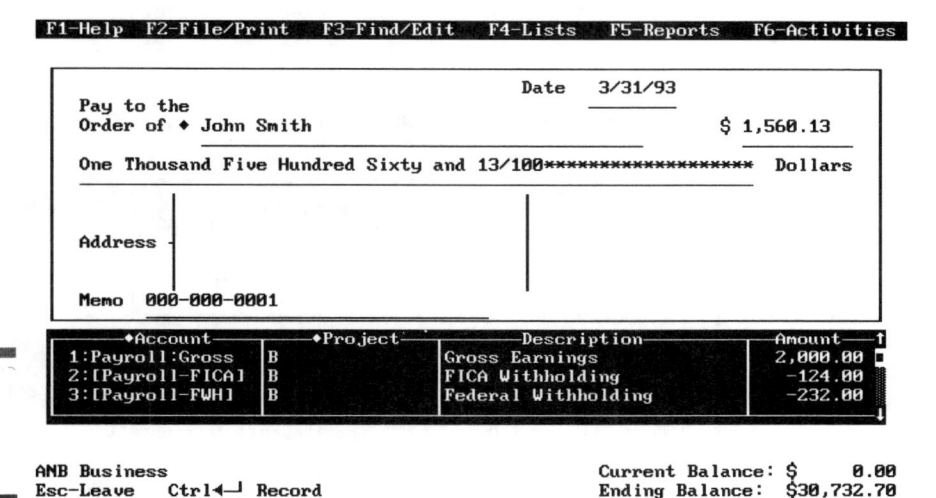

```
F1-Help  F2-File/Print  F3-Find/Edit  F4-Lists  F5-Reports  F6-Activities

                                       Date    3/31/93
   Pay to the
   Order of ♦ John Smith                               $ 1,560.13
   One Thousand Five Hundred Sixty and 13/100********************  Dollars


   Address

   Memo  000-000-0001

    ◆Account      ◆Project      Description         Amount
   1:Payroll:Gross    B       Gross Earnings        2,000.00
   2:[Payroll-FICA]   B       FICA Withholding       -124.00
   3:[Payroll-FWH]    B       Federal Withholding    -232.00


   ANB Business                       Current Balance: $      0.00
   Esc-Leave   Ctrl⏎  Record          Ending Balance:  $ 30,732.70
```

Check screen with a payroll check
Figure 8-1.

Register Entries for Payroll Transactions

The paycheck transaction shown in Figures 8-2 and 8-3 illustrates the basic payroll expenses and liabilities associated with the payment of wages. Your payroll entries will be more complex if you withhold medical insurance, pension contributions, and other amounts such as contributions to charity or deposits to savings accounts from employee checks. The basic format of the split transaction remains the same; the number of accounts in the split transaction would simply be expanded and additional current liability accounts added to cover your obligation to make payment to the parties involved.

An employee's gross earnings are entered as a positive number in the split transaction window, as are any other costs to the company, such as the company's contributions to FICA or Medicare. Negative amounts are entered for the money that needs to be deposited with the IRS or other agencies, such as the employee's FICA withholding and federal, state (abbreviated as SWH), and local income tax withholdings. If you switch the register for these other accounts, you can see how much has been or will be deposited with the government agencies for each type of withholding or tax.

QuickBooks for Profit: Making the Numbers Work

```
F1-Help        File/Print        Find/Edit        Lists        Reports        Activities
 DATE   NUM   ◆PAYEE    ·   MEMO    ·   ◆ACCOUNT    PAYMENT  C  DEPOSIT       BALANCE
 3/31         John Smith                             1,560 13                 34,499 92
 1993  SPLIT  000-000-0001
                                    Split Transaction
            ◆Account           ◆Project            Description              Amount
         1:Payroll:Gross        B           Gross Earnings                  2,000.00
         2:[Payroll-FICA]       B           FICA Withholding                 -124.00
         3:[Payroll-FWH]        B           Federal Withholding              -232.00
         4:[Payroll-SWH]        B           State Withholding                 -54.87
         5:[Payroll-MCaRE]      B           Medicare Withholding              -29.00
         6:Payroll:Comp F→      B           Payroll Taxes-FICA                124.00
         7:Payroll:Comp M→      B           Payroll Taxes-MCARE                29.00

         Esc-Cancel     Ctrl-D Delete line    F9-Recalc transaction total   Ctrl⏎ Done

 ANB Business                                         Current Balance:  $   -520.00
                                                      Ending Balance:     $30,732.70
```

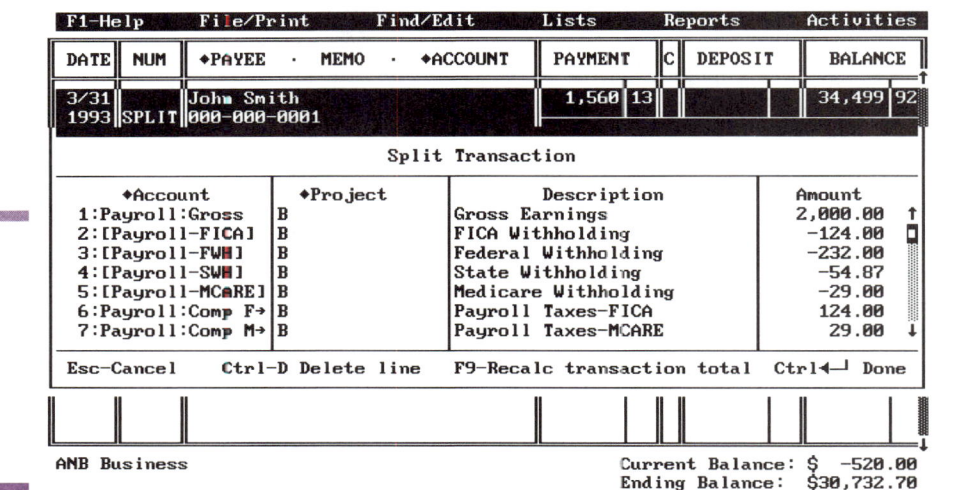

Split Transaction window showing first entries for a payroll transaction
Figure 8-2.

```
F1-Help        File/Print        Find/Edit        Lists        Reports        Activities
 DATE   NUM   ◆PAYEE    ·   MEMO    ·   ◆ACCOUNT    PAYMENT  C  DEPOSIT       BALANCE
 3/31         John Smith                             1,560 13                 34,499 92
 1993  SPLIT  000-000-0001
                                    Split Transaction
            ◆Account           ◆Project            Description              Amount
         7:Payroll:Comp M→      B           Payroll Taxes-MCARE                29.00
         8:[Payroll-FICA→]      B           FICA Matching                    -124.00
         9:[Payroll-MCARE→]     B           Medicare Matching                 -29.00
        10:
        11:
        12:
        13:
         Esc-Cancel     Ctrl-D Delete line    F9-Recalc transaction total   Ctrl⏎ Done

 ANB Business                                         Current Balance:  $   -520.00
                                                      Ending Balance:     $30,732.70
```

Split Transaction window showing last entries for a payroll transaction
Figure 8-3.

Payroll

> **TIP:** If you must pay hourly workers differing amounts each pay period use `Ctrl`-`C` to bring up the calculator in QuickBooks. Type in the hourly wage, type an asterisk for multiplication, then type the number of hours, and press `Enter`. The calculator is also useful when computing bonuses as part of a pay check.

Recording IRS Deposits

You must periodically make deposits to the IRS for the amount of FICA and federal income tax withheld from employees' pay checks, as well as your matching FICA contribution. You make your deposits to authorized banks within the Federal Reserve System. You should check with your bank to be sure they can provide this service; otherwise you must take cash or a bank check, along with the appropriate forms, to an authorized bank and make your deposit. To record the withholding deposit, you designate the Internal Revenue Service as the payee in your entry.

> **TIP:** You might want to consider opening your checking account at a bank that is a member of the Federal Reserve for convenience in making payroll withholding deposits. Without an account at the bank, you will need to obtain cash from your bank in the amount of the withholding deposits and take it to a member bank, as they are unlikely to accept a check from a credit union or savings and loan.

There are specific guidelines concerning the timing of the payments. These rules are spelled out in the special "IRS Deposit Rules" section in this chapter. For the ANB Company with just John Smith and a second employee, the monthly total tax liability is $1379. This company is required to make a withholding deposit under Rule 3 of the IRS. Rule 3 states that you must make a deposit for social security taxes and withheld federal income tax by the fifteenth or sixteenth of the following month (depending on whether the month has 30 or 31 days), if the total tax liability for any month is $500 or more but less than $3000. (This can be more than one month's worth.) You should consult your accountant or read IRS Form 941 for a full explanation of the other deposit rules. Depending on the size of your payroll, you may have to make periodic payments throughout the month in order to comply with the regulations.

The entry shown in Figure 8-4 demonstrates how you would record a payment for your business's federal tax liabilities for social security taxes, Medicare, and federal withholding taxes. You record the transaction in your checkbook account register when you pay the federal government the amount of the liabilities for FICA, Medicare, and federal income tax withholding. You follow these same steps to record the payment of the state withholding tax liability when the required payment date arrives.

All three accounts are liability accounts. Notice that no expense account is charged in the Split Transaction window shown in Figure 8-4. This is because the IRS deposit reduces the liability account balances that were established when payroll checks were written on 1/31/93. If you look at those transactions in your register like the payroll transaction shown in Figures 8-2 and 8-3, you can see that the gross earnings were charged to the Payroll:Gross account and your matching FICA contribution as an employer is charged to the Payroll:Comp FICA account. Both of these accounts are classified as expenses and will be shown on your business's profit and loss

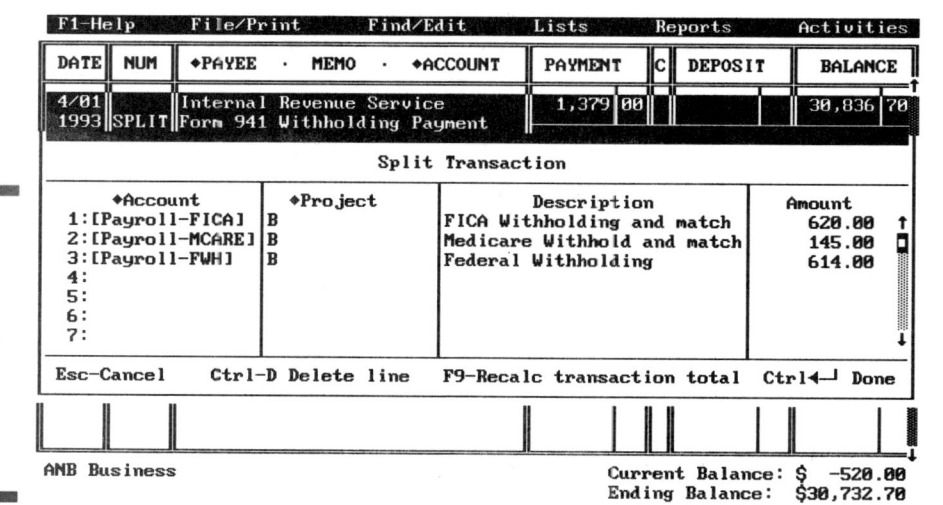

Split Transaction window showing a deposit to the IRS for withholding liabilities
Figure 8-4.

Payroll

IRS Deposit Rules

The frequency with which you must make deposits of social security and federal income taxes is dependent on the amount of your liability. Effective January 1, 1993, the IRS has simplified the rules that affect when you must make these deposits. Each November, the IRS will tell you which rule you should use throughout the upcoming year. Since the penalties for noncompliance can be steep, it is important to strictly follow the rules. Notice 931 describes the new rules in detail, but a quick summary is provided here:

Rule 1   Tax liability for last year $50,000 or less — Monthly filing

Rule 2   Tax liability for last year greater than $50,000 — Semi-weekly filings

Through the end of 1993 you can continue to use the old rules, following the instructions that come with Form 941 for the transition. The old rules are summarized as follows:

Rule 1   Tax liability for the quarter less than $500 — No deposit required

Rule 2   Tax liability for the month less than $500 — Carry forward to the next month

Rule 3   Tax liability for the month between $500 and $3000 — Deposit within 15 days from the end of the month

Rule 4   Tax liability at the end of any of the eight monthly periods (the 3rd, 7th, 11th, 15th, 19th, 22nd, 25th, and the last day) greater than $3000 and less than $100,000 — Deposit within three banking days

Rule 5   Tax liability at the end of any of the eight monthly periods greater than $100,000 — Deposit by the end of the next banking day

statement. On the other hand, the amounts withheld for payroll taxes owed by your employee and you are charged to liability accounts that will be paid at a future date. Thus, when you pay these liabilities, as you just did, you are meeting your financial obligation to the government, not incurring additional expenses.

Memorizing Payroll Transactions

Since you pay your employees on a regular basis and make regular withholding deposits, it is a good idea to memorize these entries to simplify future recording of the transactions. For salaried employees, the only changes needed each pay period are new dates and check numbers on each transaction. All of the split transaction detail will be accurate. For hourly employees or salaried employees making more than the FICA cap amount (the upper limit of earnings that owes taxes), some pay periods will require changes to the entries in the split transaction detail.

Your regular withholding deposits will also be easier to record if you use memorized transactions. When your employees are salaried, the amounts are approximately the same each period. If your employees are paid hourly, their withholdings will vary, and you will need to change some of the split transaction detail for the withholding deposits.

Establishing Transaction Groups

In Chapter 4 you learned to establish a transaction group for regular transactions. The object of this is to batch together similar transactions that occur around the same time each month so that QuickBooks can automatically record them for you the next time they need to be made. Remember, only memorized transactions can be batched into transaction groups.

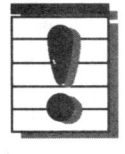

TIP: If you use an outside service bureau to handle your payroll, you might find that transaction groups make the task so easy that you no longer need to spend the money on this service.

Payroll

If you are paying higher rates of unemployment taxes than other local businesses in your field, you may want to learn whether you can change your classification to one with a lower rate.

State Unemployment Tax Transactions

In addition to withholding tax liabilities, employers must pay unemployment taxes. This program is mandated by the federal government but administered by the individual state governments. Because of this method of administration, you must make payments to both the state and federal governments. At the time of this writing, you must contribute .008 percent to the federal government to cover administrative costs and up to .054 percent to the state agency that administers the program. These percentages apply to the first $7000 of earnings for each employee. In some states, the salary cap on earnings may be higher; however, the example in this chapter uses a $7000 limit for both federal and state employer payroll tax contributions. You must make deposits to the federal government whenever your contribution liability reaches $100. These deposits are made in the same manner as the FICA, Medicare, and federal income tax withholding payments discussed earlier in this chapter.

Your actual contributions to the state agency will be based on historical rates for your business and industry classification. You may qualify for a percentage rate lower than the maximum rate allowed by law. Generally, payments to the state agency that administers the program are made quarterly. Each quarter, you are required to complete an Employer's Report of Wages form, summarizing your employees' total earnings during the quarter and the amount of your FUTA and SUTA liabilities.

When you want to include the amounts you owe for FUTA and SUTA, you can enter these amounts two ways. You can include the amounts you owe in the split transaction. You have expense amounts for the FUTA and SUTA amounts, and you have those same amounts as negative amounts in the liability accounts you set up for the state and federal government payments. This method is repeated for every payroll transaction you record; it uses the liability account to keep track of the accumulated liability.

The second method for recording your FUTA and SUTA liabilities is to record a transaction in the accounts payable register for the amount of the liability, as you will learn how to do in the next chapter.

Workers' Compensation Payments

As an employer, you make workers' compensation payments for your employees. Rates vary from state to state and also depend on your industry and your company's safety record. To record these payroll expenses, you need another account called "Payroll:Comp WCOMP." The same amount is added to the liability account for the governmental agency you owe this amount to.

Payroll Reports

Through the use of filters and customization features, you can obtain a substantial amount of the payroll-related information you need to prepare the various federal, state, and local payroll tax and withholding forms. However, as you will see in the following sections, there are some functions you must perform manually, such as totaling amounts from several QuickBooks reports to determine the numbers to place in some lines of tax forms.

You can gather information to assist in preparing such quarterly reports as: the FUTA form, SUTA form, workers' compensation report, and federal, state, and local withholding tax reports. You will find that QuickBooks can also help in the preparation of year-end W-2s, W-3s, 1099s, annual forms for federal, state, and local tax withholding, and other annual tax forms required for unemployment and workers' compensation purposes.

Payroll Report Overview

The payroll report in QuickBooks summarizes all your payroll activities in any period for which you need information—that is, you can prepare the report for weekly, monthly, quarterly, or yearly payroll summary information. You can gather information for all employees in one report, or you can limit the report to information concerning one employee at a time.

An important point to remember is that QuickBooks' payroll report is preset to use only the payroll account and subaccounts. As mentioned early in the chapter, all payroll-related charges are charged against the

Payroll

Dates for Filing Federal Payroll Tax Returns

Form 941, Employer's Quarterly Federal Tax Return	
First Quarter (Jan - Mar) If deposit required with filing If you deposited all taxes when due	April 30 May 10
Second Quarter (April - June) If deposit required with filing If you deposited all taxes when due	July 31 August 10
Third Quarter (July - Sept) If deposit required with filing If you deposited all taxes when due	October 31 November 10
Fourth Quarter (Oct - Dec) If deposit required with filing If you deposited all taxes when due	January 31 February 10
Form 943, Employer's Annual Tax Return for Agricultural Employees	
Calendar Year Filing If deposit required with filing If you deposited all taxes when due	January 31 February 10

main payroll account. You establish subaccounts for Payroll:Gross and Payroll:Comp FICA, and so on, to keep track of specific types of payroll charges.

All the reports prepared in this section are based on selecting 6 Payroll Report from the Reports menu. If you don't use this format, you must select 8 Other Reports from the Reports menu; then select 1 Summary Report and customize your summary report to gather the information necessary for tax-reporting purposes.

Employer's Quarterly Federal Tax Return

Let's now examine how you can use QuickBooks to assist you in preparing Form 941 (shown in Figure 8-5) to meet your quarterly filing requirements. Consult the special section, "Dates for Filing Federal Payroll Tax Returns," for the deadlines for filing quarterly Form 941 and annual Form 943.

To create the report shown in Figure 8-6, you select 6 Payroll Report from the Reports menu. Specify the beginning and ending dates of the quarter for which you want the report and select [Ctrl]-[Enter] to create the report. Press [Ctrl]-[P] to print the report.

Report Discussion

The finished report is shown in Figure 8-6. (Note that unless you use a wide-carriage printer, the payroll report will print on several pages instead of just one.) Let's take a look at the information gathered and discuss how you can use it to complete the appropriate lines of the Employer's Quarterly Federal Tax Return form, shown in Figure 8-5.

Line 2 This line shows the total wages subject to federal withholding. The Gross Earnings line in the payroll report shows that John Smith and Mary McFaul earned a total of $15,000 during the quarter.

Line 3 This line shows the amount of total income tax withheld from employee wages. On the payroll report, the row, FROM Payroll-FWH-Federal Withholding, shows that the total federal income tax withheld from employees was $1842. Note that $696 was paid by Smith and $1146 was paid by McFaul.

Line 6a The amount of social security taxes accumulated during the quarter totals $1860. You obtain the FICA taxes owed by totaling the amounts from the Transfers FROM Payroll-FICA-FICA Withholding and Transfers FROM Payroll-FICA-Co-FICA rows. To verify this: the gross earnings for the quarter are subject to both FICA withholding and matching contributions. This means the total in the Gross-Gross Earnings row of the report, $15,000, is multiplied by .124 to get the amount on line 6a. This should equal the total calculated in the preceding paragraph—$1860—which it does.

Form **941** (Rev. January 1992) Department of the Treasury Internal Revenue Service

4141

Employer's Quarterly Federal Tax Return

▶ **See Circular E for more information concerning employment tax returns.**

Please type or print.

Your name, address, employer identification number, and calendar quarter of return. (If not correct, please change.) ▶

Name (as distinguished from trade name) | Date quarter ended

Trade name, if any | Employer identification number

Address (number and street) | City, state, and ZIP code

OMB No. 1545-0029 Expires 5-31-93

T
FF
FD
FP
I
T

IRS Use: 1 1 1 1 1 1 1 1 1 1 2 3 3 3 3 3 3 4 4 4 / 5 5 5 6 7 8 8 8 8 8 8 9 9 9 10 10 10 10 10 10 10 10 10 10

If address is different from prior return, check here ▶ ☐

If you do not have to file returns in the future, check here . ▶ ☐ Date final wages paid . . . ▶ ______

If you are a seasonal employer, see **Seasonal employers** on page 2 and check here . . ▶ ☐

Line	Description		No.	Amount
1	Number of employees (except household) employed in the pay period that includes March 12th ▶		1	
2	Total wages and tips subject to withholding, plus other compensation . . . . ▶		2	
3	Total income tax withheld from wages, tips, pensions, annuities, sick pay, gambling, etc. . ▶		3	
4	Adjustment of withheld income tax for preceding quarters of calendar year (see instructions) . ▶		4	
5	Adjusted total of income tax withheld (line 3 as adjusted by line 4—see instructions) . . .		5	
6a	Taxable social security wages (Complete line 7)	$ × 12.4% (.124) =	6a	
b	Taxable social security tips	$ × 12.4% (.124) =	6b	
7	Taxable Medicare wages and tips	$ × 2.9% (.029) =	7	
8	Total social security and Medicare taxes (add lines 6a, 6b, and 7)		8	
9	Adjustment of social security and Medicare taxes (see instructions for required explanation) .		9	
10	Adjusted total of social security and Medicare taxes (line 8 as adjusted by line 9—see instructions) . ▶		10	
11	Backup withholding (see instructions)		11	
12	Adjustment of backup withholding tax for preceding quarters of calendar year		12	
13	Adjusted total of backup withholding (line 11 as adjusted by line 12)		13	
14	**Total taxes** (add lines 5, 10, and 13)		14	
15	Advance earned income credit (EIC) payments made to employees, if any . . . . . . ▶		15	
16	Net taxes (subtract line 15 from line 14). **This should equal line IV below** (plus line IV of Schedule A (Form 941) if you have treated backup withholding as a separate liability) . . .		16	
17	**Total deposits for quarter**, including overpayment applied from a prior quarter, from your records . ▶		17	
18	**Balance due** (subtract line 17 from line 16). This should be less than $500. Pay to Internal Revenue Service . . ▶		18	

19 **Overpayment**, if line 17 is more than line 16, enter excess here ▶ $ ______ and check if to be: ☐ Applied to next return **OR** ☐ Refunded.

Record of Federal Tax Liability (You must complete if line 16 is $500 or more and Schedule B is not attached.) See instructions before checking these boxes.

If you made deposits using the 95% rule, check here ▶ ☐ If you are a first time 3-banking-day depositor, check here . . ▶ ☐

▶ DO NOT Show Federal Tax Deposits Here ▶

Date wages paid	Show tax liability here, **not deposits.** The IRS gets deposit data from FTD coupons. First month of quarter		Second month of quarter		Third month of quarter	
1st through 3rd	A		I		Q	
4th through 7th	B		J		R	
8th through 11th	C		K		S	
12th through 15th	D		L		T	
16th through 19th	E		M		U	
20th through 22nd	F		N		V	
23rd through 25th	G		O		W	
26th through the last	H		P		X	
Total liability for month	*I*		*II*		*III*	

IV Total for quarter (add lines *I*, *II*, and *III*). **This should equal line 16 above** . . . . . . ▶

Sign Here Under penalties of perjury, I declare that I have examined this return, including accompanying schedules and statements, and to the best of my knowledge and belief, it is true, correct, and complete.

Signature ▶ Print Your Name and Title ▶ Date ▶

For Paperwork Reduction Act Notice, see page 2. Cat. No. 17001Z

Form 941, Employer's Quarterly Federal Tax Return
Figure 8-5.

8

QuickBooks for Profit: Making the Numbers Work

```
                       SUMMARY REPORT
                       Kirk Enterprises
          1/ 1/93 Through 3/31/93                          Page 1
Kirk Enterprises-Selected Accounts
4/15/93
        Inc/Exp Description         Internal Revenue
                                        Service            John Smith
-------------------------------------  --------------      -----------
INCOME/EXPENSE
  EXPENSES
    Payroll-Payroll Expense:
      Comp FICA-Payroll Taxes-FICA        0.00              372.00
      Comp MCARE-Payroll Taxes-MCARE      0.00               87.00
      Gross-Gross Earnings                0.00            6,000.00
                                        -------           ---------
    Total Payroll-Payroll Expense         0.00            6,459.00
                                        -------           ---------
  TOTAL EXPENSES                          0.00            6,459.00
                                        -------           ---------
TOTAL INCOME/EXPENSE                      0.00           -6,459.00

TRANSFERS
  TO Payroll-FICA-FICA Withholding   -1,240.00               0.00
  TO Payroll-FWH-Federal Withholding -1,228.00               0.00
  TO Payroll-MCARE-Medicare Withholdin  -290.00              0.00
  FROM Payroll-FICA-Co-FICA Matching      0.00             372.00
  FROM Payroll-FICA-FICA Withholding      0.00             372.00
  FROM Payroll-FWH-Federal Withholding    0.00             696.00
  FROM Payroll-MCARE-Medicare Withholding 0.00              87.00
  FROM Payroll-MCAREco-Medicare Matching  0.00              87.00
  FROM Payroll-SWH-State Withholding      0.00             164.61
                                       --------          ---------
TOTAL TRANSFERS                       -2,758.00           1,778.61
                                       ========          =========
OVERALL TOTAL                         -2,758.00          -4,680.39
                                       ========          =========
```

```
                       SUMMARY REPORT
                       Kirk Enterprises
          1/ 1/93 Through 3/31/93                          Page 2
Kirk Enterprises-Selected Accounts                         OVERALL
4/15/93                                Mary McFaul          TOTAL
-------------------------------------  ------------       ----------
INCOME/EXPENSE
  EXPENSES
    Payroll-Payroll Expense:
      Comp FICA-Payroll Taxes-FICA       558.00             930.00
      Comp MCARE-Payroll Taxes-MCARE     130.50             217.50
      Gross-Gross Earnings             9,000.00          15,000.00
                                       --------          ---------
    Total Payroll-Payroll Expense      9,688.50          16,147.50
                                       --------          ---------
  TOTAL EXPENSES                       9,688.50          16,147.50
                                       --------          ---------
TOTAL INCOME/EXPENSE                  -9,688.50         -16,147.50

TRANSFERS
  TO Payroll-FICA-FICA Withholding        0.00           -1,240.00
  TO Payroll-FWH-Federal Withholding      0.00           -1,228.00
  TO Payroll-MCARE-Medicare Withholdin    0.00             -290.00
  FROM Payroll-FICA-Co-FICA Matching    558.00              930.00
  FROM Payroll-FICA-FICA Withholding    558.00              930.00
  FROM Payroll-FWH-Federal Withholding 1,146.00           1,842.00
  FROM Payroll-MCARE-Medicare Withholding 130.50            217.50
  FROM Payroll-MCAREco-Medicare Matching  130.50            217.50
  FROM Payroll-SWH-State Withholding    312.84              477.45
                                       --------          ---------
TOTAL TRANSFERS                        2,835.84           1,856.45
                                       ========          =========
OVERALL TOTAL                         -6,852.66         -14,291.05
                                       ========          =========
```

Payroll report
Figure 8-6.

Line 7 The amount of Medicare taxes accumulated during the quarter totals $435. You obtain this amount from adding the Transfers FROM Payroll-MCARE-Medicare Withholding and the Transfers FROM Payroll-MCARECo-Medicare Matching rows of the report. To verify this: the gross earnings for the quarter are subject to Medicare withholding and matching contributions. This means the total in the Gross-Gross Earnings row of the report, $15,000, is multiplied by .029 to get the amount on line 7.

Line 17 This line shows the total deposits made to the IRS during the quarter. This amount can be obtained from the Internal Revenue Service column in the payroll report. The Overall Total row shows that $4137 was the amount deposited with the IRS during the quarter. When you complete your IRS deposit slip, you designate the quarter for which the payment applies. In this case, the payment was made for the first quarter; as a result it is included in this report.

Notice that the bottom portion of Form 941 requires the calculation of tax liabilities at specified time intervals during the deposit periods. If you make your payments in a timely fashion during the quarter, you do not need to complete this portion.

Other Quarterly Reports

In addition to the federal quarterly return, you must complete several other quarterly tax returns and reports, depending on the state where your business is located. These additional reports and tax forms may include state and local withholding tax reports, state unemployment tax reports, and a report for workers' compensation payments. Figure 8-6 provides information needed to prepare some of these reports. For example, the FROM Payroll-SWH-State Withholding row shows that $477.45 was withheld from employee wages for state withholding. You also need to monitor individual employees' gross earnings when completing several of the other forms. Determining the total earnings for an employee for a given time period and determining your FUTA and SUTA contributions are discussed in the section, "Other Annual Tax Forms and Reports," later in this chapter.

Preparing W-2 Forms

At the end of the year, you must give each employee who worked for you during the year a W-2 form. In the example shown in this chapter, assume that John Smith left your business at the end of March and received no further pay checks. The payroll report prepared in this case is customized for John Smith, to provide payroll information about John Smith only, by modifying the Filter Report Transactions window, as shown in Figure 8-7. To display this window, from the Create Payroll Report window, press F8 for the Create Summary Report and press F9 for the Filter Report Transactions window. QuickBooks is limited in the preparation of this report to the entries in the ANB Business checkbook account register since this is the account from which the payroll checks are written. Thus, all the information concerning John Smith's earnings are included in this account.

Notice that QuickBooks automatically limits all payroll reports to payroll account transactions, because the Account contains field is PAYROLL. (Earlier in the chapter, you were told to record all payroll activity in the payroll account or in its subaccounts. Otherwise, QuickBooks' payroll report cannot gather your payroll transactions in this report. In that case, you would need to prepare your reports from the Summary Report option.) You only need to enter the name of the employee you want to summarize by typing his or her name in the Payee contains field or by selecting the name from the Payee list. At

```
                      Filter Report Transactions
     ─────────────────────────────────────────────────────────
     Restrict report to transactions meeting these criteria
           ♦Payee contains    : John Smith
            Memo contains     :
           ♦Account contains  : PAYROLL
           ♦Project contains  :
            Number contains   :
     ─────────────────────────────────────────────────────────
     Select Inc/Exp accounts to include... (Y/N): N
     Select projects to include... (Y/N): N

     Include only Below/Equal/Above (B/E/A):   the amount:
     ──────────────── Checking/CCard Reconciliation Filters ──────────
     Show Payments/Deposits/Unprinted checks/All (P/D/U/A) : A
     Cleared status is blank (Y/N): Y       *: Y       X: Y

     Esc-Cancel                Ctrl-D Reset             Ctrl↵ Done
```

Filtering the payroll report
Figure 8-7.

Payroll

```
                    Federal Tax Liability for John Smith
                              Kirk Enterprises
                          1/ 1/93 Through 12/31/93
Kirk Enterprises-Selected Accounts                                    Page 1
1/15/93

                Inc/Exp Description                          Other
         -----------------------------------------    -----------------
         INCOME/EXPENSE
           EXPENSES
             Payroll-Payroll Expense:
               Comp FICA-Payroll Taxes-FICA              372.00
               Comp MCARE-Payroll Taxes-MCARE             87.00
               Gross-Gross Earnings                    6,000.00
                                                     -----------
             Total Payroll-Payroll Expense                          6,459.00
                                                                 -----------
           TOTAL EXPENSES                                           6,459.00

                                                                 -----------
           TOTAL INCOME/EXPENSE                                    -6,459.00

         TRANSFERS
           FROM Payroll-Co-FICA Matching                              372.00
           FROM Payroll-FICA-FICA Withholding                         372.00
           FROM Payroll-FWH-Federal Withholding                       696.00
           FROM Payroll-MCARE-Medicare Withholding                     87.00
           FROM Payroll-MCARECo-Medicare Matching                      87.00
           FROM Payroll-SWH-State Withholding                         164.61
                                                                 -----------
           TOTAL TRANSFERS                                          1,778.61

                                                                 -----------
           OVERALL TOTAL                                           -4,680.39
                                                                 ===========
```

Annual payroll report for John Smith
Figure 8-8.

this point, press Ctrl-Enter to return to the Create Summary Report. Next, modify the Report Title field to include the employee's name. The payroll report shown in Figure 8-8 provides the payroll history for John Smith in 1993.

Report Discussion

You can use a summary payroll report like the one shown in Figure 8-8 to create an employee's W-2 Wage and Tax Statement. To complete the form that appears in Figure 8-9, use the following lines in the report:

Gross-Gross Earnings is the amount ($6000) reported in the Wages, tips, other compensation box. It is also the amount in the Social security wages box, up to the $55,500 ceiling, and in the Medicare wages and tips income, up to the $130,200 ceiling.

FROM Payroll-FWH-Federal Withholding is the amount ($696) reported in the Federal income tax withheld box.

FROM Payroll-FICA-FICA Withholding is the amount ($372) reported in the Social security tax withheld box. Notice this is equal to the company FICA contribution (Comp FICA-Payroll Taxes-FICA), since the company matches employee FICA contributions dollar for dollar up to $55,500 of gross earnings.

FROM Payroll-MCARE-Medicare Withholding is the amount for the Medicare tax withheld. Notice that this is equal to the company Medicare contributions (Comp MCARE-Payroll Taxes-MCARE) since the company matches the employee's Medicare contribution dollar for dollar up to the first $130,200 of gross earnings.

FROM Payroll-SWH-State Withholding is the amount ($164.61) reported in the State income tax box.

Any account for the local taxes will fill in the Local income tax box, although the report in Figure 8-8 does not list any. If you do business in an area where local income taxes are withheld, you need to add the appropriate liability accounts to accumulate this information.

Other Annual Tax Forms and Reports

The information provided in the preceding reports can also be used to prepare other year-end tax reports. For example, payroll reports for the full year, similar to those shown in Figures 8-6 and 8-8, can be used to complete sections of the following reports:

Form W-3, Transmittal of Income and Tax Statements

Form 940, Employer's Annual Federal Unemployment (FUTA) Tax Return

Payroll

1 Control number	22222	For Official Use Only ▶ OMB No. 1545-0008				
2 Employer's name, address, and ZIP code **Kirk Enterprises**			6 Statutory employee ☐	Deceased ☐	Pension plan ☐	Legal rep ☐	942 emp. ☐	Subtotal ☐	Deferred compensation ☐	Void ☐
			7 Allocated tips		8 Advance EIC payment
3 Employer's identification number	4 Employer's state I.D. number		9 Federal income tax withheld 696.00	10 Wages, tips, other compensation 6000.00
5 Employee's social security number			11 Social security tax withheld 372.00	12 Social security wages 6000.00
			13 Social security tips	14 Medicare wages and tips 6000.00
19a Employee's name (first, middle initial, last) **John Smith**			15 Medicare tax withheld 87.00	16 Nonqualified plans
			17 See Instrs. for Form W-2	18 Other
19b Employee's address and ZIP code			22 Dependent care benefits	23 Benefits included in Box 10
20	21		27 Local income tax	28 Local wages, tips, etc.	29 Name of locality
24 State income tax 164.61	25 State wages, tips, etc. 6000.00	26 Name of state **OHIO**			

Copy A For Social Security Administration Cat. No. 10134D Department of the Treasury—Internal Revenue Service

Form **W-2 Wage and Tax Statement** 1992 (Rev. 4-92)

For Paperwork Reduction Act Notice and Instructions for completing this form, see separate instructions.

W-2 form completed using payroll report
Figure 8-9.

Various state and local withholding and state unemployment tax (SUTA) reports

FUTA and SUTA Contributions

When completing your quarterly and annual reports, you can use the Filter option in QuickBooks to prepare a report showing the total FUTA and SUTA contributions paid during the quarter or year. This would be accomplished by preparing a summary report and using QuickBooks' Filter Report Transactions window to complete the account matches: Payroll:Comp FUTA. Then prepare a second report and complete the account matches: Payroll:Comp SUI. Figures 8-10 and 8-11 show filtered reports prepared from your account register to show FUTA payments of $104 and SUTA payments of $520.

Reports filtered in this manner can be prepared to determine the total federal and state payments for unemployment withholding during the entire year. That information could then be used in completing Part II,

```
                              FUTA Payments
                             Kirk Enterprises
                         1/ 1/93 Through 12/31/93
Kirk Enterprises-All Accounts                                        Page 1
1/15/93
                                                        1/ 1/93-
                        Inc/Exp Description            12/31/93
                   --------------------------------   -----------
                   INCOME/EXPENSE
                     EXPENSES
                       Payroll-Payroll Expense:
                         Comp FUTA-Company FUTA contribution   104.00
                                                              --------
                         Total Payroll-Payroll Expense         104.00
                                                              --------
                       TOTAL EXPENSES                          104.00

                                                              --------
                       TOTAL INCOME/EXPENSE                   -104.00
                                                              ========
```

Report showing FUTA payments
Figure 8-10.

Payroll

```
                          SUTA Payments
                         Kirk Enterprises
                    1/ 1/93 Through 12/31/93
Kirk Enterprises-All Accounts                                  Page 1
1/15/93
                                                  1/ 1/93-
                   Inc/Exp Description            12/31/93
          -------------------------------------  ----------
          INCOME/EXPENSE
             EXPENSES
                Payroll-Payroll Expense:
                   Comp SUI-Company SUI contribution   520.00
                                                      --------
                Total Payroll-Payroll Expense           520.00
                                                      --------
             TOTAL EXPENSES                             520.00

                                                      --------
             TOTAL INCOME/EXPENSE                      -520.00
                                                      ========
```

Report showing SUTA payments Figure 8-11.

line 4 of federal Form 940 and the corresponding line of your state's SUTA form.

Form 1099

The last payroll-related statement discussed here is Form 1099. You must provide a Form 1099 to all individuals who are not regular employees and to whom you have paid more than $600 during the tax year. The easiest way to record transactions for payments of this nature is to type **1099** in the memo field when you record the transactions in your business account register during the year. Then, to gather the information needed to prepare 1099s for each payee, you can prepare a transaction report for the year filtered by payee and memo field matches. If you are not certain of all the payees to whom you have paid miscellaneous income, you may want to filter the memo field for 1099 first and print all these transactions. You can use that information to group your 1099 information by payee matches. You could also assign all 1099 payments to an account (for example, Consult-1099) and screen a summary or transaction report by payee and account to accumulate the necessary 1099 information.

> **NOTE:** It is necessary to adhere to the IRS guidelines regarding individuals who are employees and individuals who are outside contractors. Among other things, contractors are hired to do a specific job and are not directed by your personnel. Temporary employees can also be hired for a single job, but they are directed by you or your staff and are usually required to perform all work on site. You cannot classify a temporary employee as a contractor to avoid the paper work needed for employees.

CHAPTER

9

MORTGAGES, CREDIT CARDS, AND OTHER LIABILITIES

Most businesses have some level of debt. For some businesses the only debt might be short term; for others, there is long-term debt for office facilities, trucks, or other equipment.

QuickBooks provides the tools that you need to manage short- and long-term debt. For short-term debt, QuickBooks can help you manage your cash flows, paying bills at the latest possible time to still receive discounts. This is a better approach than writing a check as soon as you receive the bill or waiting until after the discount period is over and losing the discount you could have received with prompt payment. For long-term debt, QuickBooks lets you look at the cost of interest on the debt and the reduction of principal over time.

In this chapter you learn how to set up liability accounts to keep track of what you owe and to monitor account activity. You will have an opportunity to look at paying vendor bills, sales tax, payroll taxes, a credit card bill, and a mortgage.

Short- Versus Long-term Liabilities

Short-term liabilities are generally considered to be liabilities that are paid back in less than one year. These include your accounts with suppliers, accrued payroll taxes, accrued sales taxes, and short-term loans. You can use QuickBooks accounts payable features to handle your short-term liabilities with suppliers. You can use special features to help you manage your cash flow. Although credit card accounts are short-term liabilities, always set them up as accounts separate from other short-term liabilities; you can, however, set up one liability account to monitor two short-term loans.

You can stretch QuickBooks' limit of 255 accounts for assets and liabilities if you group like assets or liabilities into one account.

Long-term liabilities are those liabilities that will take longer than one year to pay back These might include loans for equipment, machinery, or a mortgage on the company's headquarters.

QuickBooks allows you a maximum of 255 asset and liability accounts. Even if every asset and liability has a separate account, this is an adequate number for many businesses. If you think you have more, plan to group assets and liabilities to ensure that 255 is sufficient. You can make adjustments to your liability accounts to show principal reductions when you write the check for the payment.

Accounts Payable

Accounts payable (A/P), is the term used to refer to recording and tracking all of your business bills. These bills may be from suppliers of goods that you are reselling, consultants who are providing business advice, or any other vendor who supplies you with goods and services. From a business standpoint, it is in your best interest to record bills as

Mortgages, Credit Cards, and Other Liabilities

you receive them, so that you can project the level of cash flows necessary to pay them in a timely fashion. You will want to match payments with outstanding bills in order to tell which bills have not been paid.

You might be wondering why you even need accounts payable, since you have already seen two ways to handle bills. You learned how to write checks with QuickBooks and document your payments with automatic register entries. You also learned that you could write manual checks and record the transactions in your register. However, you still need accounts payable because it offers additional advantages in tracking due dates for you, and it can help you run a more efficient business operation.

QuickBooks' accounts payable features allow you to complete a transaction for each bill using the contents of the vendor list to supply a name and address. QuickBooks can group several invoices from one vendor and write one check for their payment. You can use QuickBooks to track the sales taxes you must pay, as you will see later in this chapter. Also, as you will learn in Chapter 12, you can use QuickBooks' accounts payable features to create 1099s.

The accounts payable features can be used whether you use a cash or accrual basis accounting system in your business. Businesses that ue a *cash basis* accounting system record expenses when they pay them and record income when they receive it. Businesses that use an *accrual basis* accounting system record expenses at the time that they make a commitment to incur them; they record income when a customer commits to buying their goods and services (rather than when they pay). If you do not need to record 1099s and you use a cash basis accounting system, you may wish to stay with the checkbook rather than use accounts payable. Of course, you can use accounts payable if you prefer.

You can use QuickBooks whether you use a cash or an accrual basis accounting system.

Entering Bills

Entering the bills you have to pay in QuickBooks has several advantages, including the following:

◆ *You don't accidentally misplace bills* The bills you enter in QuickBooks accounts payable remain in QuickBooks and are available for reference at any time.

♦ *You know when you want to pay bills* QuickBooks remembers when the bills are due and reminds you to pay them.

♦ *You have the information to write the check* QuickBooks has the vendor list that includes the address and other information you want handy when you pay the vendor. QuickBooks will even write the check for you when you tell QuickBooks that you want to pay the bill.

When you enter a bill in QuickBooks, you tell QuickBooks who you owe, how much you owe, when the bill is due, and what you owe the money for. To enter the bills, follow these steps:

1. Select 3 Accounts Payable from the Main Menu.
2. Select 1 A/P Register to display an accounts payable window, as shown here:

F1-Help	F2-File/Print	F3-Find/Edit	F4-Lists	F5-Reports	F6-Activities
DATE	INV NUM	♦VENDOR · MEMO · ♦ACCOUNT		PAY DATE	OWED	PAID
		BEGINNING				
11/ 5/93		Memo: ♦Acct		11/15/93		

The date is the current date since QuickBooks assumes you are recording the payables you have received today. You can change the date to another when the date you want the invoice recorded is not the current one.

3. Move to the Vendor field and select the vendor you need to pay.

This field has a diamond, so you can press Ctrl-L and select a vendor from the vendor list. Of course, you can always type the vendor name and add it to the vendor list.

4. Enter the due date of the bill in the Pay Date field.

QuickBooks automatically supplies a date for the Pay Date field by adding a specific number of days to the date in the Date field. By default this number is ten, but you can change it in the company setting that sets the default interval between the date of a bill and when it is paid. (See the section, "Changing the Payment Interval," later in this chapter.) You can also replace the date with a new one.

5. Enter the amount to pay in the Owed field.

Mortgages, Credit Cards, and Other Liabilities

6. Select the account that the payment is for in the Account field.

   Since this field has a diamond, you can press Ctrl-L to select an account. When the payment is for an asset, such as equipment, you select the account for the asset. Most of the time, you will select an expense account such as COGS (cost of goods sold).

7. Press Ctrl-Enter to finish recording the bill and enter the next bill.

To see an example of how easy it is to enter a payment, suppose you have a bill from Keri Imports for $6,000. Assuming Keri Imports is in your vendor list, you can move to the Vendor field, press Ctrl-L, and select Keri Imports from the list. Next, move to the Owed field and type **6000** for the Owed field. Move to the Account field and press Ctrl-L to list the accounts. Select COGS for cost of goods sold. You do not need to supply the date and payment date since QuickBooks assumes the current date for the Date field and a date ten days away for the Pay Date field. If you want, you can enter Keri Imports' invoice number in the Inv Num field. The completed entry for the bill looks like this:

```
F1-Help  F2-File/Print   F3-Find/Edit   F4-Lists   F5-Reports   F6-Activities
 DATE   |INV NUM| ◆VENDOR · MEMO · ◆ACCOUNT |PAY DATE|   OWED   |   PAID
10/26/92|       |Keri Imports               |11/ 5/92| 6,000|00 |
        |Memo:  |                           |        |      |   |
        |◆Acct  |COGS                       |        |      |   |
```

At this point, you are ready to press Ctrl-Enter to finish entering the bill and continue with the next one. When you are finished entering bills, press Esc to return to the prior menu.

If you use a cash basis of accounting, you don't enter the bills you receive through the accounts payable register. When you write the check to pay the bill, the account you select is the same account you would select in the accounts payable register. Writing a check to pay the bill rather than letting QuickBooks write the check for you means an entry is never made in the accounts payable register.

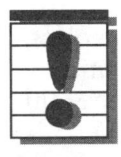

TIP: Put your bills in a folder in date order so when you pay them you have the remittance slips that should accompany the bills. If a remittance slip accompanies the payment, vendors will be sure to correctly credit your account.

> **TIP:** When a supplier offers a discount for early payment, record the date for the early payment as the payment date. QuickBooks will remind you to pay the supplier in time to receive the discount.

Editing Bill Entries

After you have entered bills into your accounts payable register, you can return to a bill and make changes. To change the bill information, move to the fields you want to change and make new entries. When you move to another record in the accounts payable register, select 1 Record transaction to have the changes to the bill applied.

There are some exceptions to making changes in a bill when it is partially or completely paid. When you have completely paid a bill, you cannot change the Pay Date field. With either partial or complete payment, you cannot reduce the amount of the bill. If you must reduce a bill that you have completely or partially paid, you must first remove the transaction that paid the bill. To do this, go to the accounts payable register. Move to the transaction by highlighting the bill, then pressing Ctrl-H, selecting the line with the PMT type, and pressing Enter. Once at the payment transaction, you can press Ctrl-Del, and then select 1 Delete transaction to remove the payment transaction from the accounts payable register.

> **TIP:** When you plan to pay a bill within the discount period, record the amount of the bill as the discounted amount. If you do not pay the bill within the discount period, you can edit the bill's transaction to increase the amount you owe, even if you have partially paid the bill.

> **TIP:** If you are not seeing reminders about scheduled bills, invoices, and checks and you have installed Bizminder, check the settings for Customize QuickBooks in the Set Up/Customize option in the Main Menu to ensure that Bizminder is active.

Bizminder

If you have installed QuickBooks with Bizminder, it will remind you that you have bills to pay every time you start your computer. A sample reminder looks something like this:

```
                    QuickBooks Bizminder
────────────────────────────────────────────────────────
You have:

       ■ Checks to print.
       ■ An overdue transaction group.
       ■ An overdue A/P bill.
       ■ An overdue A/P group.
       ■ An overdue invoice.



                                              ←┘ Continue
```

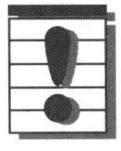

TIP: If you are planning to take a vacation and want to pay bills in advance, you can change the Customize QuickBooks option, Days in advance to remind of scheduled bills, to a higher number. The bills will all be listed ahead of their normal time. QuickBooks supports any number of days from 0 to 30.

If Bizminder is not installed, you can add it by reinstalling QuickBooks. You will also see a reminder below the Main Menu when you have bills to pay. This reminder, seen here, appears when you first start QuickBooks or when you change companies:

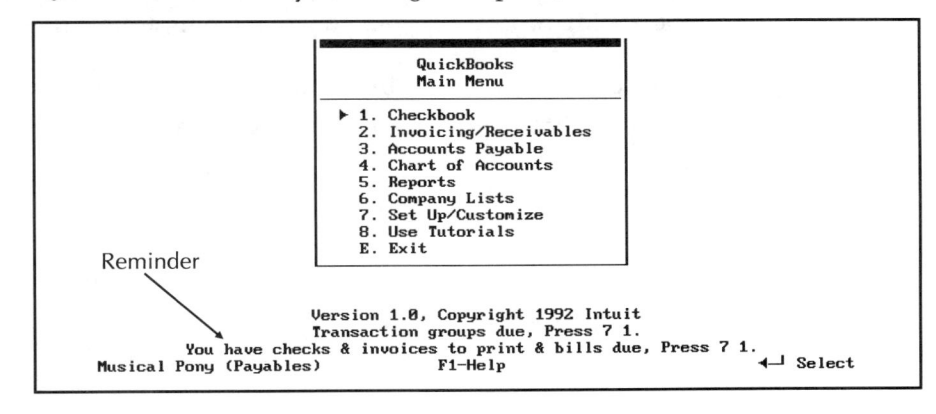

```
                           QuickBooks
                           Main Menu

                     ▶ 1. Checkbook
                       2. Invoicing/Receivables
                       3. Accounts Payable
                       4. Chart of Accounts
                       5. Reports
                       6. Company Lists
                       7. Set Up/Customize
                       8. Use Tutorials
                       E. Exit


               Version 1.0, Copyright 1992 Intuit
               Transaction groups due, Press 7 1.
        You have checks & invoices to print & bills due, Press 7 1.
  Musical Pony (Payables)          F1-Help              ←┘ Select
```

Reminder

> **TIP:** Make sure any services or goods that you contract for allow for the last payment after you receive merchandise or services without defects. If you have paid in full for services that you have a problem with, you have no leverage to correct the problem.

Changing the Payment Interval

If you do not pay your bills ten days after they are recorded, you may want to change the default date interval between the date and the payment date. Changing the default date interval does not prevent you from overwriting the date in the Pay Date field of the bills you record. To change the number of days QuickBooks adds to the date for the Pay Date field, follow these steps:

1. Select 7 Set Up/Customize from the Main Menu.
2. Select 4 Customize Current Company.
3. Select 2 Options.
4. Type the number of days between the date and bill date for the option, Default number of days between DATE and PAY DATE in Accounts Payable.
5. Press [Ctrl]-[Enter] to finish choosing options.

Recording Payments

After the bills are entered, you need to pay them. You can pay them using menu selections. Using QuickBooks to pay bills automates the check-writing process for you. To pay the bills, follow these steps:

1. Select 3 Accounts Payable from the Main Menu.
2. Select 2 Pay Bills to display the Pay Vendors window seen in the following:

Mortgages, Credit Cards, and Other Liabilities

```
┌─────────────────────────────────────────────────────┐
│                    Pay Vendors                      │
├─────────────────────────────────────────────────────┤
│  Pay bills with Pay Dates through: 11/ 4/93         │
│  ♦Checking account to use:                          │
│  Pay All/Selected bills (A/S): A                    │
├─────────────────────────────────────────────────────┤
│  Esc-Cancel                            Ctrl↵  Done  │
└─────────────────────────────────────────────────────┘
```

You can also display this window from the accounts payable register by pressing [F6] for the Activities menu and selecting 2 Pay Bills, or by pressing [Ctrl]-[Y]. In the Pay Vendors window, QuickBooks displays the current date for the Pay bills with Pay Dates through field, so all the unpaid bills with dates up until today's date are included. You can change the date to another when you want to pay bills for a different set of dates. For example, if you are taking tomorrow off, you may want to change the date to tomorrow's date so you can take care of tomorrow's bills now.

3. Move to the Checking account to use field and select the checking account that you will use to pay the bills.

   This field has a diamond, so you can select a checking account from any of those you may have available.

4. Type **A** for All or **S** for Selected to tell QuickBooks you plan to either pay all of the bills listed, or just selected amounts of selected bills.

5. Press [Ctrl]-[Enter] to finish with the window.

   QuickBooks displays a Choose Bills to Pay window like the one shown in Figure 9-1. This window lists all of the unpaid bills that have a Pay Date field of the date you entered in the previous window, or earlier. Any bills that are not due until later do not appear in the list. The difference between All and Selected for the Pay All/Selected bills field is how much of the bills QuickBooks assumes you want to pay. When All is selected, QuickBooks

QuickBooks for Profit: Making the Numbers Work

```
                    Choose Bills to Pay

        Vendor         Invoice  Pay Date    Balance    Payment

   Acme Supplies                10/25/93    2,500.00   2,500.00   ↑
   Keri Imports                 11/ 5/92    6,000.00   6,000.00   ▯




   Checking Balance $24,436.52              TOTAL      8,500.00
                                                                  ↓
   Esc-Cancel          F9-Pay in full/Don't pay        Ctrl⏎ Done

Musical Pony (Payables)
```

Figure 9-1. Recorded bills ready for payment

assumes you want to pay all of the listed bills. When Selected is chosen, QuickBooks assumes you want to pay $0 of the listed bills, so you must enter the payment amounts for the bills you want to pay. You can change these assumptions by moving to a bill and pressing F9 to switch between paying the bill in full or not paying it at all. You can also make a partial payment by typing the amount you want to pay in the Payment column.

6. Press Ctrl-Enter after selecting the bills to pay.

   The next window prompts whether you want to print a payment summary. A payment summary looks like this:

```
                       PAYMENT SUMMARY
              Paid from Checking (Balance = $24,436.52)

     Vendor         Invoice  Inv Date  Pay Date   Balance   Payment
     ---------------------   --------  --------   --------  --------
   Acme Supplies             10/15/93  10/25/93   2,500.00  2,500.00
   Keri Imports              10/26/92  11/ 5/92   6,000.00  6,000.00
                                                  ========  ========
                             Totals:   2 item(s)  8,500.00  8,500.00
```

7. Select 1 Don't print payment summary or 2 Print payment summary.

Mortgages, Credit Cards, and Other Liabilities

8. Type the date you want to appear on the printed checks or leave the current date in place.

   The date is the date that appears on the checks and the accounts payable register. Preparing the checks lets QuickBooks handle printing them using the vendor information you have stored in the vendor list.

9. Press Ctrl-Enter to prepare the checks.

After preparing the checks, you can print them. As you learned in Chapter 3, you select 1 Checkbook from the Main Menu and 1 Write/Print Checks. Next, press Ctrl-P and then Ctrl-Enter. An example of the checks and how QuickBooks gets the information for the check is shown in Figure 9-2. If you entered an invoice number in the accounts payable register, the invoice number would appear in the memo field of the check.

> **TIP:** The person preparing the checks should not be the one signing them (unless the business owner is doing both). Having two people involved in preparing checks prevents either one from writing a check to themselves or a friend.

After making the payments, when you look at the accounts payable register, you will see transactions for the payments of those bills. You will also notice that the Pay Date fields now contain "PAID" for the bills you have paid. For example, after paying the Keri Imports bill, the accounts payable register looks like this:

DATE	INV NUM	◆VENDOR · MEMO · ◆ACCOUNT	PAY DATE	OWED	PAID
10/26/92		Keri Imports COGS	PAID	6,000 00	
11/ 4/93		Keri Imports [Checking]			6,000 00

If you need to make a change to the payment of the bill, you can edit the payment. To do this, move to the transaction for the payment, then press F3 for the Find/Edit menu, and select A Edit Payment. You can also press Ctrl-E. From the first window displayed, you can switch to

QuickBooks for Profit: Making the Numbers Work

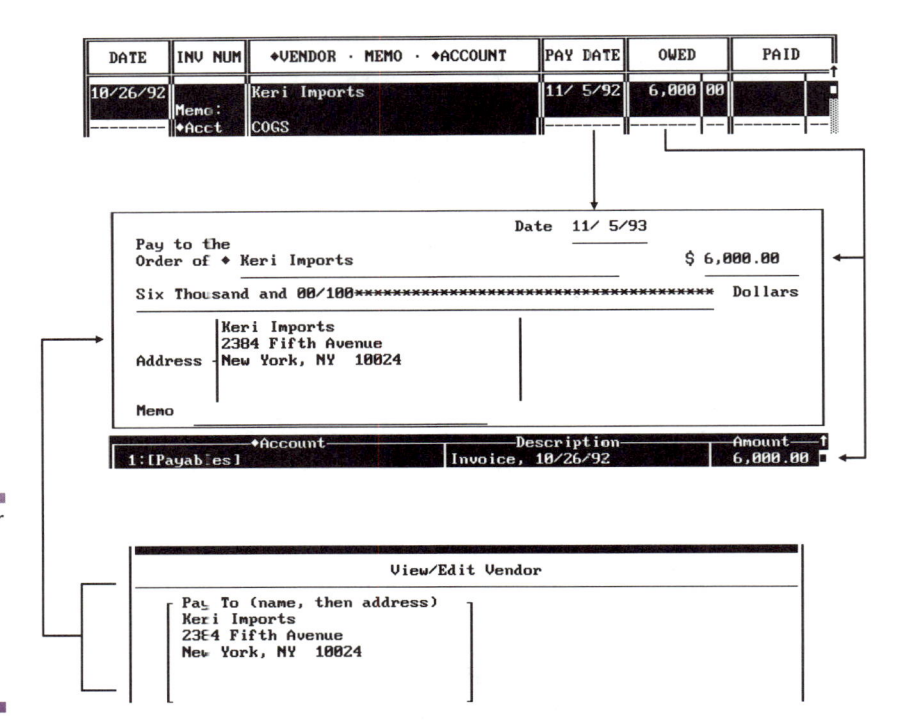

Bill and vendor information used to create the check to pay a bill
Figure 9-2.

another checking account by making a selection in the Checking account to use field. After pressing Ctrl-Enter, you will see the same Choose Bills to Pay window you saw earlier when you paid the bill. Now, however, only the bills that are paid by the payment are shown. Once you have printed the check, you cannot edit the transaction that pays the bills.

Recording Bills Paid Directly by Checks

If you are paying bills that you have not recorded in QuickBooks, the process is different. In these cases, you pay the bill by writing the check. You learned how to write checks in Chapter 3. When you look at the accounts payable register, you do not see the bill because you did not use the accounts payable register to record the bill and payment.

Mortgages, Credit Cards, and Other Liabilities

If you plan to prepare a 1099 for the payee at the end of the year, you must enter the bill in the accounts payable register with the current date in the Pay Date field. Then use QuickBooks to prepare the check. Recording the bill through the accounts payable register gives you a record of the payment, which you can use to create a report that will help you prepare the 1099. (You will learn how to do this in Chapter 12.)

NOTE: If you use a cash basis of accounting, you may think you should not use accounts payable. However, you can benefit from using it by setting report options to show reports on a cash basis.

Other Short-term Liabilities

Taxes are another short-term liability that you need to pay. In the last chapter, you were introduced to taxes that you pay and collect from your employee. In Chapter 6, you learned about adding sales tax items to your item list. These taxes collected as part of sales and payroll are liabilities because you owe these amounts to governmental agencies. Sales taxes have their own sales tax account, and payroll taxes have different accounts for the different taxes you collect. You enter these amounts in different ways, through invoices for sales taxes or checks for the payroll. Some other short-term liabilities you may have are deposits received from customers and gift certificates.

Sales Taxes

Sales taxes are added through the invoices you create. When you add sales tax to an invoice, you add a sales tax item code to the invoice. The sales tax item code you create uses the sales tax item type so QuickBooks knows to make an accounts payable account for it. QuickBooks adds a transaction to this sales tax account for the amount that you owe the governmental agency. You do not make entries in the sales tax account, since QuickBooks makes the entry for you as you create invoices. You will also notice that QuickBooks groups sales taxes collected from invoices for each day in groups of 30 for a single transaction. This means that a transaction in the sales tax account contains the sales taxes collected for up to 30 different invoices on the same day.

Another special feature of the sales tax account is the Pay Date field. The Pay Date field for the sales tax transaction is not 10 days or another number you specify from the current date. Sales taxes are due monthly, quarterly, or yearly. The transactions for sales taxes have their Pay Date field set to the last date of the month, quarter, or year. You can change the payment from monthly to quarterly or yearly in the company options. Type **Q** or **A** in place of the M after the option, Sales Tax collected is payable Monthly, Quarterly, or Annually.

To tell QuickBooks that you want to pay these bills, change from the accounts payable account to the payable account for the taxes. Follow these steps:

1. Select 4 Chart of Accounts.
2. Select the A/P account for the other liabilities you want to use.

QuickBooks will combine sales tax amounts for you so you know exactly how much to pay at the end of the month, quarter, or year.

As an example, if you select a sales tax account you have set up to keep track of the taxes you have collected in invoices, the account might look like Figure 9-3. This looks just like the standard accounts payable account. You can add other amounts due, but you usually do not have to because the transactions for the account are created when you make other entries.

At this point, you can press [Esc] and then select 2 Pay Bills from the menu. The window looks like Figure 9-4. When you owe a vendor several bills, QuickBooks combines the amounts from the different bills into a single amount. So, in the sales tax due shown in Figure 9-4, you will only have one check for the City of Madison and another for the State of Ohio. In the sales tax example, you would not want to write separate checks for the sales tax you collected for each sale. When you want to return to working with the standard accounts payable account, select the accounts payable account after selecting 4 Chart of Accounts from the Main Menu.

Mortgages, Credit Cards, and Other Liabilities

```
F1-Help  F2-File/Print  F3-Find/Edit  F4-Lists  F5-Reports  F6-Activities
```

DATE	INV NUM	♦VENDOR · MEMO · ♦ACCOUNT	PAY DATE	OWED	PAID
10/13/93 SPLIT		City of Madison [Receivables]	10/31/93	15 99	
10/20/93 SPLIT		State of Ohio [Receivables]	10/31/93	4,285 50	
10/20/93 SPLIT		City of Madison [Receivables]	10/31/93	857 10	
10/22/93 SPLIT		State of Ohio [Receivables]	10/31/93	81 97	
10/22/93 SPLIT		City of Madison [Receivables]	10/31/93	16 39	
11/ 4/93	Memo: ♦Acct		11/14/93		

Sales Tax
Esc-Leave   Ctrl⏎ Record   Ending Balance: $5,336.90

Register entries for sales taxes
Figure 9-3.

```
                    Choose Bills to Pay

       Vendor          Invoice   Pay Date    Balance     Payment

    City of Madison              10/31/93      16.39       16.39
    City of Madison              10/31/93      15.99       15.99
    City of Madison              10/31/93     857.10      857.10
    State of Ohio                10/31/93   4,285.50    4,285.50
    State of Ohio                10/31/93      81.97       81.97
    State of Ohio                10/31/93      79.95       79.95


    Checking Balance $23,565.21             TOTAL        5,336.90

    Esc-Cancel         F9-Pay in full/Don't pay       Ctrl⏎ Done
```

Musical Pony (Sales Tax)

Sales taxes owed and ready to be paid
Figure 9-4.

Payroll Taxes

Payroll taxes are collected every pay day. It is a good idea to set up separate accounts for each governmental agency you must pay. These accounts are created like other accounts. When you create the account, select Current Liability as the account type. The fields for the name, description, beginning balance, and account number are just like the information you supplied when you created other accounts. As with the sales tax payable account, you will not make entries into the accounts payable register for this account. When you write the check to record the payable, the transaction that writes the check also handles adding the amount to the accounts for the payroll taxes.

When you want to pay the bill for these payroll taxes, write a check for it or record the transaction in the check register. For example, if you owe $1746.84 to the IRS for social security taxes collected from the employee, your check register entry (assuming the transfer of funds is made by your bank) might look like this:

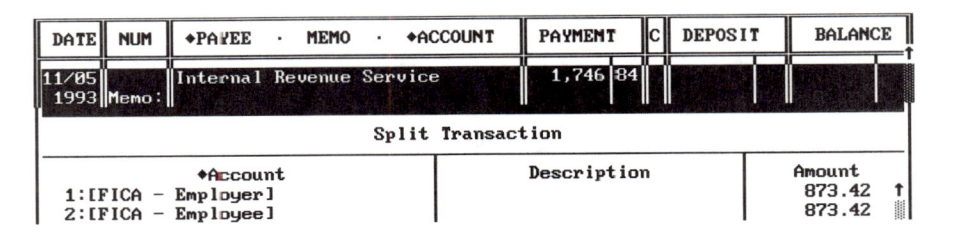

DATE	NUM	♦PAYEE · MEMO · ♦ACCOUNT	PAYMENT	C	DEPOSIT	BALANCE
11/05 1993	Memo:	Internal Revenue Service	1,746 84			

Split Transaction

♦Account	Description	Amount
1:[FICA - Employer]		873.42
2:[FICA - Employee]		873.42

Deposits and Gift Certificates

Two other current liability accounts you may need are for deposits and gift certificates. When you receive deposits from customers—for example, a security deposit if you are a landlord—the deposit needs to be saved, since you will later return it to the customer or apply it to a sale. Until the deposits are used for another purpose, the deposit is still an amount you owe the customer. With gift certificates, you do not have a sale when a customer buys one; the sale occurs when the customer uses the gift certificate to purchase merchandise or services. You will want separate accounts for deposits and gift certificates.

The item code you create to add a deposit or gift certificate to the invoice has the liability account for the Account field. You may want to

Mortgages, Credit Cards, and Other Liabilities

have separate item codes: one for the charging of the deposit or purchase of the gift certificate, and one for the return of the deposit or redemption of the gift certificate.

Figure 9-5 shows what happens when a gift certificate is purchased and redeemed. When the gift certificate is purchased, the customer receives the invoice that shows they have paid for the certificate. This invoice has an item code, "Gift Certificate Purchased," which uses the account of Gift Certificates. After this gift certificate is purchased, you owe the amount of the certificate to the bearer. When the gift certificate is redeemed, the customer's invoice shows an item code of a negative amount for the amount of the gift certificate. This item has the same account, Gift Certificates, but the "Gift Certificate Redeemed" item has a

Customer buys gift certificate

Invoice

Item Code	Description	Price Each	Amount
Gift Purch	Gift Certificate Purchased (added as a liability)	50	50
Total			50

Customer redeems gift certificate

Invoice

Item Code	Description	Price Each	Amount
Merchand	Merchandise	75	75
Gift Purch	Gift Certificate Redeemed (removing the liability)	(50)	(50)
Total			25

Invoices for purchasing and redeeming a gift certificate
Figure 9-5.

negative price that reverses the amount previously entered. The effect of a deposit is the same.

Credit Card Accounts

If you maintain a credit card account and enter each transaction, you can reconcile the account in much the same way you reconcile bank statements.

A business credit card provides another method of paying your company's bills. A credit card account is especially useful when you have a significant amount of business travel. It offers the advantage of an interest-free loan for a short period (as long as you pay the bill in full), and it means that you do not have to travel with cash.

If you use a credit card for your business, you can have QuickBooks record the charges you make to the account. You can also use QuickBooks to quickly reconcile the credit card statement with the account. The account you use for a credit card is a liability account because it is money you owe to the credit card issuer.

A credit card account is set up just like other accounts, but you can supply different optional information. You can enter a credit limit, account number, and vendor for the issuer of the credit card. Once the credit card account is created, you can select the account from the chart of accounts to view its register. Figure 9-6 shows an example of a credit card register. Notice how each of the charges has an account selected for the transaction; for example, Chenelle Gas Supply's account is "Auto." These accounts are the same accounts you use when you enter the bill that you subsequently pay by check.

With the credit card account, you can either enter each charge you make with the card, as in Figure 9-6, or you can enter a single amount for all charges made during a month. Enter each charge you make with the card if you want to be able to look at the credit card account in between billings and know the total charged to date.

TIP: Safely keeping track of your credit card and your charge slips is just as important for a business as for your personal charging activities.

Mortgages, Credit Cards, and Other Liabilities

```
F1-Help   F2-File/Print   F3-Find/Edit   F4-Lists   F5-Reports   F6-Activities
```

DATE	REF	♦PAYEE · MEMO · ♦ACCOUNT	CHARGE	C	PAYMENT	BALANCE
10/10 1993		Chenelle Gas Supply Auto	10 67			10 67
10/11 1993		Macaretti's Designs Materials	107 78			118 45
10/13 1993		WTMF - Promotions Advert	500 00			618 45
10/14 1993		Davis Supplies Off Supp	175 34			793 79
10/16 1993		Wyse Lock & Key Repairs:Bldg	75 00			868 79
10/18 1993	Memo: ♦Acct	U. P. S. Shipping costs for prior week Freight	78 74			947 53

Massive Charge
Esc-Leave   Ctrl⏎ Record

Credit Remaining: $4,052.47
Ending Balance: $ 947.53

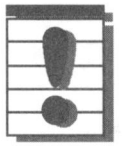

Register for a credit card account
Figure 9-6.

> **TIP:** Keep personal charges off your company credit card and your business charges off your personal credit card. If you include personal items on your business credit card, do not include them in the list of items. You will want to write a separate check for the personal items, using your personal checking account.

Paying the Credit Card Bill

When you receive a bill for your credit card purchases, you need to reconcile the credit card charges you have recorded to the statement. Also, you need to record any finance charges or other charges. To pay the credit card bill, follow these steps:

1. Press [F6] for the Activities menu and then select 2 Reconcile/Pay Bill to display the window in Figure 9-7.

   You can also press [Ctrl]-[Y]. The information you enter in the Credit Card Statement Information window is information you get from the statement, not the register.

Credit Card Statement Information window **Figure 9-7.**

```
         Credit Card Statement Information

    Charges, Cash Advances:
      (other than finance charges)
    Payments, Credits      :
    New balance            :

    ——————Transaction to Be Added (Optional)——————
        Finance Charges:
      ◆Account:
        Date: 11/ 4/93

              Enter statement information.
    Esc-Cancel          F1-Help          Ctrl◄┘ Done
```

2. Type the amount for charges and cash advances you have received through the credit card.

3. Type the amount of any credit applied to the bill from a previous period or any interim payment.

    You will type **0** if you have no payments or credits.

4. Type the remaining amount due.

5. Type any finance charge in the Finance Charges field.

6. Select the account to register any finance charges by pressing Ctrl-L and selecting the account.

    Many of the initial chart of accounts have a "Fin" account with the description, "Finance Charge," for this purpose.

7. Type the date of the statement in the Date field and press Ctrl-Enter to finish the window.

    QuickBooks displays the reconciliation summary like the one shown in Figure 9-8.

8. Mark in the reconciliation summary the charged items that appear in the statement.

    For each item in the statement, move to the same item in the summary and type * or press the Spacebar. Also, check that the amount in the statement matches the amount in the summary. If an item does not match, highlight the item in the list and press F9 to edit the transaction. If the error is with the credit card, you will need to contact the credit card's issuer. Ideally, when you are finished, the Difference field will equal zero.

Mortgages, Credit Cards, and Other Liabilities

```
F1-Help        File/Print        Find/Edit        Lists        Reports        Activities
┌──────┬───┬──────────┬──────────┬──────────────────────┬─────────────────────────┐
│ REF  │ C │  AMOUNT  │   DATE   │        PAYEE         │          MEMO           │
├──────┼───┼──────────┼──────────┼──────────────────────┼─────────────────────────┤
│      │   │    10.67 │ 10/10/93 │ Chenelle Gas Supply  │                         │
│      │   │   107.78 │ 10/11/93 │ Macaretti's Designs  │                         │
│      │   │   500.00 │ 10/13/93 │ WTMF - Promotions    │                         │
│      │   │   175.34 │ 10/14/93 │ Davis Supplies       │                         │
│      │   │    75.00 │ 10/16/93 │ Wyse Lock & Key      │                         │
│      │   │    78.74 │ 10/18/93 │ U. P. S.             │ Shipping costs for pr   │
│      │ * │     2.52 │ 11/ 4/93 │ Finance charges      │                         │
└──────┴───┴──────────┴──────────┴──────────────────────┴─────────────────────────┘
  ■ To mark cleared items, press ↵        ■ To add or change items, press F9.

                         RECONCILIATION SUMMARY
           Items You Have Marked Cleared (*)
           ─────────────────────────────────    Bal per register (X,*)     2.52
             1    Charges, Debits      2.52     Bal per card statement   871.31
             0    Payments, Credits    0.00     Difference              -868.79

  F1-Help          F8-Mark range        F9-View as register       Ctrl-F10 Done
```

Reconciliation summary Figure 9-8.

9. Press Ctrl-F10 when you finish marking cleared charges.

    If Difference does not equal zero, you will see the Adjust Register to Agree with Statement window. You can select the accounts the adjustments use and see the adjusting entries QuickBooks makes.

10. Select the checking account you want the check written from in the Make Credit Card Payment window.

    You can also tell QuickBooks that you will be writing out the check yourself, by typing **Y** in the Handwritten check field.

11. Make any changes you want to the check displayed as part of the check register. Then print the check just as you have printed other checks, assuming QuickBooks is writing the check for you.

    If you choose to write the check yourself, return to the register to complete the transaction by entering the payment you are making.

Mortgages and Other Long-term Liabilities

The most common long-term liability for a business is a mortgage. The mortgage may be for property, land, or a building, but they all work the same way. A mortgage payment has at least two parts—interest and principal repayment. The *principal repayment* is the part of the loan that reduces the amount you still owe. Using QuickBooks to track your mortgage payments keeps you informed of how much interest and principal repayment you have paid.

To add a mortgage, add an account to the chart of accounts the same way you add other accounts. For the mortgage account, you can supply the name, description, beginning balance, and any notes. Make the beginning balance the balance of the loan before the next payment.

When you are ready to make a payment on the loan, write a check, or make an entry in the check register if QuickBooks is writing the check for you. Assuming you let QuickBooks write the check, fill out the payee information (the financial institution) and amount. In the bottom half of the check, enter the different parts of the loan payment. To fill in this section, you need an *amortization schedule* that you can get from your bank. Sometimes the remittance slips for the loan payments will separate the payment into its components, which you can use in lieu of an amortization schedule. Figure 9-9 shows an amortization schedule. Each payment has a different amount of interest depending on which one you are making. The amount of the interest

Amortization Schedule
For a $10,000 loan at 10% interest and for 3 years. Monthly payments are $968.02

Period	Balance Still Due	Interest Payment	Amount Applied to Principal	Period	Balance Still Due	Interest Payment	Amount Applied to Principal
1	$30,000.00	$250.00	$718.02	19	$16,118.17	$134.32	$833.70
2	$29,281.98	$244.02	$724.00	20	$15,284.47	$127.37	$840.65
3	$28,557.98	$237.98	$730.04	21	$14,443.82	$120.37	$847.65
4	$27,827.94	$231.90	$736.12	22	$13,596.17	$113.30	$854.72
5	$27,091.82	$225.77	$742.25	23	$12,741.45	$106.18	$861.84
6	$26,349.57	$219.58	$748.44	24	$11,879.61	$99.00	$869.02
7	$25,601.13	$213.34	$754.68	25	$11,010.59	$91.75	$876.27
8	$24,846.45	$207.05	$760.97	26	$10,134.32	$84.45	$883.57
9	$24,085.48	$200.71	$767.31	27	$9,250.75	$77.09	$890.93
10	$23,318.17	$194.32	$773.70	28	$8,359.82	$69.67	$898.35
11	$22,544.47	$187.87	$780.15	29	$7,461.47	$62.18	$905.84
12	$21,764.32	$181.37	$786.65	30	$6,555.63	$54.63	$913.39
13	$20,977.67	$174.81	$793.21	31	$5,642.24	$47.02	$921.00
14	$20,184.46	$168.20	$799.82	32	$4,721.24	$39.34	$928.68
15	$19,384.64	$161.54	$806.48	33	$3,792.56	$31.60	$936.42
16	$18,578.16	$154.82	$813.20	34	$2,856.14	$23.80	$944.22
17	$17,764.96	$148.04	$819.98	35	$1,911.92	$15.93	$952.09
18	$16,944.98	$141.21	$826.81	36	$959.83	$8.00	$951.83

Amortization schedule
Figure 9-9.

Mortgages, Credit Cards, and Other Liabilities

from the amortization schedule is the amount you enter as an expense interest. This amount is part of the cost of running your business. The principal repayment is the amount you select for the long-term liability account. Usually the principal repayment amount is the difference between the loan payment and the interest payment. The payment you send to the bank may be higher than the loan payment because it includes amounts for insurance and property taxes. Figure 9-10 shows a check written to make the first payment of a loan.

If loan amortization seems confusing, you may want to look at it from another angle. As an example, you have just borrowed $30,000 for three years with monthly payments of $968.02, assuming an interest rate of 10 percent annually or 0.83 percent per month. Another way to look at this loan is that the bank will lend you a decreasing amount every month for the next three years so at the end of the three years, you have paid off the loan. In the first month, you have borrowed $30,000. The first month's interest expense is $250, or $30,000 × .0083. Since you are paying $968.02, you have $718.02 left over to reduce the principal. In the second month, you are only borrowing $29,281.98 ($30,000 − 718.02). In the second month, the interest is only $244.02. The interest is less because you are borrowing less. Also, since less of the

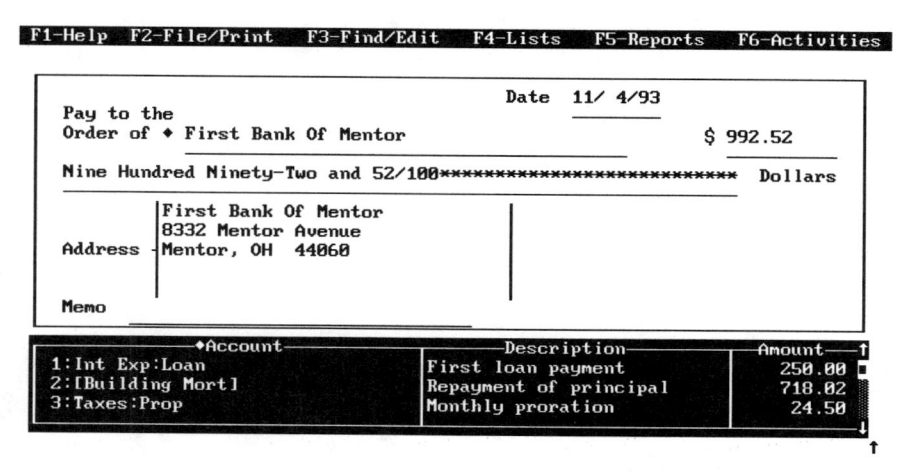

Check for making a loan payment
Figure 9-10.

loan payment goes to interest, more of the loan is paid off. At the end of the second month, you only owe $28,557.98 ($29,281.98 – 724). With the third month, $237.98 is applied to the interest and $730.04 is applied to the principal, so only $27,827.94 is left at the end of the third month.

As this example shows, the amount of the payment that is for interest decreases as the loan ages, and the amount of the payment that is for reducing the amount you are borrowing increases as the loan ages. The effect is more noticeable as the loan gets older. At the bottom of the amortization table in Figure 9-9 you can see how the loan gets paid off during the term of the loan.

PART 4

GETTING INFORMATION FROM YOUR SYSTEM

CHAPTER

10

REFINING YOUR FINANCIAL PICTURE

In prior chapters, you learned about all the day to day transactions that you record to keep your financial records up to date. Businesses without any long-term assets, such as a service business, need no further records to maintain an accurate financial picture. Other businesses have equipment that must be depreciated each year to reflect their true costs of doing business. Also, businesses that maintain inventory for resale must know the cost of their inventory before they can determine the cost of goods that they have sold and make an assessment of how the business is doing.

There are three distinct types of business organizations: sole proprietorships, partnerships, and corporations. QuickBooks works with all three types. The details of how they differ are covered later in this chapter. You will learn that each type of business organization looks at the ownership or equity in the business in slightly different ways. You will have an opportunity to assess your equity in any of the three types of business organizations using the profit and loss statement.

If your business does not maintain inventory for resale and has no equipment or other assets that must be partially written off as expenses each year, you can skip to the last section of this chapter, "Looking at Your Equity."

Inventory Valuation

If you have a retail business, the inventory of merchandise that you have on hand is an asset. You will have a record of the inventory that was available when you started the accounting period as well as any purchases that you made. Since it is unlikely that you will reduce inventory with each sale, you must determine the amount of inventory on hand at the end of the period. You can then use the beginning and ending inventory numbers, and the purchases you made, to determine how much inventory was sold during the period. The value of this sold inventory is referred to as the cost of goods sold (COGS). Determining the cost of goods sold allows you to determine if you have made a profit from your sales during the period.

Look at an example using real numbers to make this clearer: Suppose your beginning inventory is 100 notebooks that cost $5 each, giving you $500 in beginning inventory. During the accounting period you purchase 100 additional notebooks at $6 each. At the end of the period you have $1800 in receipts, but it is not clear how much is profit and how much is the cost of the goods that you have sold. If you count the remaining notebooks and find that you still have 50 notebooks on hand, which cost $6 each, your ending inventory would be valued at $300.

The cost of all the goods available for sales during the period was $500 for the original notebooks plus $600 for the additional notebooks, or $1100. You still have $300 in inventory, so you must have sold $800

Refining Your Financial Picture

worth of inventory. When you subtract this cost of goods sold from the $1800 in revenue, you find that you made $1000 in profit. These computations are illustrated in Figure 10-1.

In order to have QuickBooks make this determination for your company, you must enter a beginning inventory balance, record your purchases as expenses, value your remaining inventory, and then update the inventory balance.

NOTE: QuickBooks is not suitable for recording inventory measurements for a manufacturing firm, since you must keep finished goods, raw materials, and work in progress inventories.

When you use QuickBooks to record your inventory, you record how much the inventory is worth at the beginning of an accounting period. The beginning of the period is the beginning of the month, quarter, or

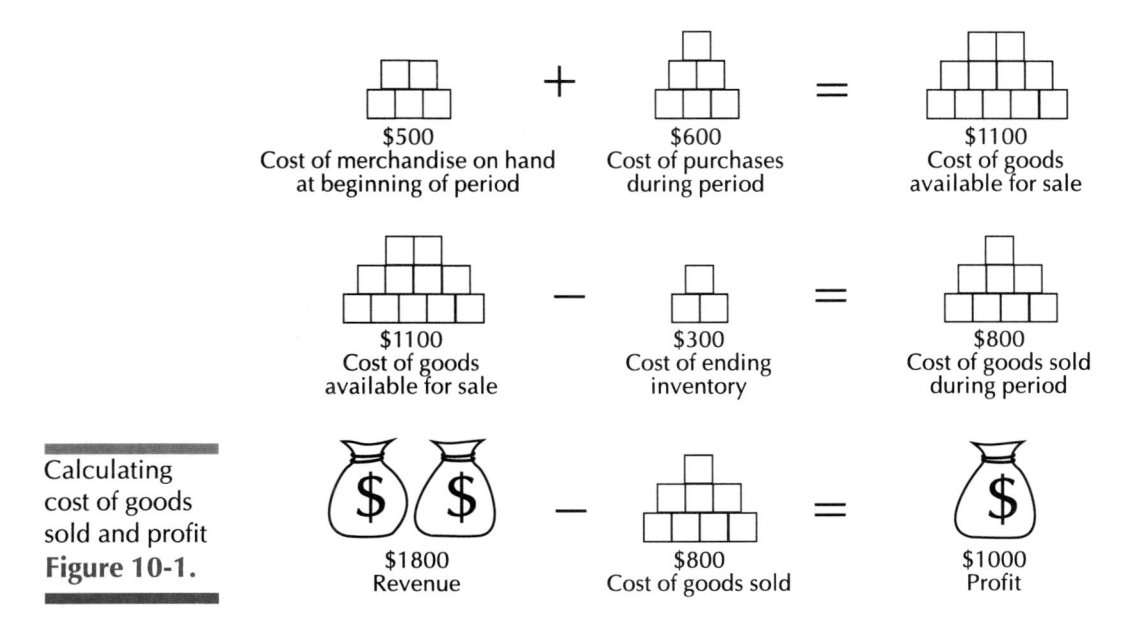

Calculating cost of goods sold and profit
Figure 10-1.

year that you want to use as the measurement period. During the period, as you record the payables to the vendors for the items in your inventory, the account you select is the COGS expense account for cost of goods sold. At the end of the period, you again record your current inventory. The difference between the beginning and ending inventory is the amount you increase or decrease the COGS account. You increase the COGS and decrease inventory when you have sold more goods than you bought. You decrease COGS and increase inventory when you have more in inventory at the end of the period than when you started. Figure 10-2 shows a diagram of this process.

At the end of the fiscal period take a physical inventory, and adjust the inventory account so that the correct balance will be reflected in this asset account. You can use QuickBooks to record inventory that you update on a periodic basis. When you update your inventory, QuickBooks adjusts the accounts so your inventory and COGS accounts are correct.

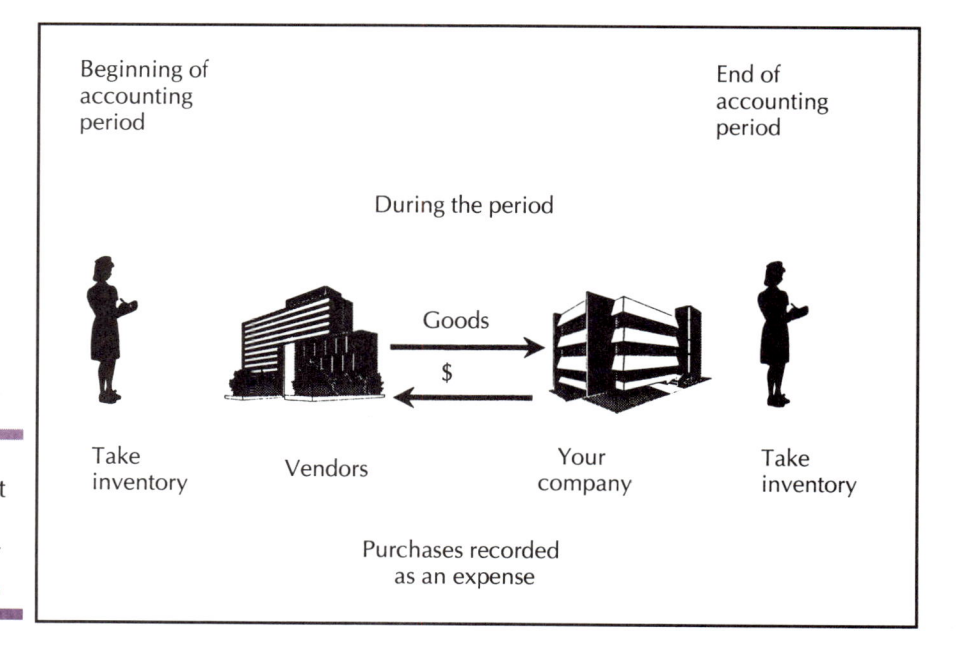

Process of recording cost of goods sold and inventory
Figure 10-2.

Entering the Inventory's Initial Value

The first time you take an inventory, you need to tell QuickBooks what the inventory you are starting off with is worth. Use the Open Bal Equity account because you are not changing what you have sold. Instead you are setting how much inventory and how much equity in the inventory you are starting with. Follow these steps to establish a beginning inventory value:

1. Select 4 Chart of Accounts from the Main Menu.
2. Press ⬇ until Inventory is highlighted, then press Enter.
3. Press F6 for the Activities menu from the Inventory account register and select 2 Update Acct Balance.

   You can also press Ctrl-Y to update the account's balance.
4. Type the correct balance in the Update this account's balance to field.
5. Press Ctrl-L for the Account for adjustment field and select the Open Bal Equity account.

Recording Inventory

When you take an inventory, you record the items and the quantities you have in inventory. You need to go back after you finish your inventory and add prices. You might use a manual ledger for these entries and show a price *extension* for each item to the right after multiplying units by price. A spreadsheet package will help with calculations like this. Although you can use QuickBooks' calculator to do an extension, QuickBooks makes no provision for recording the detail physical inventory counts. Figure 10-3 shows a record of inventory. Later, you can use QuickBooks to calculate the totals for the items.

What Are the Items Worth?

Accountants use many methods to value inventory, but you want something simple. One way you can measure the cost or value of the inventory is to use the last price you paid for the items. This inventory valuation method is called *FIFO* for *first in, first out*; it assumes that the

Recording inventory on hand
Figure 10-3.

Musical Pony, Inc.		
Item Code	**Item**	**# in Stock**
BigBop	Big Bopper music box	25
Carousel	Carousel music box	39
Ferris	Ferris wheel music box	23
Hound Dog	Hound dog musical ornament	40

first item you add to inventory is the first item you sell. The only items remaining in the ending inventory are the last items you purchased.

For example, assume you are in the business of selling widgets. You start the month with 100 widgets. You purchase 2000 at $1.95 each and 1000 at $2.00 each and have 1500 left at the end of the period. The value of the widgets remaining is (500 * $1.95) + (1000 * $2.00), or $2975. This step is repeated for all of the items you have in stock.

Other inventory valuation methods are LIFO (last in, first out), averaging methods, or lower of cost or market. Discuss these with your accountant and decide which one to use. Once you have chosen a method you must stay with it, as the Internal Revenue Service (IRS) disapproves of random changes among inventory valuation methods.

When you have counted the items in your inventory and valued them, multiply the cost by the items in stock for the total inventory value. Figure 10-4 shows the inventory sheet after counting the stock and determining the price. You can use QuickBooks' calculator to compute the totals. For example, multiply the price by quantity for each item and then calculate the total value of the inventory of $1000.19. Performing the inventory at the beginning of a period is the same as performing it at the end. The ending inventory of one period is the beginning inventory of the next period.

Refining Your Financial Picture

Calculating inventory at the end of the period
Figure 10-4.

Musical Pony, Inc.				
Item Code	Item	# in Stock	Price	Total
BigBop	Big Bopper music box	25	12.78	319.50
Carousel	Carousel music box	39	5.65	220.35
Ferris	Ferris wheel music box	23	4.78	109.94
Hound Dog	Hound dog musical ornament	40	8.76	350.40

Updating the Inventory Balance

Once you know what the ending inventory should be, you can update the balance. Updating the inventory balance also updates the cost of goods sold balance. After updating the inventory and COGS balance, the COGS expense account properly reflects the goods you have sold and the inventory account reflects the goods you have on hand to sell. To update these two accounts, follow these steps:

1. Select 4 Chart of Accounts from the Main Menu.
2. Press the ⬇ until Inventory is highlighted, then press Enter.
3. Press F6 for the Activities menu from the Inventory account register and select 2 Update Acct Balance.

   You can also press Ctrl-Y to update the account's balance.
4. Type the correct balance in the Update this account's balance to field.

   In the inventory shown in Figure 10-4, you would type **1000.19**.
5. Press Ctrl-L for the Account for adjustment field and select the COGS account.

Figure 10-5 shows the inventory register after making this adjustment. The COGS account is increased by $1499.81, and the inventory went

QuickBooks for Profit: Making the Numbers Work

```
F1-Help  F2-File/Print   F3-Find/Edit   F4-Lists   F5-Reports   F6-Activities
 DATE  REF  ♦PAYEE  ·  MEMO  ·  ♦ACCOUNT    DECREASE  C  INCREASE    BALANCE

                        ▬▬ BEGINNING ▬▬
 1/01       Opening Inventory                          2,500 00    2,500 00
 1993                    [Open Bal Equi→

 3/31       Balance Adjustment              1,499 81               1,000 19
 1993 Memo:
      ♦Acct COGS
 1/01
 1993
                           ▬▬ END ▬▬

 Inventory
 ■Esc-Leave   Ctrl↵ Record                           Ending Balance:  $1,000.19
```

Transactions to set inventory account balance
Figure 10-5.

from $2500.00 to $1000.19. If you do not make this adjustment, the cost of your sales is too low, your profit is too high (because you did not record all of the expenses), and your inventory is too high (because you included items that you have sold).

Producing the Inventory

If you are producing the items that appear in the inventory, you can follow the same steps given previously to update your accounts. Although QuickBooks is not designed to handle product costing, you can still use QuickBooks to record the value of your inventory at the beginning and end of accounting periods. You cannot use QuickBooks to track how well you are controlling the costs that go into making the product.

Accounting systems that can keep track of product costing may be more complex than you want. For a simple recording of your business's production, use QuickBooks.

TIP: If you own the business and are overseeing the different parts of production, you will know from observing work flow how productive your employees are, and controlling costs may be less important.

Refining Your Financial Picture

Asset Depreciation

The assets you use in your business range from the building you are in, to the sign you use to advertise, the equipment you use to produce goods, and the display equipment you use to sell the goods. These assets last longer than the items that you record as expenses—usually longer than one year. The cost of these assets cannot be expensed in the year that you buy them since they benefit the business over a period of time longer than the current year. They also should not be totally written off as expense in the last year that they are used. A better way to more accurately reflect the cost of doing business is to apportion the cost of these assets as an expense over their useful life. This means that if you use your building for 30 years, you want part of the cost of the building to reduce profits for each of the 30 years you use the building. This amount representing a portion of the asset's cost that reduces profit for the years that you use it is called *depreciation*.

> **Tip:** The IRS establishes the rules for asset depreciation. You cannot arbitrarily decide to depreciate the cost of a building over five years or a truck over two years. Although these actions would increase your expense and reduce your profits, the IRS would not allow depreciation to be accelerated in this way, and you would be liable for back taxes on higher profits than you reported plus penalties.

Following are four points to remember about depreciation:

✦ Depreciation is matching the cost of the asset with the period that you use the asset.

✦ Depreciation is an expense since it reduces your company's profit. However, you do not pay out the expense (you will never write a check to depreciation).

✦ Depreciation is usually recorded only at the end of the year.

✦ Depreciation reduces the balance in the asset account and shows on your reports as depreciation expense.

Certain assets do not depreciate; for example, land. Unless you live on an eroding coastline, the land that you start out with is the land that you have in the end. Assets that depreciate are only those that become worth less as time progresses.

There are several terms that you need to understand in order to compute depreciation. To illustrate these different terms, suppose you have a glass display case that you bought for $5000. The $5000 is its *original cost,* or what you initially paid. Assume that you have already recorded depreciation expense during the last two years of $1000 a year. This $2000 is the *accumulated depreciation* or the depreciation you have recorded for the asset as an expense for the prior years. The difference between the original cost of the glass display case and the accumulated depreciation, $3000, is the asset's *book value*. The length of time you expect to use an asset is the asset's *life*. When you expect the asset to have a value at the end of its useful life, that value is the asset's *salvage value*. In this example, if you assume that after five years (as long as you plan to use it), you will sell the case for $300, the $300 is the salvage value of the display case.

TIP: The IRS allows expensing Section 179 property. Section 179 property is property other than buildings, air conditioning units, and structural components of a building. Up to $10,000 of this property purchased in the current year can be treated as an expense. This is designed to reduce record keeping for small businesses that purchase few long-term assets.

Depreciation Methods

You can depreciate assets in different ways. The different depreciation methods vary in how much of the asset is depreciated at different periods of the asset's life. You can use the *straight-line* method to evenly spread depreciation over the asset's life, or use an *accelerated* method that depreciates more over the beginning of the asset's life than the end. Accelerated depreciation methods reduce the amount of income tax you pay on your company's earnings in the early years. Table 10-1 shows some of the depreciation methods that the IRS allows. You can also get IRS Publication 534, which lists rules about when you can use the different types of depreciation.

Refining Your Financial Picture

Depreciation Methods
Table 10-1.

Depreciation Method	Description
ACRS	The Accelerated Cost Recovery System is an accelerated depreciation method that can be used for assets that you started using in your business after December 31, 1980 and before December 31, 1986.
Declining-Balance	This method allows the deduction of depreciation expense at a faster rate than straight-line. You can use different percentages to compute this type of depreciation, although 150 percent of straight-line depreciation is the most common.
MACRS	The Modified Accelerated Cost Recovery System is an accelerated depreciation method for assets you started using in your business after December 31, 1986.
Straight-Line	This method is the easiest to compute since the cost of the asset is depreciated evenly over the life of the asset.

Straight-Line Depreciation

You use straight-line depreciation to evenly distribute depreciation for the asset's cost over the life of the asset. With this method you calculate the difference between the original cost and the salvage value, then divide the difference by the number of years you expect to use the asset. For the display case example discussed earlier, the depreciation is $940, or $4700 divided by 5. The display case's asset life is 5 years, and $4700 is the difference between the original cost of $5000 and the salvage value of $300.

TIP: The IRS has rules about minimum life expectancies for equipment and the types of depreciation you can use for different types of assets. You must follow these rules when reporting to governmental agencies.

MACRS and ACRS

Two other depreciation methods you can use to calculate depreciation are the Modified Accelerated Cost Recovery System (MACRS) and Accelerated Cost Recovery System (ACRS). The system you use depends on when you place the asset in service (when you start to use it in your business). MACRS is used for assets that you start to use after 1986 and ACRS is used for assets that you started to use between 1980 and 1986. Both cost recovery systems depreciate more than the straight-line method at the beginning of the asset's life, so you pay less in taxes earlier in the asset's life. With MACRS or ACRS, assets are divided into classes or types of property, and you use a chart provided by the IRS to get the percentages for each type of property. There are different percentages for each year of the life of the asset, so have the chart handy when computing depreciation expense.

Your most recently acquired assets will use MACRS. Older assets use ACRS and earlier depreciation methods.

As an example, assume the glass display case is a five-year asset. The MACRS percentages for this asset are 20 percent, 32 percent, 19.2 percent, 11.52 percent, 11.52 percent, and 5.76 percent. There are six percentages because the IRS assumes all assets are only used for half of the year, whether purchased on January 1 or December 1 of the year they are placed in service. The other half of a year's depreciation is taken in the sixth year. For this asset, the depreciation expenses for the six years is $1000, $1600, $960, $576, $576, and $288. You use the following calculations to compute the depreciation:

$5000 * 20.00% = $1000
$5000 * 32.00% = $1600
$5000 * 19.20% = $ 960
$5000 * 11.52% = $ 576
$5000 * 11.52% = $ 576
$5000 * 5.76% = $ 288

Total depreciation = $5000

Since the IRS has published many rules about the ACRS and MACRS methods of depreciation, it is a good idea to consult with your accountant or read IRS Publication 534 before you use them.

Refining Your Financial Picture

> **TIP:** Write down the schedule of depreciation for assets when you purchase them and file it away safely. You can use a table of the entire depreciation to check that you have calculated the correct amounts, and it makes your year-end preparations easier.

Entering Assets and Depreciation into QuickBooks

When you enter assets and their depreciation into QuickBooks, you have three different types of entries you can make:

- You make entries that record the assets you are starting off with.
- You record assets that you purchase during the year.
- You record depreciation for the assets for the current year.

A fourth special case of transactions you enter is the sale or other disposal of an asset.

Entering Existing Assets

When you start using QuickBooks, you can add the assets and depreciation that you have recorded to date. Including the assets in QuickBooks means your balance sheet reports (you will learn how to create them in the next chapter) include the assets your business owns. If you have few assets, you can add an account for each fixed asset. If you have many, you will probably have one account for all of the equipment.

To enter the asset and any depreciation accumulated so far, you can enter the book value of the asset. This produces the same results as entering the book value of the asset as the account balance when you add the account to record your asset.

You can also add the asset's original cost as one transaction and the accumulated depreciation as a separate transaction. The account used in both transactions is Open Bal Equity. To enter the asset and its accumulated depreciation, follow these steps:

1. Select 4 Chart of Accounts from the Main Menu.
2. Select the account containing the asset you want to add.
3. Type a description for the asset, such as "Display Cases - Initial Cost," in the Payee field.
4. Type the cost of the asset in the Increase field.
5. Select Open Bal Equity for the Account field.
6. Select 1 Record transaction to record the asset's cost.
7. Type a description for the asset's depreciation, such as "Display Cases - Accumulated Depreciation," in the Payee field.
8. Type the accumulated depreciation for the asset in the Increase field.
9. Select Open Bal Equity for the Account field.
10. Select 1 Record transaction to record the asset's cost.

As an example, if you have display cases that you purchased a few years ago and you want to enter their cost of $50,000 and accumulated depreciation of $20,000, after following the steps above, your entries will look like this:

		BEGINNING			
10/27 1993		Display Cases - Initial Cost [Open Bal Equi→]		50,000 00	50,000 00
10/27 1993		Display Cases - Accumulated Dep [Open Bal Equi→]	20,000 00		30,000 00
10/27 1993	Memo: ◆Acct				

These two transactions—adding the original cost and then the accumulated depreciation—can be repeated for the other equipment you want to record in your equipment account. The account balance is the value of the assets you use in your business. Making entries for nondepreciable assets (like land) follows the same procedure, but you do not have a second entry for the accumulated depreciation.

Refining Your Financial Picture

Purchasing an Asset

The entry you make to record paying for the asset, or to record the liability incurred for the asset, is the entry that adds the asset to your long-term asset account.

When you purchase an asset, you record a transaction that adds the original cost to the asset account. You can enter the transaction for purchasing an asset from the checking account when you record the check used to pay for the asset, or you can use the accounts payable register to record the purchase of the asset. The Account field in either transaction references the fixed asset account that stores your transactions for the asset.

As an example, suppose you want to buy a new neon sign for your store. You pay $10,000 for this sign. The check entry for this purchase looks like Figure 10-6. When you record this check you have also made an entry in your equipment account that increases the balance by $10,000 for your new sign.

When the asset is paid through a loan, set up an account for the payee of the loan as a liability account; then add a transaction that adds the asset to the fixed asset account and the amount due to the lender. With long-term loans, you will want to use an amortization schedule to determine how much of each payment is transferred from the liability account to the accounts payable and how much is interest expense. When

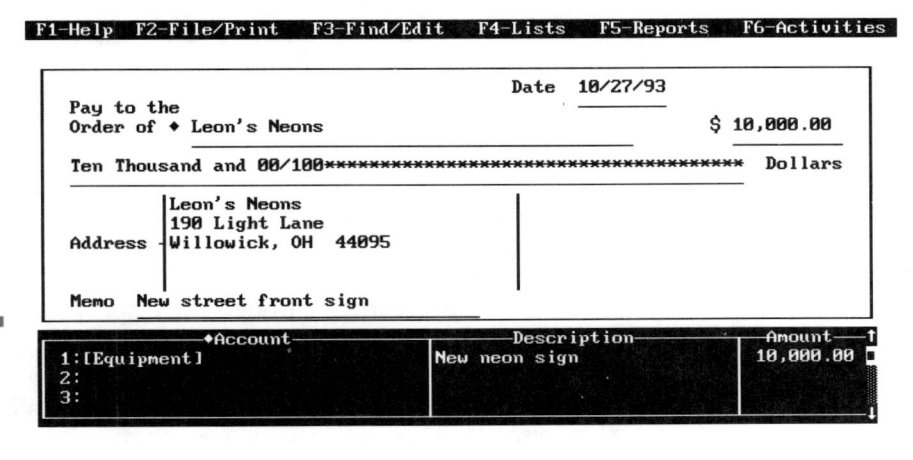

Check to record purchase of an asset
Figure 10-6.

you write a check for the loan payment, the voucher area will show two accounts: the loan's liability account for the reduction in the loan's principle, and the expense account for the interest you are paying.

Recording Depreciation Expense

At the end of the year, you need to calculate and record depreciation expense. This depreciation expense is recorded in the equipment register since you are not writing a check or receiving a payment. To enter the depreciation, follow these steps:

1. Select 4 Chart of Accounts from the Main Menu.
2. Select the account containing the asset for which you want to record depreciation.
3. Type a description, such as "1993 Depreciation," in the Description field.
4. Type the amount of depreciation in the Decrease field.
5. Select Deprec Exp for the Account field.
6. Select 1 Record transaction to record the depreciation expense.

The depreciation expense for the neon sign in the previous example is $4000 (assuming a five-year property and MACRS depreciation). The transaction looks like this:

10/27 1993	1993 Depreciation - Neon Sign Deprec Exp	4,000 00		36,000 00

Selling an Asset

When you sell a depreciable asset or you lose it through fire or theft, you must tell QuickBooks that you no longer own the asset. Removing an asset from QuickBooks' records also removes the depreciation and records any profit or loss earned through the disposition. To remove an asset from the asset's register, follow these steps:

1. On a separate piece of paper or on the calculator, calculate the total amount of depreciation expense you have recorded on an asset. Subtract the depreciation taken on the asset from the cost of the asset.

Refining Your Financial Picture

2. Select 4 Chart of Accounts from the Main Menu.
3. Select the account containing the asset which you want to remove.
4. Type a description, such as "Sale of Display Case," in the Description field.
5. Type the asset's book value in the Decrease field.

   This is the amount you calculated in step 1—the difference between the asset's cost and depreciation.
6. Press `Ctrl`-`S` for the Account field since you want a split transaction.
7. Select the account that will receive the proceeds from disposal of the asset—usually your checking account.
8. Type a description, such as "Sale of Display Case," in the Description field.
9. Type the amount you received from disposing of the asset in the Amount field.

   This is the cash or check you received from sales or insurance proceeds.
10. Press `Ctrl`-`L` to add an account, and press `Ctrl`-`Ins` to create a new account since you will need an account to record the gain or loss of the asset.
11. Select Income from the Select Type of Account to Add window.
12. Type a title for the added account's name, such as "Selling Assets," in the Name field.
13. Type a title for the new account's name, such as "Gain/loss-sale of assets," in the Description field.
14. Press `Ctrl`-`Enter` twice to create the account to record the gain or loss and to add it to the split transaction.
15. Type a description, such as "Sale of Display Case," in the Description field for the gain or loss.

    You do not have to worry about whether the correct sign is in front of the amount. Also, QuickBooks calculates the gain or loss for you. Gains are negative numbers and losses are positive numbers.
16. Press `Ctrl`-`Enter` twice to finish the split transaction and record the overall transaction.

An example of following these steps when you sell a display case for $2500 that has a book value of $2000 is shown in Figure 10-7.

You want the gain or loss from selling assets reported separately from the income you receive from your regular business. When you record another gain or loss from disposing of an asset, you will not need to repeat steps 10 through 14 in the previous procedure because you already have the account. You only need to press Ctrl-L and select the account you have set up for this purpose ("Selling Assets" in this example). If you are recording a loss of an asset when you have no proceeds, such as losing an uninsured asset, you can skip steps 6 through 9, since you have no proceeds to record.

REMEMBER: You can move through the equipment register, and as you find the transactions that relate to the asset you are getting rid of, you can display the calculator and add the amount of the transaction to the current calculation. This lets you flip through screens of transaction records to list the depreciation and original cost.

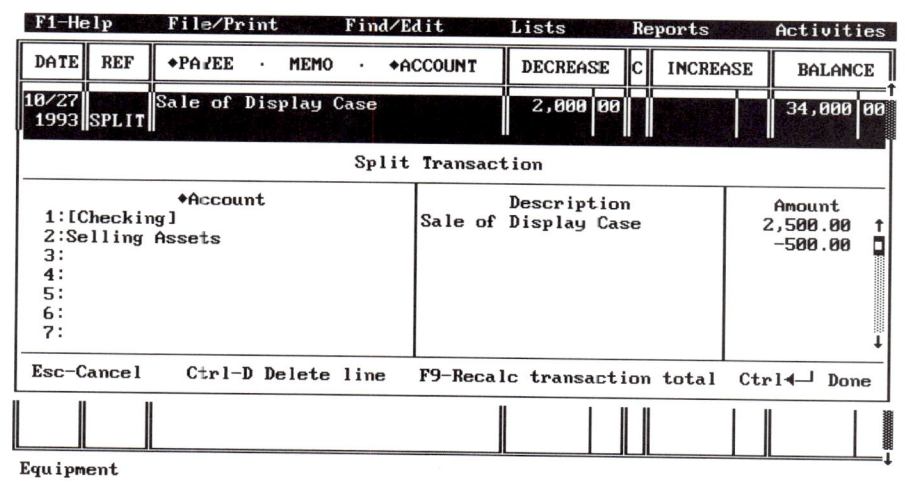

Transaction for selling an asset
Figure 10-7.

```
 F1-Help      File/Print      Find/Edit       Lists      Reports       Activities
 DATE   REF   ◆PAYEE  ·  MEMO  ·  ◆ACCOUNT   DECREASE  C  INCREASE    BALANCE
 10/27        Sale of Display Case            2,000 00                34,000 00
 1993  SPLIT
                              Split Transaction
            ◆Account                   Description              Amount
   1:[Checking]                    Sale of Display Case       2,500.00
   2:Selling Assets                                            -500.00
   3:
   4:
   5:
   6:
   7:
   Esc-Cancel    Ctrl-D Delete line    F9-Recalc transaction total   Ctrl⏎ Done

 Equipment
                                                    Ending Balance:   $34,000.00
```

Looking at Your Equity

From your perspective as an owner in a company you are always interested in whether or not the company is making a profit, but you are also interested in whether or not your *equity* has increased or decreased over the accounting period. In other words, is your ownership within the company growing or shrinking? There are a number of factors involved in looking at your equity, with some variation in terminology for the accounts used depending on the type of business organization.

You will want to examine the three business organization possibilities—sole proprietorships, partnerships, and corporations—in a little more detail to determine which situation matches your company. First, take a quick look at the profit and loss report, since this is where you look to determine the income or loss that will affect the equity account balance. Also, take a closer look at the way that QuickBooks handles equity accounts in order to be aware of the special account that it sets up for you when you start any new company.

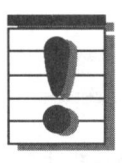

TIP: The equity presented by QuickBooks does not necessarily represent what your business is worth to others. Your business may have additional positive value created by a prime location or a good reputation.

Creating a Profit and Loss Statement

A profit and loss statement is designed to present the net profit or loss for an accounting period. It is one of the two reports considered essential for all businesses, whether it is handwritten, typed, or produced by QuickBooks. The other essential report is the balance sheet, which allows you to look at the balances in asset, liability, and owner's equity accounts at a particular time.

The profit and loss report shows all of the various revenues earned and expenses incurred. Your accountant might refer to the profit and loss report as an income statement or earnings statement.

A profit and loss statement can be created quite easily with QuickBooks by following these steps:

1. Select 5 Reports from the Main Menu.
2. Select 1 Profit & Loss to display this window:

```
                    Create Profit & Loss Statement

   Report title (optional):

   Report on months from:   1/93 through: 11/93


   Esc-Cancel      F1-Help   Ctrl-M Memorize   F8-Customize   Ctrl⏎ Done
```

3. Type the title you want to see at the top of the report in the Report title field.
4. Type the dates that you want the profit and loss report to cover.

    For both dates, you only need to enter the month and year since QuickBooks includes all transactions from the first day of the first month to the last day of the second month. Initially, QuickBooks assumes you want the dates to be the first day of the current year to the last day of the current month.

5. Press [Ctrl]-[Enter] to create the report.

    After searching the transactions, QuickBooks generates the report. Figure 10-8 shows this report created for the Sample Data Company from 1/92 to 12/92. At this point, you can press [Ctrl]-[P], select the printer to use, and press [Enter] to print the report.

6. Press [Esc] until you return to the Main Menu.

TIP: Use a consistent accounting period for all your reports. If you produce them quarterly, always use a quarter as a basis. If you create the next one in four months rather than three, it is not possible to compare the two reports.

Equity Accounts in QuickBooks

When you first start a new company with QuickBooks, the package automatically creates an equity account named Open Bal Equity. As you establish balances for your asset and liability accounts, Open Bal Equity contains an amount equal to the difference of all the assets and liabilities. This account therefore represents the initial investment in

Refining Your Financial Picture

```
                      Sample Data Company
Sample Data Company-All Accounts  1/ 1/92 Through 12/31/92              Page 2
11/ 2/93
                                      1/ 1/92-
Inc/Exp Description                  12/31/92

Rent:
   Building                           6,000.00
   Total Rent                                        6,000.00
T&E:
   Meals                                 31.23
   TOTAL T&E                                            31.23
Tel:
   Local                                415.45
   Long dist                            313.48
   Total Tel                                           728.93
Utilities:
   Gas & elec                           563.61
   Total Utilities                                     563.61
                                                   ----------
TOTAL EXPENSES                                      46,720.23
                                                   ----------
TOTAL INCOME/EXPENSE                                68,014.12
                                                   ==========
```

```
                      Sample Data Company
Sample Data Company-All Accounts  1/ 1/92 Through 12/31/92              Page 1
11/ 2/93
                                      1/ 1/92-
Inc/Exp Description                  12/31/92

INCOME/EXPENSE
INCOME
   Interest inc                         104.21
Sales:
   Consult                           12,400.00
   Design                            66,010.00
Pass-thru:
   Cost                             -69,747.36
   Receive                           87,582.50
   Total Pass-thru                   17,835.14
   Production                        18,385.00
                                                  ----------
   Total Sales                                    114,630.14
                                                  ----------
TOTAL INCOME                                      114,734.35

EXPENSES
Auto:
   Gas & Oil                            276.68
   Total Auto                                         276.68
Bank fees:
   Serv                                   9.00
   Total Bank fees                                      9.00
Ben:
   Health Ins                         2,250.00
   Total Ben                                        2,250.00
Interest exp:
   Loan                                 221.70
   Total Interest exp                                  221.70
Maint:                                                 200.22
   Kitchen                              360.00
   Janitor                            4,000.00
   Total Maint                                        360.00
Owner's Draw                                       4,000.00
Payroll:
   Comp FICA                          1,331.94
   Comp FUTA                            150.42
   Comp MCARE                           311.50
   Comp SUI                             365.27
   Gross                             21,482.50
   Total Payroll                                   23,641.63
Prof fee:
   Outside cons                       8,437.23
   Total Prof fee                                   8,437.23
```

Profit and loss statement
Figure 10-8.

Since you have more factors to consider than just using QuickBooks, consult your accountant and your lawyer before deciding on the business form you will use.

the business. For example, when you start a business with $5000 cash, $15,000 of equipment, $5000 of inventory, and $10,000 of payables, the Open Bal Equity account equals $15,000 as the difference between assets ($25,000) and liabilities ($10,000). To add the assets, create accounts for them and provide the amounts as their balance on the beginning date. The payables are recorded as other payables, except you select Open Bal Equity as the account rather than an expense account because the payment is for an expense from a previous time period. After adding the assets and liabilities, QuickBooks adjusts the balance of the Open Bal Equity account. After adding these accounts, the chart of accounts looks like Figure 10-9.

Once you add the existing assets and liabilities to QuickBooks, you can transfer the balance of the Open Bal Equity account to other equity accounts, or you can rename the Open Bal Equity account to another name, such as "Initial Investment." Usually the Open Bal Equity account represents what you or other owners have transferred to the business. You will want to transfer the Open Bal Equity balance to the equity account you have created for recording the initial investment you and any other owners have contributed.

The equity accounts that you add can monitor the parts of equity that represent your investment in the business. The number, names, and use of these equity accounts differ with the various types of business organizations. You can also use equity accounts that monitor your earnings.

Accounts after setting up initial amounts
Figure 10-9.

Account	Type	Description	Balance
	Balance Sheet		
Cash In Bank	Checking	Admiral Federal Bank	5,000
Receivables	A/R	A/R Account	0
Inventory	Cur Asset	In-store Inventory	5,000
Equipment	Fxd Asset		15,000
▶ Payables	A/P	A/P Account	10,000
Sales Tax	A/P	Sales Tax Payable	0
Open Bal Equity	Equity	Opening Bal Equity	15,000
	Income/Expense		
Int Inc	Income	Interest Income	

Chart Of Accounts — Company: The First Day

Refining Your Financial Picture

After you determine the amount of the profit or loss for the year, you want your equity accounts to reflect this amount. QuickBooks uses a different approach than traditional accounting practice. If you have studied accounting, QuickBooks' approach may even seem bizarre, but it accomplishes its objective and allows you to use the package without the traditional closing process that is required to transfer profit or loss to retained earnings.

With QuickBooks you set up an expense account in order to transfer the difference between income and expenses to equity. If you have a profit for the year, you set up an expense account called, for example, "1993 Profit," in order to enter a transfer which increases your retained earnings equity account. If you have a loss, you can set up an expense account with a name like "1993 Loss" and enter a transaction which decreases retained earnings by placing a negative value in the expense account.

Although sole proprietorships do not separate the business from the owner, you will want to use QuickBooks for the business transactions in order to keep them separate from your personal expenses.

Sole Proprietorships

A sole proprietorship is a business owned by one person. It is the simplest form of business organization. There are several different ways to set up your equity accounts with QuickBooks. Each of them is correct; the selection of a method depends on how much detail you want to be able to show in the balance sheet. The equity account that represents a sole proprietor's initial investment in the business is called "Owner's Equity" or "Capital" account. Company profits can be added to this account or you can set up a second equity account called "Retained Earnings." It is perfectly acceptable to use one account for the full amount of equity with a sole proprietorship. Withdrawals that you make from the business are entered into Retained Earnings if you choose to set up this second account. Figure 10-10 provides a diagram of the process from startup to the end of the year.

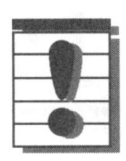

> **TIP:** If you enter all your transactions in one account you may want to consider using projects to reflect withdrawals, additional investments, and so on.

Setup:

Asset accts setup → QuickBooks transfers the net amt → Open Bal Equity account

Liability accts setup

Open Bal Equity Acct → You transfer to appropriate equity accts after setup → Owner's Equity or Capital acct

During the year:

Account update during the period → You create a P&L report to determine profit or loss → P&L Report

End of year:

P&L Report / Amount of profit or loss → You transfer from expense acct to retained earnings → Expense acct 1993 Profit or Loss

Recording equity in a sole proprietorship Figure 10-10.

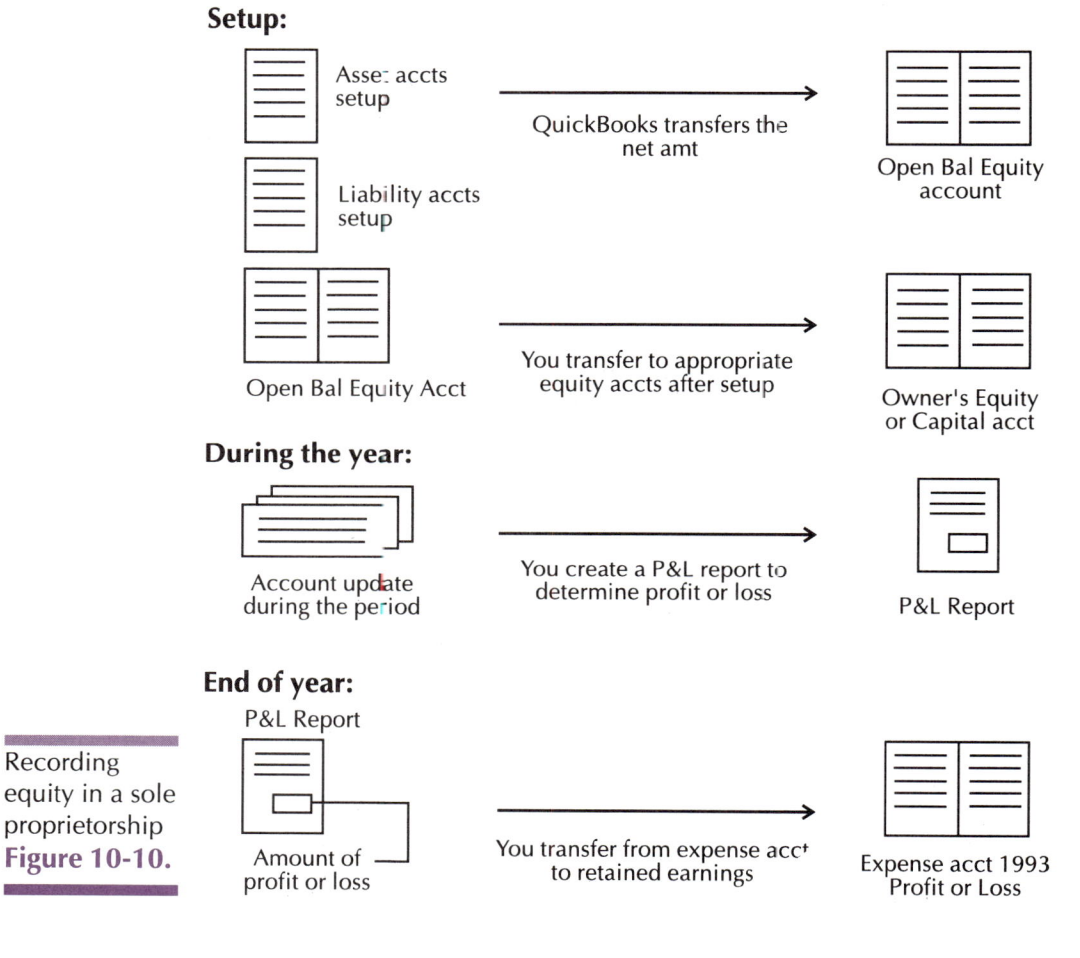

NOTE: Withdrawals in both sole proprietorships and partnerships are reductions in capital or equity accounts, not expenses of the business.

If you use QuickBooks as soon as you start your business, you can transfer all of the balance from the Open Bal Equity account to the

Refining Your Financial Picture

Owner's Equity account that you create. When you start using QuickBooks at a different point and want to maintain the Owner's Equity and Retained Earnings as separate accounts you will only want to transfer the amount of the initial investment. Retained Earnings should reflect the profit to date less any withdrawals that have been made by the owner.

> **NOTE:** For consistency with the QuickBooks manual the terms Owners' Equity and Retained Earnings are used. Typically, in sole proprietorships and partnerships, the term "Capital" is used, as in Mary Smith, Capital.

At the end of the year, you will want to transfer the profit you have made for the year to the Retained Earnings account. QuickBooks can calculate this amount for you when you create a profit and loss report. After looking at the profit and loss report to determine the profit, you can add the profit to your retained earnings by setting up an expense account, as shown in these steps:

1. Select 4 Chart of Accounts from the Main Menu.
2. Select the Retained Earnings account.
3. In the Date field type the last date of the accounting period for the earnings you are recording.

    You usually enter a different date than the current one when you enter this transaction. For example, when you are making the entry for the end of 1993's profit, the date will be 12/31/1993. However, there may be times when you enter the transaction after this date, such as when you do not finish entering year-end transactions.

4. Type a description, such as "1993 Profit," in the Description field.
5. Type the profit in the Increase field.
6. Press [Ctrl]-[L] to add an account, and press [Ctrl]-[Ins] to create a new account since you will need an account to record the gain or loss of the asset.
7. Select Expense from the Select Type of Account to Add window.

8. Type a title for the account's new name, such as "1993 Profit," in the Name field.
9. Type a description, such as "Acct used to transfer profit," in the Description field.
10. Press Ctrl-Enter twice to finish adding the account and to add it to the transaction.
11. Select 1 Record transaction to record the retained earnings.

The expense part of the transaction performs two functions: first, it balances the transaction; second, it returns the current earnings for the year to zero. If the current year has a loss, the transaction is entered the same way except the amount is entered in the Decrease field, and it results in a negative entry in the expense account used to facilitate the transfer. The entry for a sole proprietorship with earnings of $11,500 and a previous balance of $-2000 might look like this:

2/01 1993	John Jacobs Owner Withdrawal [1st Federal]	BEGINNING		2,000 00	-2,000 00
3/10 1993	Earnings 1993 Profit		11,500 00		9,500 00
1/02 1993	Memo: ♦Acct				

To give you an example of the differences in business types, Figure 10-11 shows Retained Earnings accounts for a sole proprietorship as well as for a partnership and corporation. Assuming that profits are $68,014.12, the owner withdrew $20,000, and there are no previous earnings, the Retained Earnings account has a balance of $48,014.12. The profit is recorded following the steps just described. When the owner withdraws the $20,000, he or she writes a check using the Retained Earnings account for the account.

Partnerships

Partnerships are two or more individuals operating a business together. In a partnership, there is an agreement between the co-owners that specifies how profits, losses, and salaries are shared. When a partnership agreement is lacking, usually the partners share profits and losses

Refining Your Financial Picture

Profit is $68,014.12
$20,000 is distributed to the business's owners

Sole proprietorship:

Retained Earnings	
Profit	$68,014.12
Withdrawals	-$20,000.00
Balance	$48,014.12

Partnership (50/50 split of profit and losses):

Retained Earnings, Partner Ace	
Profit	$32,007.06
Withdrawals	-$15,000.00
Balance	$17,007.06

Retained Earnings, Partner Blue	
Profit	$32,007.06
Withdrawals	-$5,000.00
Balance	$27,007.06

Corporation:

Retained Earnings	
Profit	$68,014.12
Dividends	-$20,000.00
Balance	$48,014.12

Retained earnings for different types of businesses
Figure 10-11.

equally and no one receives a salary. Also, both you and your partners are equally responsible for the business's liabilities.

In a partnership, you need separate accounts to record the contributions and withdrawals made by each partner. Just as in a sole proprietorship, withdrawals are the money a partner withdraws from the business. You can have a single equity account for each partner or you can have separate accounts for contributions, earnings, salaries, and withdrawals for each partner. Whether you use one or several depends on how much detail you want in your reports. If you would like to use a single account, you can use project entries to differentiate among the types of entries.

Transactions for the partner accounts are similar to those for a sole proprietorship. Initially the difference between the company's assets and liabilities is placed in the Open Bal Equity account. You can distribute this amount among the various partners' capital accounts. When you pay a salary to a partner you need to decrease his or her equity account. You should use a project named "Salary," unless you set up salaries for each partner in separate accounts. Withdrawals are likewise recorded to both the Draws account and the checking account, or they can be reductions against the Equity account (in which case they should have a project entry of "Draws"). You distribute the profit or loss of the company to the various partner accounts using the same technique created for the sole proprietorship. However, you will need to add special expense accounts for the sole purpose of transferring the profit or loss to the appropriate equity accounts.

As an example of how the earnings and withdrawals in a partnership are shown, suppose you have two partners, Ace and Blue, who share profits and losses equally, but Ace withdraws $15,000 from the business and Blue withdraws $5000. The partnership section of Figure 10-11 shows the equity account transactions for each partner. The profit is entered following the steps described previously for a sole proprietor. You go to each partner's Retained Earnings account and increase it by $32,007.06, with the profit expense account as the other half of the transaction. When Ace withdraws the $15,000, you write a check using the Retained Earnings, Partner Ace account. For Blue's $5,000, you write a check using Retained Earnings, Partner Blue as the account. Also notice how each partner has a separate account. These separate accounts allow you to see how much each partner has contributed and withdrawn from the business.

TIP: If your business is a partnership, make sure you have a partnership agreement that includes each partner's contribution to the business and how much they receive from it. Without a partnership agreement, you are held by the partnership laws of your state.

Corporations

A corporation is legally considered to have an existence separate and apart from the owners of the business. Unlike a sole proprietorship or partnership, where you can have one or two equity accounts for all entries, you have several accounts for the equity paid in by stockholders and earned for stockholders in the corporation. Larger corporations will even have different accounts for the different types of stocks. When the common stock of the company has a *par value* (the stated value of the stock), the par amount of each share is included in the common stock while the difference between what the stockholders paid when the shares were issued is in an Excess Over Par equity account. When the

Refining Your Financial Picture

stock has no par value, the entire amount the stockholders paid for the stock is in the common stock account. When you are setting up QuickBooks for use in an existing business, most of the initial value of the common stock equity account is transferred from the Open Bal Equity account.

Like sole proprietors, you will have a Retained Earnings account to amass the profits and losses of the company. All of these accounts are created like other equity accounts. Entering transactions for these accounts is just like entering other transactions. These transactions set up the balance in the account and transfer balances from one account to another. At the end of the year, transferring the year's earnings to the Retained Earnings account is identical to transferring earnings to Retained Earnings accounts in a sole proprietorship, as described earlier in the chapter. One special difference is that corporations return money to their investors through dividends.

A special form of a corporation is an S corporation that retains the corporation business form but shares some of the tax rules followed by sole proprietorship.

Look again at Figure 10-11 to see an example of the difference between business types. In the corporation section, the profit is added to the Retained Earnings account at the end of the year the same way it is for a sole proprietorship. The withdrawals are done as a dividend that decreases cash and retained earnings. The dividends go to the shareholders who are not necessarily the same people who run the business.

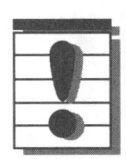

> **TIP:** States have different laws about separating capital accounts. For example, you may need to separate the paid-in capital accounts (accounts for the amounts shareholders have paid for their stock) from the other accounts when your state has rules prohibiting you from issuing dividends greater than the retained earnings. You can learn more about these rules from your accountant.

Now that you have had a quick look at some of the reporting that QuickBooks can do for you, you should be anxious to explore the reporting options in more detail. Chapter 11 presents additional standard reports as well as some of the customizing options that QuickBooks provides.

CHAPTER

11

CREATING STANDARD AND CUSTOM REPORTS

Periodically you will want to step back from the detail of the QuickBooks registers and take a look at reports that the package can create for you. QuickBooks reports present your data in an organized format that can help you analyze how your business is doing. You can view any of the reports onscreen or print them out to share with others.

QuickBooks provides many standard reports that are just as easy to create as the profit and loss statement that you looked at in Chapter 10. For many users these standard reports provide all of the information they need. However, as you become more familiar with QuickBooks, you may want to customize reports to meet your individual needs. In this chapter, you first learn how to create and print a standard report. Then you look at some specific reports in more detail to see how you might customize them and use the information in them to help you manage your business. To save time, you learn how to memorize the reports that you use most frequently. Some of the reports that were introduced in previous chapters, such as payroll and budget, will not be discussed here.

TIP: If you do not feel comfortable using your own data when trying different options, use the sample company as the examples in this chapter do. The best way for you to discover which reports are most useful to you is by trying different settings with reports and looking at the results. Creating reports does not affect the company's data, so you cannot damage your entries by trying another option in a report.

Creating a Standard Report

A *standard* report is one that is created automatically by QuickBooks. It has a fixed layout to present your data. QuickBooks provides 13 standard reports that you can select from the Reports menu or one of its submenus. Table 11-1 provides a list of the standard QuickBooks reports along with some ideas for how you can use them. Two of the reports, the profit and loss statement and payroll report, are variations of the summary report.

Follow these simple steps to create any of the standard reports:

1. Choose 5 Reports from the Main Menu.
2. Choose the report or the report group that you want. If you choose an option such as A/R Reports, A/P Reports, or Other Reports, a submenu displays, and you can make another selection to refine your specification.

   A report window like the Create Cash Flow Forecast Report window in Figure 11-1 appears. The report window options will vary depending on the type of report that you are creating. The

Creating Standard and Custom Reports

Report Type	Purpose
Balance sheet	Displays the company's current assets and liabilities
Profit and loss statement	Displays earnings for a specific time period
Sales	Lists sales separated by item code, which provides you with an itemized listing of your company's sales
A/R aging	Shows how promptly your customers pay their bills and whether you need to adopt policies to encourage prompt payment
Collections	Reports customer names, phone numbers, and balances so you can call and remind customers to pay their bills
A/P aging	Shows vendors with the bills you still owe, broken down by their age, so you are aware of vendors you have not paid
Sales tax	Reports the sales tax you have collected, which helps you prepare the reports needed when you remit the collected sales tax
1099	Sums payments made to independent contractors in the vendor list during an accounting period, which helps you prepare Form 1099s at the end of the year
Cash flow forecast	Reports expected cash inflows and outflows to help you judge whether you have the cash on hand to pay your bills promptly
Payroll	Lists totals for various payroll accounts amassed during an accounting period, which helps you prepare reports such as W-2s, W-3s, and Form 941
Budget	Prepares and lets you enter a budget so you can review expenses that are out of line or income projections that do not meet expectations

Report Types and Their Uses
Table 11-1.

Report Type	Purpose
Summary	Shows totals for the group of transactions you select, which gives you an overview of your income, expenses, and transfers
Transaction	Shows individual transactions that are part of a group so you can review items in specific expense accounts
Itemized income/ expense account	Lists individual transactions for one or more accounts so you can review accounts that you want to reduce
Project	Reports on incomes and expenses separated by project

Report Types and Their Uses *(continued)*
Table 11-1.

full title of this window will change from report to report, but in all cases it is the first window that you see after selecting a specific report.

3. Complete any options such as report title or dates in the report window.
4. Press Ctrl-Enter to display the report.

```
                    Create Cash Flow Forecast Report

   Report title (optional):

   From:  4/10/92 through:  5/31/92

   Delay receipts for how many days after due date: 0

   Report at intervals of: 7    days.


   Esc-Cancel     F1-Help   Ctrl-M Memorize   F8-Options      Ctrl⏎ Done
```

Window for creating a report
Figure 11-1.

Viewing a Report on the Screen

Viewing a report onscreen before you print allows you to verify that the report is the one you want printed.

QuickBooks first displays your selected report on the screen. This allows you to look through it and decide if you need to make any changes before printing the report. Since some reports are wider or longer than the screen, you will want to learn the techniques for scrolling the information on the screen.

With a mouse, use the horizontal or vertical scroll bar at the bottom or right edge of the screen. You can drag the small rectangle in the scroll bar or click the arrows at either end.

With the keyboard, use the ← or → to scroll a column to the left or right. The Tab key or Ctrl-→ moves a full screen to the right. Shift-Tab or Ctrl-← moves a screen to the left. Pg Dn moves down one screen and Pg Up moves up one screen. Home moves to the upper-left corner and End moves to the lower-right corner.

Although F9 does not exactly scroll, it can affect the displayed information. On some transaction-oriented reports, the display shows half of the column width to maximize the number of columns that displays. Pressing F9 shows the full column width. When you want to set the column display back to half of the width, just press F9 a second time.

Printing a Report

Once you display a report, all you need to do is press Ctrl-P to print it. The Print Report window appears, allowing you to specify the printer you want to use. Press Ctrl-L to select another printer if your current setting is not correct. You can simply pick an option from the Available Printers window. Press F9 if the printer that you want is not represented. Once your changes are made, pressing Enter starts the printing.

You can also save reports as files. This is useful if you want to transfer the report data to a spreadsheet or database program, or edit the contents and appearance with a word processing or desktop publishing package. The file formats supported are ASCII (.TXT), a comma-delimited ASCII file (.PRN), and a Lotus 1-2-3 worksheet file (.WKS).

To save the data to a file, change the Print to field in the Print Report window to a file format. When you finalize this window, another window will appear where you can specify the filename and an existing directory if you want the file in a location other than C:\QBOOKS.

TIP: Print a report to a .TXT file when you want to subsequently incorporate it into a report. The .TXT file QuickBooks creates can be read by most word processors.

Options for Customizing Reports

QuickBooks provides several ways to customize a report. You can use a Filter feature on most reports to limit the transactions used in creating the report. You can choose a Customize option on some report windows by pressing [F8]. From other windows you can access a smaller group of options by pressing [F8], but it is labeled Options on the screen rather than Customize. For several reports you decide whether you want to use cash or accrual basis accounting. You will learn the difference in this chapter so you can make the best selections for your business.

Filtering Report Data

Sometimes you want to include all the transactions you have entered into QuickBooks when you create reports; other times you would like the reports for specific payee names, vendors, or accounts. QuickBooks has a Filter feature, which can be used with some reports, that allows you to include only a portion of your QuickBooks transactions in a report. For example, filtering allows you to look at a single expense account, payee names that begin with W, or transactions above a specific amount. To filter the transactions, press [F9] when F9-Filter appears at the bottom of a window.

Filter Report Transactions Window

To tell QuickBooks what transactions to include in your report, you complete a Filter Report Transactions window. You can perform either partial matches, where the transaction will contain what you type for a field, or an exact match. You can also use this window to specify

Creating Standard and Custom Reports

income or expense accounts or projects. You can screen for entries above or below a certain amount; check the Cleared status; or show payments, deposits, or unprinted checks using a Filter Report Transactions window like the one for the summary report shown in Figure 11-2.

Specifying Matching Entries

QuickBooks supports partial and exact matches.

The top part of the Filter Report Transactions window lets you limit report transactions depending on the contents of specific fields. These are the same fields that you see when you look at an account register. Your entries in the fields in the Filter Report Transactions window require a transaction to have a matching entry in the account register to be included in the report. Several rules apply to your entries:

✦ QuickBooks assumes that you are looking for a transaction that contains the entry in the field with or without other information.

✦ To limit QuickBooks to an exact match with the entry, precede the entry by the equal sign (=).

✦ Press Ctrl-L to provide a list of entries if you see a diamond next to the field in the Filter Report Transactions window.

✦ Use .. on either side of the entry to indicate other unspecified characters in that position. For example, typing **sims..** matches with Simsfield or Simson and typing **..field** matches with Smithfield or Summerfield.

✦ Precede your entry with a tilde (~) to look for any transaction that does not include the entry.

✦ Use ? to substitute for any single unknown character.

The middle part of the Filter Report Transactions window allows you to select specific income or expense accounts. You can also use this section to search for entries for specific projects. If either of these two fields has a Y, when you leave the Filter Report Transactions window, you have a window for selecting the specific income and expense accounts or the projects that the report will include. This window is just like the windows you use for printing tasks, such as selecting which checks to print or which customers in the customer list to print. The next field in the Filter Report Transactions window lets you limit

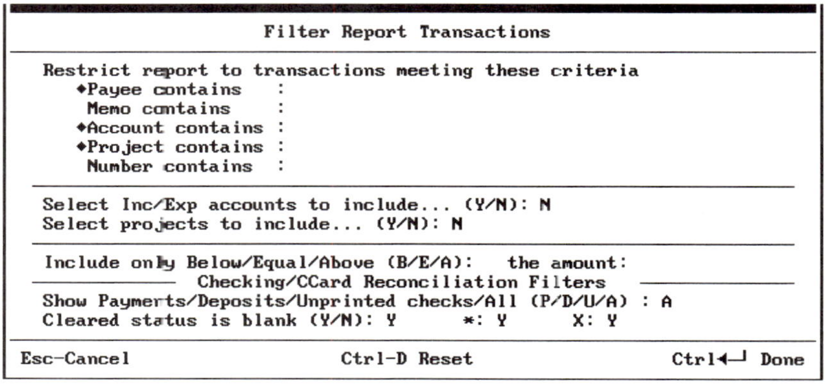

QuickBooks for Profit: Making the Numbers Work

```
┌─────────────────────────────────────────────────────────────────┐
│                    Filter Report Transactions                   │
│  Restrict report to transactions meeting these criteria         │
│        ◆Payee contains    :                                     │
│         Memo contains     :                                     │
│        ◆Account contains  :                                     │
│        ◆Project contains  :                                     │
│         Number contains   :                                     │
│  ─────────────────────────────────────────────────────────────  │
│  Select Inc/Exp accounts to include... (Y/N): N                 │
│  Select projects to include... (Y/N): N                         │
│  ─────────────────────────────────────────────────────────────  │
│  Include only Below/Equal/Above (B/E/A):    the amount:         │
│  ──────────────── Checking/CCard Reconciliation Filters ─────── │
│  Show Payments/Deposits/Unprinted checks/All (P/D/U/A) : A      │
│  Cleared status is blank (Y/N): Y       *: Y       X: Y         │
│                                                                 │
│  Esc-Cancel           Ctrl-D Reset              Ctrl⏎ Done      │
└─────────────────────────────────────────────────────────────────┘
```

Filter Report Transactions window
Figure 11-2.

included transactions to those above, below, or equal to an amount that you set.

The last section of the Filter Report Transactions window is used only for checking accounts and credit card accounts. It lets you choose to show one or all of the following: payments, deposits, and unprinted checks. You can also choose to look at a cleared check status, a transaction with a check number, or a check with an X in the Cleared status.

Using F8 for Customize or Options

Because QuickBooks reports differ so much, there are different ways to customize them. With some reports, you can make most of the changes you need right from the report window that displays when you select the report. Figure 11-3 shows the options in the report window for the profit and loss statement. For some reports you press F8 to select Customize and choose from additional options. Sometimes the customize window offers an F8 Options choice with additional changes that you can make. Sometimes F8 Options is offered from the report window with no opportunity to select Customize. The F8 Options window typically allows you to round to the nearest dollar and may also offer options such as including transfers in the report.

Look at the changes that appear on the report window first, then look at the bottom of the screen to see if additional changes can be made by

Creating Standard and Custom Reports

pressing `F8`. An example of the changes you can make using `F8` Options might look like this (shown for the transaction report):

```
                         Report Options
    Transfers to include: 1
         1. Include all transfers.    2. Exclude all transfers.

    Round amounts to nearest dollar            (Y/N): N
    Detail level: None/Transactions/Splits     (N/T/S): T
    Show Memo/Account/Both                     (M/A/B): B

    Esc-Cancel            Ctrl-D Reset              Ctrl⏎ Done
```

Cash Versus Accrual Basis Accounting

For your reports and your business you must decide on the timing of recording financial transactions. You can record a transaction as soon as you know that it will occur, or you can wait until cash changes hands. The former is accrual basis accounting, and the latter is cash basis accounting. There is a third method, called *modified cash basis,* discussed shortly. If your business is organized as a corporation, the accrual method *must* be used.

Some small businesses use the cash basis because it corresponds to their tax-reporting needs and because the financial reports prepared provide information summarizing the cash-related activities of the business. With cash basis accounting, you report income when you receive cash

```
                       Create Summary Report

    Report title (optional): Profit & Loss Statement

    Restrict transactions from:  1/ 1/92 through:  4/30/92

    ♦Row headings (down the left side): Income/Expense Account

    ♦Column headings (across the top): Totals only

    Report on Cash (received) or Accrual (billed) basis (C/A): A

    Use Current/All/Selected balance sheet accounts...(C/A/S): A

    Esc-Cancel    Ctrl-M Memorize    F8-Options    F9-Filter  Ctrl⏎ Done
```

Sample window displayed when you press `F8` to customize your report
Figure 11-3.

from customers for services you provide. For example, if you are in the plumbing business, you would recognize income when a customer makes payment for services. You might provide the services in December and not receive the customer's check until January. In this case, you would record the income in January, when you received and deposited the customer's check. Similarly, you recognize your expenses when you write your checks for the costs you incur. Thus, if you order supplies in December but don't pay the bill until January, you would deduct the cost in January, when you write a check to the supplier.

The basic difference between cash basis accounting and accrual basis accounting is the timing for the recognition of income and expenses.

With the accrual basis, you record your revenues and expenses when you provide services to your customer or incur expense, regardless of when the cash flow occurs. Using the plumbing example from the preceding paragraph, you would recognize the income from the plumbing services in December, when you provided the services to the customer, even though the cash is not received until the next year. Likewise, if you purchase supplies in December and pay for them in January, the cost of the supplies would be recorded in December, not in January when they were actually paid for. The same information is recorded under both the cash and accrual methods.

The basic difference between the cash and accrual basis accounting is what accountants call *timing* differences. When a cash basis is used, the receipt of cash determines when the transaction is recorded. When the accrual basis is used, the time the services are provided determines when the revenue and expenses are recorded.

A third method of reporting business revenues and expenses is the modified cash basis approach mentioned previously. This method uses the cash basis as described, but modifies it to report depreciation on certain assets over a number of years. In this case, you must spread the cost of trucks, computer equipment, office furniture, and similar assets over the estimated number of years they will be used to generate income for your business. The IRS has rules for determining the life of an asset. In addition, the tax laws allow you to immediately deduct the first $10,000 of the acquisition cost of certain qualified assets each year without worrying about depreciation. Once again, these are areas where your accountant can be of assistance in setting up your QuickBooks accounts.

Whether you use the cash, accrual, or modified cash basis in recording your transactions is determined by a number of factors. Some of the considerations are listed for you in the special "Cash Versus Accrual Methods" section.

> ## Cash Versus Accrual Methods
>
> A number of factors determine whether you use a cash or accrual basis for accounting in your business. These are a few of the considerations:
>
> - *Tax requirements* You must decide what your tax reporting obligations are and whether those requirements alone will dictate the method you select for reporting. For most small businesses, this is the overriding factor to consider. For instance, if inventories are part of your business, you must use the accrual method for revenues and purchases. If inventories are not a part of your business, you will probably find it best and easiest to use the cash basis for accounting.
>
> - *Users of your financial reports* The people who use your financial reports can have a significant influence on your reporting decisions. For example, do you have external users such as banks and other creditors? If so, you may find they require special reports and other financial information that will influence how you set up your accounting and reporting system.
>
> - *Size and type of business activity* The kind of business you have will influence the type of financial reports you need to prepare and the method of accounting you adopt. Are you in a service, retail, or manufacturing business? Manufacturing businesses use the accrual method since they have sales that will be billed and collected over weeks or even months, and they carry inventories of goods. Retail stores such as small groceries would also use the accrual method of accounting, at least for sales and purchases, since they have inventories that affect the financial reports they will prepare. On the other hand, a small landscaping business would probably use the cash basis; there are no inventories, and the majority of the cost associated with the business is payroll and other costs generally paid close to the time services are performed. In this case, the use of business equipment calls for the modified cash basis to record depreciation on the property.

Memorizing Reports

You can memorize any setting changes that you make to a report except the date. This allows you to select a certain account, select a row or column heading, or make other changes, and use them each time you create the report. The data that you use for the report is not saved when you memorize a report.

Let's say that you just created a report with all of the filter entries and other custom changes. If you think you might like to create this report again in the future, you can memorize it by pressing [Ctrl]-[M] from the report, filter, or customize windows or while you are looking at the report on your screen. All you need to do is follow these steps:

1. Press [Ctrl]-[M] to display the Memorizing Report window.
2. Type a name to identify the information you have already entered that QuickBooks will memorize, and press [Enter] to memorize your entries.

TIP: To change a memorized report in any way other than altering the name it is saved under, you will need to delete the memorized report and resave a report with the entries that you need.

Recalling a Report You Have Memorized

The whole point of memorizing a report is to be able to create it again quickly. If you have assigned meaningful names to the reports that you have memorized, you will find this quite easy. You can display the list of memorized reports using either 5 Reports from the Main Menu or by pressing [F5] from any register, the Write Invoices, or Write Checks screen. Just follow these steps:

1. Select 5 Reports from the Main menu or press [F5] from a register.
2. Select 9 Memorized Reports to display a list that might look something like the following:

Creating Standard and Custom Reports

```
        Memorized Reports List
▸ 1099 Report for Contractors
  Balance Sheet Compared to Yr Beginning
  Profit & Loss by Quarter
  Transaction Report by Customer
  Transaction Report by Vendor
```

3. Select the desired report.
4. Change the title or dates or make customizing changes with `F8` if the option is presented.
5. Press `Ctrl`-`Enter` to display the report.

A Closer Look at Some of the Reports

In this section, you examine some of the QuickBooks reports in greater detail. Ideas for customizing these reports and ways that you can change them to make them work better for you will also be covered. In Chapter 12, you will have an opportunity to examine reports again but with the emphasis on preparing year-end tax returns and payroll reports.

TIP: Consider what you want to do with a report before creating it. QuickBooks creates reports for every possible need. If you create every possible report you will have more information than you can effectively work with.

Balance Sheet

Chapter 10 covered the profit and loss statement; the other essential business financial statement is the balance sheet. The term *balance sheet* comes from the fact that the total of your assets must balance with your liabilities and owner's equity.

The balance sheet shows the balances of asset, liability, and equity accounts at a particular time, in separate sections of the report. These three sections of the report are further subdivided. The assets section shows current assets, such as checking account balances and receivables, and the fixed asset section shows plant and equipment. Liabilities are also split into current liabilities, such as payroll, vendor payables, and credit card purchases, and long-term liabilities, such as mortgages. The equity section shows equity accounts and current earnings for the accumulated earnings since the last time profits or losses were transferred to the appropriate equity accounts.

A balance sheet report covers a point in time.

Figure 11-4 shows the first page of a balance sheet created for the sample company. This balance sheet was created by pressing `F8` for Customize, then typing **1/1/92** as the Date of first balance sheet field and **3/31/92** as the Date of last balance sheet field. The only difference between this balance sheet and the balance sheet that would be created with the default settings is that this report includes the balance sheet for two separate dates.

Another change you might want to make is to the Intermediate intervals field. This field sets how the date range is broken into smaller units, which are reported on separately. The list QuickBooks displays when you press `Ctrl`-`L` includes None, Day, Week, Two weeks, Half month, Month, Quarter, Six months, and Year. For example, if you change the Intermediate interval field to Month for the balance sheet in Figure 11-4, you would have balance sheet columns for 1/1/92, 1/31/92, 2/29/92, and 3/31/92.

Changing the Standard P&L Report

In Chapter 10, you created a profit and loss statement using the default settings. The default settings use accrual basis, income and expense accounts for row headings, and totals for the columns. You can easily change to a cash basis if you want to, or make other changes such as using only whole dollars. Figure 11-5 shows a profit and loss statement for the sample data company using the cash basis and rounding numbers to the nearest dollar. The Total Income/Expense is lower than it would be when you use the accrual basis because some of the customers have not paid for their goods.

A P&L report covers a period of time.

In a profit and loss report, the most important setting you make is the Report on months from ... through fields. These two dates select the boundaries of the transactions QuickBooks looks at to create the P&L report. Any effects on profit that occur before the first date and after the last one are treated as if they do not exist.

Creating Standard and Custom Reports

```
                              Balance Sheet
                              As of 3/31/92
Sample Data Company-All Accounts                                    Page 1
1/10/93
                                         1/ 1/92        3/31/92
                   Account               Balance        Balance
       ---------------------------------  ------------   ------------
       ASSETS
          CURRENT ASSETS
             Checking                     3,248.62       29,454.56
             Petty Cash                     114.64           93.19
             Receivables                 8,836.44       94,246.05
             Undeposited received payments     0.00            0.00
                                         ------------   ------------
             TOTAL CURRENT ASSETS        12,199.70      123,793.80

          FIXED ASSETS
             Fixed Assets                43,000.00       43,000.00
                                         ------------   ------------
             TOTAL FIXED ASSETS          43,000.00       43,000.00

                                         ------------   ------------
          TOTAL ASSETS                   55,199.70      166,793.80
                                         ============   ============


       LIABILITIES
          CURRENT LIABILITIES
             Payables                     4,551.58       44,118.16
             Payroll-FICA                   302.26          163.88
             Payroll-FUTA                    17.06           25.42
             Payroll-FWH                    343.00          116.00
             Payroll-MCARE                   70.70           48.00
             Payroll-SDI                     24.38           14.85
             Payroll-SUI                     41.44           20.27
             Payroll-SWHCA                   70.34           23.94
             Sales Tax                      106.68        2,243.36
             Texaco Card                      0.00          129.36
                                         ------------   ------------
             TOTAL CURRENT LIABILITIES    5,527.44       46,903.24

          LONG TERM LIABILITIES
             Auto Loan                    8,949.26        8,470.96
                                         ------------   ------------
             TOTAL LONG TERM LIABILITIES  8,949.26        8,470.96

                                         ------------   ------------
          TOTAL LIABILITIES              14,476.70       55,374.20

       EQUITY
          EQUITY ACCOUNTS
             Earnings                    28,405.48       28,405.48
             Open Bal Equity                  0.00            0.00
             Peggy's Equity              15,000.00       15,000.00
                                         ------------   ------------
             TOTAL EQUITY ACCOUNTS       43,405.48       43,405.48

          CURRENT EARNINGS               -2,682.48       68,014.12
                                         ------------   ------------
```

Balance sheet showing two dates
Figure 11-4.

QuickBooks for Profit: Making the Numbers Work

```
                  Profit & Loss Statement
                  1/ 1/92 Through 12/31/92
Sample Data Company-All Accounts                              Page 1
1/10/93
                                          1/ 1/92-
     Inc/Exp Description                 12/31/92

INCOME/EXPENSE
  INCOME
    Partial Payment                                          83,709
    Interest inc                                                104
    Sales:
      Consult                                 150
      Design                                3,280
    Pass-thru:
      Cost                               -37,326
      Receive                              3,952
                                        --------
        Total Pass-thru
        Production                                          -33,373
                                                                605
                                                           --------
        Total Sales                                         -29,338
                                                           --------
  TOTAL INCOME                                               54,475
  EXPENSES
    Auto:
      Gas & Oil                              277
                                        --------
      Total Auto                                                277
    Bank fees:
      Serv                                     9
                                        --------
      Total Bank fees                                             9
    Ben:
      Health Ins                           1,500
                                        --------
      Total Ben                                               1,500
    Interest exp:
      Loan                                   222
                                        --------
      Total Interest exp                                        222
    Kitchon                                                     145
    Maint:
      Janitor                                240
                                        --------
      Total Maint                                               240
    Owner's Draw                                              4,000
    Payroll:
      Comp FICA                            1,332
      Comp FUTA                              150
      Comp MCARE                             312
      Comp SUI                               365
      Gross                               21,482
                                        --------
      Total Payroll                                          23,642
    Rent:
      Building                             4,000
```

```
                  Profit & Loss Statement
                  1/ 1/92 Through 12/31/92
Sample Data Company-All Accounts                              Page 2
1/10/93
                                          1/ 1/92-
     Inc/Exp Description                 12/31/92

    Total Rent                                                4,000
    T&E:
      Meals                                   31
                                        --------
      TOTAL T&E                                                  31
    Tel:
      Local                                  331
      Long dist                              210
                                        --------
      Total Tel                                                 541
    Utilities:
      Gas & elec                             417
                                        --------
      Total Utilities                                           417
                                                           --------
  TOTAL EXPENSES                                             35,024
                                                           --------
TOTAL INCOME/EXPENSE                                         19,451
                                                           ========
```

Profit and loss statement using cash basis

Figure 11-5.

Some other changes you can make to a profit and loss report include

- Changing the Column headings field to Project when you want the income statement broken down by projects. If you want to be selective about which projects are included, press `F9` to add a filter, type **Y** for the Select projects to include field, then press `Ctrl`-`Enter` and select the projects you want to appear on the statement.
- Changing the Row headings field to Project when you want a mini-profit and loss report on each project.
- Changing the Column headings field to a time period, such as Quarter or Month, to break down expenses and earnings into smaller time periods. For example, when you look at last year's profit and loss on a monthly basis, you may decide that increased summer sales justifies hiring summer help.

Monitoring Accounts Receivable

QuickBooks allows you to create three different reports from the information in your accounts receivable accounts. You can focus on sales with the sales report. You can create an accounts receivable aging report similar to the one that you saw in Chapter 7. The last accounts receivable report is a collections report to help you collect delinquent bills by providing names and phone numbers for delinquent accounts.

Sales Report

The sales report is produced from the line item entries on your invoices. This report includes the number of line items and the total dollar value of the items sold. Line items for parts, services, discounts, and other charges are all included with the default settings. Figure 11-6 shows a sales report.

You can select which entries are listed. You might want to do this to limit the listed entries to either items or services. For example, before you count inventory at the end of the year, you may want to print the items only in the sales report, to have a hard copy of the items you will count.

The Column headings field lets you separate items into different groups. Changing the Column headings field to a time interval, for example, creates separate columns for sales of items and dollar amounts

```
                            SALES REPORT
                       1/ 1/92 Through 12/31/92
       Sample Data Company-Receivables                                Page 1
       1/10/93
                                                 1/ 1/92-    12/31/92
                                                 ------------------------

           Item Code      Description            Units         Dollars
           ---------      -----------            -----         -------

           bcard          Printing 500 business cards    84    5,460.00
           BCPKG          500 Business Cards with log     1      175.00
           cons           Consultation hours             48    2,400.00
           des adapt      Adapt design                    1    7,500.00
           des manual     Design manuals                  1   20,000.00
           des1           Design hours                   31      930.00
           des2           Design hours                  147    5,880.00
           desf           Design hours                  105    4,200.00
           desID          Corporate ID/Product logo d     1   25,000.00
           focus          Arrange focus groups and re     1   10,000.00
           illus          Illustration hours             10      500.00
           lino           Linotronic output               8      320.00
           mech           Mechanical pasteup hours       82    1,630.00
           mech ID        Mechanical art for ID packa     1   15,000.00
           mug            Custom mugs                   195      877.50
           pen            Custom ballpoint pens       2,000    1,900.00
           photo          Photography hours              40    2,000.00
           print          Printing                       13   53,150.00
           proto          Produce prototypes of desig     1   15,000.00
           refine         Refine designs based on fee     1    2,500.00
           ship           Shipping                        1      670.00
           slide          Custom slide transparencies    80      300.00
           swt            Custom sweatshirts             34      255.00
           tbag           Custom travel bag             500    3,250.00
           travel         Reimbursement for travel ex     1    2,500.00
           type           Typesetting hours              78    1,755.00
           write          Copywriting hours              35    1,400.00
                                                              ------------
                          OVERALL TOTAL                       184,552.50
                                                              ============
```

Sales report
Figure 11-6.

by that time interval. Changing the Column headings field to customer or customer type creates separate columns for these groups. For example, if you select Customer type for the Column headings field using the sample company, you will have columns labeled Corporate,

Creating Standard and Custom Reports

Financial, Food Service, Hotel/Resort, Professional, Retail, and Travel to separate the different items sold. You can also separate the columns by employee when you want to see how much each employee is contributing in sales.

Aging Report

In Chapter 7 you learned how to display a customer's aging status for their outstanding invoices. You can look at current receivables with this report as well as those that are past due. You can create an aging report that contains this information for all of your customers. The first page of a sample aging report looks like Figure 11-7, using a date of 4/12/92 and the sample company. The "Current" column includes invoices that have not reached the due date. The other columns separate the invoice amounts by how much they are overdue. The options for this report that you may want to change include changing the interval of each group of aged receivables, changing the last interval reported, or selecting which customers you want in the report. This report tells you if your customers are paying their bills very late. If they are, you may want to create policies that encourage early payment.

```
                              A/R AGING REPORT
                                As of 4/12/92
      Sample Data Company-Receivables                                Page 1
      4/12/92

           Customer         Current      1 - 30     31 - 60    61 - 90      > 90
      ------------------   ---------   ---------   ---------   ---------   ---------
      Book Nook               0.00        0.00        0.00      500.75       0.00
      Ellis Interiors         0.00        0.00        0.00      866.30       0.00
      Asset Mgmt.             0.00        0.00     3,863.73       0.00       0.00
      Franz Telecom           0.00        0.00        0.00        0.00   1,469.80
      Gee Whiz Toys           0.00        0.00        0.00      504.39       0.00
      Mari's Deli             0.00        0.00        0.00    1,597.00       0.00
      Sequoia Resort     29,136.60        0.00        0.00        0.00       0.00
      Computer USA        8,634.90   45,000.00        0.00        0.00       0.00
      Pacific Pines           0.00    1,783.13        0.00        0.00       0.00
      Uhl & Sone              0.00        0.00      889.45        0.00       0.00
                         ---------   ---------   ---------   ---------   ---------
      OVERALL TOTAL      37,771.50   46,783.13    4,753.18    3,468.44   1,469.80
                         =========   =========   =========   =========   =========
```

Aging report showing overdue receivables
Figure 11-7.

Collections Report

Use a collections report when you need phone numbers and contacts to arrange collection of overdue monies.

When you know you need to remind customers to pay their bills, you want to be able to call them and tell them how much they owe and what they owe the money for. QuickBooks makes this process easier through the collections report. When you create this report, QuickBooks lists the customer, the contacts and their phone numbers, the invoice, when it was sent, when it was due, and its amount. This report gives you all the information you need to make your phone calls. One of the segments of the report might look like this:

```
         Customer               Invoice   Issued    Due      Balance Due

Book Nook                        1011     1/ 3/92  2/ 2/92      500.75
   Linda Hafezi
   (415) 555-8682 ext                     Total Book Nook       500.75
```

Creating Payables Reports

Besides creating an aging report for how well your customers are paying their bills, you can also create an aging report to show how well *you* are paying your bills. An accounts payable aging report looks just like an accounts receivable aging report (like the one in Figure 11-7) except the first column contains vendors, not customers, and the amounts in the other columns are the amounts you owe. You also have the same customizing options that you have for accounts receivable aging reports. The "Current" column contains the bills that have not reached the due date. The other columns separate the bills by how much they are overdue. If your business is short of cash, you might want to use this report to select which bills you will pay.

Sales Tax Report

If you collect sales tax, you will need to report the taxable sales you have made and the sales taxes you have collected. QuickBooks' sales tax report lists the different tax agencies (they appear as separate vendors in the Sales Tax accounts payable account), the taxable revenues, and the taxes you have collected during the period. This report has an option for cash or accrual basis accounting since you want to match the basis you use to the rules your state uses. As an example, the beginning of the sales tax report for the sample company looks like the following:

Creating Standard and Custom Reports

Sales Tax District	Revenue	Sales Tax
Nevada Dept of Taxation		
Sierra County	25,110.00	1,506.60
Total Nevada Dept of Taxation		1,506.60

1099 Report

The IRS requires that companies prepare Form 1099 for non-employed people to whom they pay more than $600 a year. QuickBooks' 1099 report assists you by listing non-employee payees from the accounts payable register, their taxpayer ID number, and the total you have paid over the year. You will get to see an example of this report in the next chapter, since this is a form you complete at the end of the year.

Analyzing Cash Flows

The most common problem for a small business is inadequate cash flow. Use a cash flow report to monitor the situation.

Given all of the receipts and bills you have, you might want to know that you have enough cash to pay your bills. A cash flow report provides this analysis. A cash flow report looks like the one in Figure 11-8. In this report, the current balances of checking as well as the past due accounts receivable and accounts payable are shown. QuickBooks separates when accounts receivable are received and accounts payable are paid according to their due dates. The date intervals are set by the From ... through fields and broken into a set number of days by the Report at intervals of field. For example, you can see from the report shown in Figure 11-8 that you will receive $1783.13 from your customers and pay $8771.58 in bills during the first week of April.

The value of this report decreases as time passes because it does not take into account new transactions that occur. For example, the cash flow report in Figure 11-8 does not take into account the sales that are made in the month of April, the bills that arrive during April, or payments such as payroll that must also be made. What this report does give you is a feel for whether you have enough cash on hand to pay current bills in a timely way.

Taking a Summary Look

As its name implies, the summary report summarizes the transactions you have made. Instead of individual transactions, you see their sums.

```
                CASH FLOW FORECAST REPORT AT 7 DAY INTERVALS
                            4/ 1/92 Through 5/31/92
Sample Data Company-All Checking/AR/AP Accounts                     Page 1
6/10/92
                         Accts       Accts     Checking      Net      Projected
       Date Range         Recv      Payable     Accts      Inflow      Balance
---------------------  ----------  ----------  ----------  ----------  -------------

Checking balance                               29,454.56
Past due A/R & A/P      9,691.42  -37,589.94
                       ----------  ----------  ----------
        As of 3/31/92   9,691.42  -37,589.94   29,454.56                  1,556.04

   4/ 1/92 -  4/ 7/92   1,783.13   -8,771.58        0.00   -6,988.45     -5,432.41
   4/ 8/92 -  4/14/92  45,000.00        0.00        0.00   45,000.00     39,567.59
   4/15/92 -  4/21/92       0.00        0.00        0.00        0.00     39,567.59
   4/22/92 -  4/28/92       0.00        0.00        0.00        0.00     39,567.59
   4/29/92 -  5/ 5/92  29,136.60        0.00        0.00   29,136.60     68,704.19
   5/ 6/92 -  5/12/92   8,634.90        0.00        0.00    8,634.90     77,339.09
   5/13/92 -  5/19/92       0.00        0.00        0.00        0.00     77,339.09
   5/20/92 -  5/26/92       0.00        0.00        0.00        0.00     77,339.09
   5/27/92 -  5/31/92       0.00        0.00        0.00        0.00     77,339.09
                       ----------  ----------  ----------  ----------
   4/ 1/92 -  5/31/92  84,554.63   -8,771.58        0.00   75,783.05

                       ----------  ----------  ----------
        As of 5/31/92  94,246.05  -46,361.52   29,454.56                 77,339.09
```

Cash flow forecast Figure 11-8.

The profit and loss and payroll reports are variations of summary reports with filters created to present specific information. You use a summary report to present different information than what you see in the other reports. When you print a summary report using the default settings, the report looks just like the profit and loss statement, except the transfers between accounts are included. These transfers do not appear in a profit and loss statement because when you press `F8` for the Report Options window, the Transfers to include is 2, to exclude transfers. Figure 11-9 shows the transfer section of a summary report.

The customization options you have in the profit and loss report, such as having columns to show the amounts for different time periods, projects, employees, or vendors, are also available for summary reports.

Creating a Transaction Report

The transaction report is the most detailed report that you can create with QuickBooks. Normally, you will customize this report to narrow its scope. If you list all transactions from all accounts you will probably have more information than you can meaningfully process. On the other hand, if a particular account does not have the balance that you expect, you can use F9 Filter to look at the detail for this one account. If you are having a problem with one payee and are not certain of the history of their purchases, you can use the transaction report to look at all the detail for this one payee. You can also limit the transactions in the report to a specific balance sheet account by selecting that account from the chart of accounts and then typing C for the Use

```
TRANSFERS
    TO Auto Loan                        -478.30
    TO Checking                     -115,566.91
    TO Fixed Assets                  -51,000.00
    TO Open Bal Equity               -65,013.00
    TO Payables                      -48,630.55
    TO Payroll-FICA                   -2,500.00
    TO Payroll-FUTA                     -125.00
    TO Payroll-FWH                    -2,600.00
    TO Payroll-MCARE                    -575.00
    TO Payroll-SDI                      -200.00
    TO Payroll-SUI                      -345.00
    TO Payroll-SWHCA                    -425.00
    TO Petty Cash                       -214.64
    TO Receivables                   -13,191.18
    TO Sales Tax                      -2,218.06
    TO Texaco Card                      -147.32
    FROM Auto Loan                     8,949.26
    FROM Checking                     58,344.23
    FROM Earnings                     28,405.48
    FROM Fixed Assets                  8,000.00
    FROM Open Bal Equity              65,013.00
    FROM Payables                      4,551.58
    FROM Payroll-FICA                  2,663.88
    FROM Payroll-FUTA                    150.42
    FROM Payroll-FWH                   2,716.00
    FROM Payroll-MCARE                   623.00
    FROM Payroll-SDI                     214.85
    FROM Payroll-SUI                     365.27
```

Transfer section of a summary report
Figure 11-9.

Current/Selected/All balance sheet accounts field. You can also select the balance sheet account by typing **S** for this field and then selecting the accounts you want to include.

Figure 11-10 shows all the transactions for Barklow Custom Products. This report was created by following these steps after selecting Transaction Report:

1. Type **1/1/92** and **3/31/92** for the Restrict transactions from ... through fields.

    You will also want to check that the Subtotal by field is Totals only and the Use Current/Selected/All balance sheet accounts field has an A for All.

2. Press [F8] for the Report Options window.

3. Type **S** for the Detail Level so that split transactions show the different accounts rather than just indicating Split, which is QuickBooks' default.

4. Press [Ctrl]-[Enter] to leave the Report Options window.

```
                        TRANSACTION REPORT
                       1/ 1/92 Through 3/31/92
     Sample Data Company-All Accounts                              Page 1
     4/10/92


     Date    Acct     Num      Description      Memo       Accts    ProjectClr Amount
     -----   -------  -----    -------------    -------    -------  -------    --------

     1/24  Checkin  1022 S   Barklow Custom              Payables          X   -682.50
     1/12  Payable  5503 S   Barklow Custom   120 mugs   Sales:Pas Doell     -420.00
                                              75 mugs    Sales:Pas Baysof    -262.50
     1/24  Payable           Barklow Custom              Checking             682.50
     3/ 3  Payable  5623     Barklow Custom   2000 ballp Sales:Pas DJosep  -1,500.00
                                                                            ---------
                    TOTAL  1/ 1/92 - 3/31/92                               -2,182.50


                    TOTAL INFLOWS                                            682.50
                    TOTAL OUTFLOWS                                        -2,865.00
                                                                            ---------
                    NET TOTAL                                              -2,182.50
                                                                            =========
```

Transaction report for Barklow Custom Products **Figure 11-10.**

Creating Standard and Custom Reports

5. Press [F9] for the Filter Report Transactions window.
6. Press [Ctrl]-[L] and select Barklow Custom Products from the Payee list.
7. Press [Ctrl]-[Enter] to leave the Filter Report Transactions window.
8. Press [Ctrl]-[Enter] to create the report.

Looking at Income and Expense Transactions

Another report QuickBooks has available for looking at individual transactions is the itemized income/expense report. This report lists the individual transactions for all or selected income and expense accounts. As with other reports, you select a range of dates for the transactions that you want the report to include. Figure 11-11 shows the first page of an itemized income/expense report that focuses on the expenses involved with operating the business's office. The expense accounts that are included are selected by pressing [F9] for the Filter option, then typing Y for the Select Inc/Exp accounts to include field. When you leave the Filter Report Transactions window, QuickBooks displays a list of the income and expense accounts that are included or omitted from the report. By selecting the expense accounts from this window, the report in Figure 11-11 is reduced to only displaying information on the specific expenses.

For a close-up look at income and expenses, use QuickBooks to create an itemized income/ expense report.

The customization options for this report include all of the filtering options for summary and transaction reports. From the Create Transaction Report window, when you change the Subtotal by field to another predefined selection, you are changing how the income and expense items are divided into groups. The Subtotal by field selects the groups of the report and when the items within a group are totaled. If you want to focus on the expenses that you pay directly by check or through the accounts payable register, type S for Use Current/All/Selected balance sheet accounts. Later, select the Checking or Payables account to include in the report.

Monitoring Projects

The project report is only accessible if you have turned tracking on. In fact you will see an error message rather than a report unless you display the company's options and type Y for the Project tracking on

QuickBooks for Profit: Making the Numbers Work

```
                        Itemized Inc/Exp Account Report
                           1/ 1/92 Through 3/31/92
Sample Data Company-All Accounts                                  Page 1
4/10/92

 Date   Acct    Num        Description        Memo        ProjectClr Amount
 ----   ----    ---        -----------        ----        ---------- ------

                INCOME/EXPENSE
                EXPENSES
                  Kitchen
                  -------
 1/ 8  Petty C             Bayshore Pizzeria  Pizza, etc.              -38.38
 1/ 9  Petty C             Bagel Maven        Bagels for meet Obayas   -10.75
 1/29  Petty C             Bayshore Pizzeria  Pizza, etc               -41.09
 2/10  Payable             Green Mountain Water Monthly drinkin        -55.00
 3/10  Payable             Green Mountain Water Monthly drinkin        -55.00
                                                                     ---------
                  Total Kitchen                                       -200.22

                  Maint:
                  ------
                    Janitor
                    -------
 1/15  Payable             Gil Janitorial Servi Monthly janitor       -120.00
 2/10  Payable             Gil Janitorial Servi Monthly janitor       -120.00
 3/10  Payable             Gil Janitorial Servi Monthly janitor       -120.00
                                                                     ---------
                    Total Janitor                                     -360.00
                                                                     ---------
                  Total Maint                                         -360.00

                  Rent:
                  -----
                    Building
                    --------
 1/12  Payable             Onquit Properties    Monthly Rent        -2,000.00
 2/10  Payable             Onquit Properties    Monthly Rent        -2,000.00
 3/10  Payable             Onquit Properties    Monthly rent        -2,000.00
                                                                     ---------
                    Total Building                                  -6,000.00
                                                                     ---------
                  Total Rent                                        -6,000.00

                  Tel:
                  ----
                    Local
                    -----
 1/17  Payable             Bay Telephone        Monthly phone b       -163.04
 2/10  Payable           S Bay Telephone                              -168.38
 3/12  Payable           S Bay Telephone                               -84.03
                                                                     ---------
                    Total Local                                       -415.45

                    Long dist
                    ---------
 2/10  Payable           S Bay Telephone                              -210.05
 3/12  Payable           S Bay Telephone                              -103.43
                                                                     ---------
```

Itemized income and expense report for specific expenses **Figure 11-11.**

Creating Standard and Custom Reports

field. For the project report to provide meaningful information you must also enter a project as you record income and expenses; otherwise, QuickBooks will not be able to categorize transactions by project. Use project tracking when your business deals with identifiable projects. For example, the sample company included with QuickBooks uses project tracking because the business designs printed materials for specific clients. If your business does not have specific projects, do not use project tracking; its features will not be useful to you.

A project report is just like a profit and loss statement except each project has a separate column that shows the income and expense items for the project. Figure 11-12 shows the income section of a project report that is limited to bank projects.

```
                              PROJECT REPORT
                           1/ 1/92 Through 4/30/92
Sample Data Company-All Accounts                                   Page 1
6/10/92


                              Bank proj         Bank proj         Bank proj
   Inc/Exp Description         Brochure         Stationery           TOTAL
----------------------      -----------         ----------        ---------
INCOME/EXPENSE
  INCOME
    Sales:
      Consult                    150.00               0.00           150.00
      Design                   1,000.00               0.00         1,000.00
    Pass-thru:
      Cost                      -415.00            -216.00          -631.00
      Receive                    585.00             260.00           845.00
                              ----------         ----------        ---------
      Total Pass-thru            170.00              44.00           214.00
      Production                 545.00               0.00           545.00
                              ----------         ----------        ---------
      Total Sales              1,865.00              44.00         1,909.00
                              ----------         ----------        ---------
  TOTAL INCOME                 1,865.00              44.00         1,909.00

                              ----------         ----------        ---------
  TOTAL INCOME/EXPENSE        1,865.00              44.00         1,909.00
                              ==========         ==========        =========
```

Report showing only selected projects
Figure 11-12.

When a project has subprojects, each of the subprojects has a separate column with another column for the total of the subprojects. From the first window for this report, you can select whether you want to report on specific projects or all of them. The customization features for project reports are identical to the customization features for profit and loss reports.

CAUTION: Releases of QuickBooks prior to Release 9 *sometimes* make calculations that result in the under reporting of sales tax in a cash basis accounting system. Contact Intuit if you own one of the earlier releases.

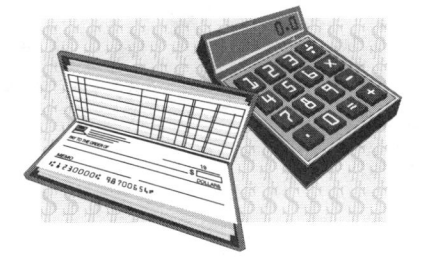

CHAPTER

12

YEAR-END REPORTS AND SPECIAL ACTIVITIES

QuickBooks is designed to make your year-end process go smoothly whether you are keeping your books on a calendar- or fiscal-year basis. There is no need to perform any special procedures at the end of the year to have the package continue to work for you in the next year, outside of transferring your profit or loss to the equity accounts. You already learned how to perform this quick procedure in Chapter 10.

The end of the year is a good time to think about doing some protective maintenance on your system. You might want to consider backing up your files at this time, and changing system passwords. You will probably also want to look at some reports that are usually needed only at the end of the year, for tax purposes. QuickBooks can provide all the information that you need to create 1099s, W-2s, Schedule C, and other tax forms.

In this chapter you take a quick conceptual look at the typical year-end process, to show you all the time that you are saving with QuickBooks. To put some of this timesavings to good use, you can institute appropriate backup procedures for the end of the year and throughout the upcoming year. You will also learn how you can use QuickBooks' existing reports to prepare the year-end tax documents that you need.

The examples assume your company's books are kept on a calendar-year basis. If they are not, you need to use a different date than the December 31 used in the examples.

The Business Cycle

Throughout this book you have learned many procedures that you can use during the year to help you run your business. You learned how to write checks, record bills, create invoices, and receive payments. The timing of each of these activities is easy to decide since they correspond to concrete tasks that you are already aware that you need to perform. The end of the year is different; you are not as likely to be aware of any special activities that must occur.

Treat the end of the year as a special time. It should be a measuring point—a time for you to create reports and prepare information for tax purposes. For example, preparing a balance sheet measures assets and liabilities; creating an income statement measures the income you have generated from the last measuring point to the current one. Since you are going to use these measurements for external reporting, such as tax returns, you want these numbers to be correct. The year-end process is a time to make sure that your assets, liabilities, expenses, and income are correct and reliable.

Year-End Reports and Special Activities

Accounting Steps at the End of the Cycle

The following is a list of the steps an accountant performs to close books versus those you must perform in QuickBooks:

Accounting Steps	QuickBooks Steps
Prepare a trial balance	End of the year entries
Prepare a worksheet	Adjust retained earnings
End of the year entries	
Close income and expense accounts	
Adjust retained earnings	
Prepare financial statements	

Avoiding the Typical Year-End Closing Process with QuickBooks

You probably have heard accountants and bookkeepers complain of everything they have to do at the end of the year to close the books. QuickBooks consolidates this process into only a few steps. The steps an accountant performs and the steps you perform with QuickBooks are summarized in the box "Accounting Steps at the End of the Cycle."

There are some tasks you must perform whether you use QuickBooks or another system. Your accountant will probably help you with these tasks, which include recording depreciation, adjusting your inventory current asset account, and recording prepaid expenses. You learned how to do the first two in Chapter 10. You will learn about prepaid expenses in the next section of this chapter. One year-end task that is different using QuickBooks than using other accounting systems is how you credit your equity accounts for the current period's earnings. You learned how to do this in Chapter 10. These year-end transactions make sure your assets, liabilities, expenses, and income accounts are correct. The expenses and income need to be correct so you can report the proper amount of income.

> **TIP:** Here is a quick way to remember whether you have any assets, liabilities, expenses, or income that may not have been recorded: imagine you closed your business at the end of the last day of the year—what money is still due and what bills must still be paid?

Accounting for Prepaid Expenses

Your accountant might suggest other year-end adjusting entries, such as prepaid expenses. As an example, you may have paid an insurance premium for a period that covers part of the upcoming year. At the end of the year, the unused portion of the insurance is an asset, since it is owed to the company (rather than an expense for something the company has consumed). The portion of the insurance premium that applies to the subsequent year should be transferred to a current asset account. You can create a current asset account for this purpose with a name like "Prepaid Expenses." Once you have the account, you can record the portions of paid expenses that apply to the upcoming year. An example of an entry for this purpose looks like this:

| 12/31 1992 | Prepaid Insurance Insur | | | 1,875 57 | 1,875 57 |

On January 1, reverse this entry, since it will all be used up in the next year, as shown here:

| 1/01 1993 | Reverse Prepaid Insurance Insur | 1,875 57 | | | 0 00 |

As a result of the two transactions, when you look at your balance sheet at the end of the year, it includes the correct amounts for prepaid insurance. Also, the insurance expense for the year that just ended is reduced to the appropriate amount so you do not deduct too much in your tax calculations. Note that if you use a cash basis of accounting, these two entries are not needed, because all of the expense is recognized when you pay it.

Adjusting the Equity Account for Earnings

When your balance sheet has all the assets and liabilities and all the income and expenses for the year recorded, you only have one more entry to make—the one to the retained earnings account. You learned about this in Chapter 10, but a quick review is appropriate at this time before you begin to produce your year-end reports.

In standard double-entry accounting—the process accountants use—you would have to close all of your income expense accounts to an income summary account. The income summary account would equal the difference between income and expenses. The entry would include each income and expense account with its balance, as shown in Figure 12-1. This can be a long and tedious process if you have many accounts, but fortunately you do not make this entry in QuickBooks. The second entry transfers the balance of the income summary to your retained earnings account.

General Journal

Date	Description	Debit	Credit
12/31	Sales	1 00 24 56 0 6	
	Fees	45 73 1 52	
	... All other income accounts		
	Advertising Expense		3 57 81 52
	Auto Expense		1 24 05 45
	... All other income accounts		
	Income Summary		3 56 00 0 0
12/31	Income Summary	3 56 00 0 0	
	Retained Earnings		3 56 00 0 0

Closing entry for double-entry accounting
Figure 12-1.

With QuickBooks, you only add one entry to retained earnings. This is the entry you learned how to make in Chapter 10. As a reminder, you add the amount from the Total Income/Expense line in the profit and loss statement to the retained earnings account. You use an expense account with a name such as "1993 Profit". The same journal entries shown in Figure 12-1 appear in QuickBooks as this single entry:

```
12/31     1993 Profit                      35,600 00           107,600 00
1993                      1993 Profit
```

Adding Taxes to QuickBooks

If your business is a corporation, you have the additional expense of income taxes. Only corporations pay income taxes since sole proprietorships and partnerships pay taxes on the business income through the owners' personal income statements. Recording taxes is just like recording any other accounts payable item with a Taxes:Fed subexpense as the account for the transaction. By entering the tax bill, QuickBooks will remind you to pay it on time. Also, the calculations of your company's earnings will include this amount so that you will transfer the correct amount to retained earnings. As an example, if you owe $21,057 in taxes, your entry looks like this:

```
12/31/92     Internal Revenue Service      2/28/93  21,057 00
             1992 Taxes        Taxes:Fed
```

Now your profit and loss statement will include the amount you owe for the year's taxes as an expense. You may need another entry for state income taxes, depending on where you live.

Performing Year-End Maintenance Tasks

After you have finished the transactions for a year, you will want to perform a few maintenance tasks to protect your data. You can protect data for the previous year by setting a password that you must supply every time you want to alter old transactions. You should also create

Year-End Reports and Special Activities 311

backup copies of data and store them in another location, in case you lose your originals.

As a final step, review your prior year's budget and prepare a budget for the next year. Comparing your budget to the year's results lets you see how well you accomplished your business's goals. Also, you can see how good your budget assumptions are, which will help you prepare next year's budget. Look at Chapter 5 for more information on budgeting.

Backing Up the Year's Transactions

Consider storing a year-end backup at an off-site location such as your safe-deposit box or at a friend's.

Backing up your QuickBooks files can save you time and anguish if you have to review the year's transactions at a later date. (This sort of review may be necessary if you are audited.) Creating year-end backups lets you return to a file if you ever need to. Year-end backups are different from regular backups, which are kept in case you lose your original data. The year-end backup ignores transactions that occur after the end of the year. You will also want to store your year-end backups in a different place than regular backups.

To create a year-end back-up, follow these steps:

1. Select 7 Set Up/Customize from the Main Menu.
2. Select 2 Back Up/Restore/Copy Company Files.
3. Select 1 Back Up Company Files.
4. Highlight the company you want to back up using the arrow keys and press [Enter].
5. Insert a formatted floppy disk in a drive. If the drive you plan to use is not the A drive, type its letter before pressing [Enter].

    QuickBooks displays windows indicating which company files QuickBooks is currently backing up. When QuickBooks is finished, it displays a window saying so.
6. Press [Enter] to return to the Select Company to Back Up window.

After you back up your company for the end of the year, put it in a safe location. You may want to make two backups, so you have one copy to put with your tax records and another copy to put with the prior year's business records.

Protecting Your Data with Passwords

With QuickBooks, you can protect your data with passwords. There are two reasons for using passwords: first, they protect your data from dishonest employees who have access to the computer; second, they protect your transactions for a prior period from being changed accidentally. This is important since using the end of the year as a measuring point is only reliable if its data does not change.

QuickBooks allows two types of passwords that protect the data in your QuickBooks data files. Using passwords is a two-step process. First you tell QuickBooks what the passwords are and then you tell QuickBooks when the passwords are required.

TIP: Adding passwords does not completely prevent other people from getting to the data. You may also want to limit access to the computer by putting the computer in a locked room or using the lock that many computers include.

Adding Passwords

To tell QuickBooks the passwords, select 4 Customize Current Company. Then select 3 Passwords from the Set Up/Customize menu. QuickBooks displays the Set Passwords window:

```
                       Set Passwords

         Owner (high-security) password:

     Bookkeeper (low-security) password:

   Date through which books are closed:  1/15/93


              Leave password blank to remove
   Esc-Cancel              F1-Help              Ctrl⏎ Done
```

In this window, you can enter two passwords. For either password, you can type up to 16 characters. (QuickBooks does not distinguish between

Year-End Reports and Special Activities

Requiring the use of an Owner password to change transactions in a previous accounting period allows you to protect the "closed" period from accidental changes.

upper- and lowercase.) The *Owner* password is the high-security password that you only want one or two people to know. This is the password you would require to edit transactions from past years. The *Bookkeeper* password is the low-security password for people who work with QuickBooks during the year. Knowing the Owner password lets you change both passwords and the level of password required for different activities. The Bookkeeper password permits you to perform those activities that require a Bookkeeper password or no password. If you only want one level of password, supply the Owner password.

In the Date through which books are closed field you can set the cutoff date that different passwords are required in order to edit transactions. Usually this will be the last date of the year. Use this feature to ensure that no one changes any old transactions.

After you type any passwords, change the date, and press Ctrl-Enter, you must enter the Owner password again. This time, and all subsequent times, the characters you type for the password appear as squares. Next, you go directly to the Password Level Assignment window, where you can assign different password levels to different activities, as described in the next section.

When you want to change or remove password protection, return to the Set Passwords window. You will need to enter the Owner password. You can remove an existing password by pressing Del to remove each character, or change the displayed passwords by typing over them.

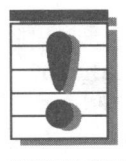

TIP: Write down your passwords and keep them in a safe place that is not accessible to your other employees. If you forget the passwords, you cannot perform the activities in QuickBooks that require a password.

Changing the Password Table

Selecting 4 Password Table, or completing the Set Passwords window and then supplying the Owner password, opens the Password Level Assignment window, shown in Figure 12-2. This window shows the activities you can set passwords for. Highlight an activity by pressing

Use the Password Level Assignment window to set passwords for certain activities
Figure 12-2.

```
                Password Level Assignment
       Program Area or Activity              Password

  ▶ Delete transactions after    1/15/93     None Req'd   ↑
    Add/Edit transactions after  1/15/93     None Req'd
    Delete transactions through  1/15/93     None Req'd
    Add/Edit transactions through 1/15/93    None Req'd
    Print checks                             None Req'd
    Print invoices                           None Req'd
    Edit printed checks/invoices             None Req'd
    Delete accounts                          None Req'd
    Add/Edit/Move accounts                   None Req'd
    Delete customers/vendors/employees       None Req'd
    Add/Edit customers/vendors/employees     None Req'd
    Modify company options                   None Req'd
    Open/Delete company                      None Req'd   ↓

              Spacebar-Change password level
  Esc-Cancel              F1-Help              Ctrl⏎ Done
```

the ↑ and ↓. Each time you press the Spacebar, the Password column's entry switches between None Req'd, Owner, and Bookkeeper. The entry you place in this column is the minimum password that you must supply to complete the activity. As an example, change the Delete transactions after 1/15/93 and Add/Edit transactions after 1/15/93 activities to Owner, so that the Owner password must be supplied to change last year's transactions. After assigning passwords to the activities, press Ctrl-Enter to close the window.

TIP: Only set password requirements for the activities you want to restrict to specific people. An activity like printing invoices, which you may want anyone to do, should not have a password. With activities such as modifying old transactions, you want the Owner password to be supplied before the entry can be changed.

Using Passwords

Once you assign passwords to activities, you can still select these activities from the menus of QuickBooks. However, when you do, a window, shown in the following, will appear requesting the appropriate password:

Year-End Reports and Special Activities

```
┌─────────────────────────────────┐
│        Password Required        │
│                                 │
│   Password:                     │
│                                 │
│   Esc-Cancel  F1-Help  ←┘ Continue │
└─────────────────────────────────┘
```

When you see a prompt like this, you can type either the Owner or Bookkeeper password. An Owner password is accepted any time QuickBooks prompts for a password. If you must supply the Owner password, the window title is Owner Password Required. If you do not provide the correct password, you will see a message that access is denied, and you will not be allowed to perform the activity.

Getting the Data You Need to Complete Year-End Tax Forms

Part of the year-end process for any business is completing tax forms. Tax forms compute the taxes you owe, and they provide government agencies with a report on your earnings and expenses.

The tax forms you fill out depend on your company's business type—sole proprietor, partnership, or corporation. See the special "Year-End Business Tax Forms" section for a list of important tax forms for the small-business owner. It shows the forms you use for different business ownership types.

Schedule C, Profit or Loss from Business

Schedule C is the tax form sole proprietorships use when reporting business income and expenses during the year. QuickBooks can provide the information you need to complete your form. If you examine Schedule C, shown in Figure 12-3, you see that it is a business profit and loss statement. You can use the profit and loss statement prepared by QuickBooks to fill it in. Figure 12-4 shows a profit and loss statement used as an example for completing Schedule C.

Year-End Business Tax Forms

Form	Title
Sole Proprietorship	
Schedule C (Form 1040)	Profit or Loss from Business
Form 4562	Depreciation and Amortization
Schedule SE (Form 1040)	Social Security Self-Employment Tax
Form 1040-ES	Estimated Tax for Individuals
Partnership	
Form 1065	U.S. Partnership Return of Income
Schedule D (Form 1065)	Capital Gains and Losses
Schedule K-1 (Form 1065)	Partner's Share of Income, Credits, Deduction, Etc.
Corporation	
Form 1120-A	U.S. Corporation Short-Form Income Tax Return
Form 1120	U.S. Corporation Income Tax Return
Form 1120-S	U.S. Income Tax Return for an S Corporation

Completing Schedule C

Because Schedule C is basically just a profit and loss statement, many of the entries can be obtained directly from your QuickBooks report. The following is a list of line numbers and how you can complete them in Schedule C.

- *Line 1* This line shows gross sales. Place the Retail Sales amount ($304,904.06) from your report on this line.

Year-End Reports and Special Activities

Schedule C to report business results for a sole proprietorship
Figure 12-3.

```
                        PROFIT & LOSS STATEMENT
                        1/ 1/93 Through 12/31/93
Musical Pony-All Accounts                                          Page 1
1/ 4/94
                                                     1/ 1/93-
                Inc/Exp Description                  12/31/93
       ---------------------------------------   ------------

       INCOME/EXPENSE
         INCOME
           Revenue-Revenue:
             Retail Sales-Retail Sales             304,904.06
                                                   ------------
             Total Revenue-Revenue                             304,904.06
             Sales Disc-Sales Discounts                         -14,249.99
                                                               ------------
           TOTAL INCOME                                         290,654.07

           EXPENSES
             Advert-Advertising                                   3,287.42
             Auto-Car and Truck Expenses                             10.67
             Charges-Charges:
               Fin-Finance Charge                     2.52
               Charges-Charges - Other                1.78
                                                   ------------
               Total Charges-Charges                                  4.30
             COGS-Cost of Goods Sold                             154,344.81
             Deprec Exp-Depreciation Expense                       4,000.00
             Freight-Freight & Delivery                           12,992.86
             Insur-Insurance                                       5,101.00
             Materials-Materials                                     107.78
             Off Supp-Office Supplies                                175.34
             Payroll-Payroll:
               Comp FICA-Company Soc. Sec. Contrib  2,328.00
               Comp FUTA-Company FUTA Contribution    420.00
               Gross-Gross Wages                   32,600.00
                                                   ------------
               Total Payroll-Payroll                              35,348.00
             Rent-Rent                                            24,613.73
             Repairs-Repairs:
               Bldg-Building Repairs                 75.00
                                                   ------------
               Total Repairs-Repairs                                  75.00
             Shipping-Shipping                                     2,413.00
             Telephone-Telephone                                   3,781.12
             Util-Utilities:
               Elect-Electricity                  3,579.15
               Gas-Gas                            5,764.14
               Water-Water                          127.45
                                                   ------------
               Total Util-Utilities                               9,470.74
                                                                 ------------
           TOTAL EXPENSES                                        255,725.77
                                                                 ------------
           TOTAL INCOME/EXPENSE                                   34,928.30
                                                                 ============
```

Profit and loss report used to complete tax forms
Figure 12-4.

Year-End Reports and Special Activities

- *Line 2* This line shows return of sales and discounts. Place the Sales Disc amount (–$14,249.99) from your report on this line.

- *Line 4* This line shows cost of goods sold. Place the COGS amount ($154,344.81) from your report on this line.

- *Lines 8 through 27* These lines list the expenses you have incurred. They are grouped into fewer categories than you have in QuickBooks, but you can use QuickBooks' calculator to total the expenses for different groups. Line 13 includes depreciation and the section 179 deduction from Form 4562, Depreciation and Amortization. Taxes for line 23 include payroll taxes the company pays (not including the portion withheld from employees' pay) as well as state, local, and foreign taxes. For Wages in line 26, the amount is the gross wages paid to employees.

    Some examples of amounts from your report are $3287.42 in line 8 for Advertising, $283.12 in line 22 for Supplies ($107.78 for materials plus $175.34 for office supplies), and $2748 in line 23 for Taxes ($2328 for FICA plus $420 for FUTA).

- *Line 28* This line shows your total deductions. This is the amount of Total Expenses ($255,725.77) less the cost of goods sold in line 4, assuming your company has no nondeductible expenses.

- *Line 29* This line shows your net profit (or loss). This is your Total Income/Expense, $34,928.30.

If you need an extra copy of schedule C or any other form, call the IRS form order line at 800-829-3676 or check your local library.

NOTE: You can round the cents to the nearest dollar when completing your tax forms.

Once you have completed Schedule C, you are ready to complete Schedule SE, Social Security Self-Employment Tax. The net profit from your Schedule C, $34,928.30, is carried to line 2 of that form, and the rest of the form can be easily completed.

When you complete line 13, Depreciation, in Schedule C, you use the total Depreciation Expense amount from your profit and loss statement. This information must be included on Form 4562, Depreciation and Amortization. After reading through Publication 534, you would have entered the appropriate amounts for section 179 property and ACRS or MACRS depreciation. This results in a total of $4000, shown on line 20 of Form 4562 and transferred to line 13 on Schedule C.

> **TIP:** The IRS has placed many limits on what may be deducted for home offices and food and entertainment expenses. If you have these types of expenses, you or your accountant should review the expenses to calculate the portion of each that is deductible and the portion that is not.

Form 1099 for Independent Contractors

When you pay non-employees more than $600 per year, you must report to the IRS the payee and the amount. You must also send the individual a 1099 form. QuickBooks handles creating this report for you by keeping track of the vendors in your accounts payable.

To create this report, complete the following steps:

1. Select 5 Reports from the Main Menu.
2. Select 4 A/P Reports.
3. Select 3 1099 Report.
4. Type a title for the report after the Report title field if you want to use a title other than 1099 Report.
5. Type **Y** for the Select vendors to include field and press [Ctrl]-[Enter].

    QuickBooks displays a vendor list that includes the names, balances, and whether or not the vendor is included in the report.

6. Move to a vendor and press the [Spacebar] for the vendors you do not want to include.

    You may want to go through the list twice—once to remove those from the list that have account balances of less than $600 and another time to remove the vendors from the list that are corporations.

7. Press [Ctrl]-[Enter] to create the report.

Year-End Reports and Special Activities 321

You should see a report like the one shown in Figure 12-5. The address and taxpayer ID number come from the vendor list.

8. Press Ctrl-P and the Print Report window appears.
9. Select the printer and press Enter.

From the printed report, you have the information necessary to prepare the 1099 and the summary 1096.

Payroll Taxes

When you have employees, you have several forms to complete for the IRS. Some of these forms are W-2, W-3, 940, and 941. Forms W-2 and W-3 report to the IRS and to your employees the total gross earnings and deductions for the year. The W-2 tells the employee what they have earned during the year, and the W-3 sums it up for all employees. At the end of the year, you must give each employee who worked for you during the year a W-2 form. In Chapter 8, you learned how you can print payroll reports for both a single employee and all employees. You also learned how to take that information and put it into a W-2.

Figure 12-5. 1099 report created by QuickBooks

```
                          1099 REPORT
                     1/ 1/93 Through 12/31/93
                  Musical Pony-All A/P Accounts
                  1/ 4/94

                     Vendor                    1993

              Ellen Mercaidy                  2,787.42
                 4340 Chillecothe Road
                 Chesterland, OH  44032
                 Taxpayer ID Num: 123-45-6789

              Keith Landmark                 24,613.73
                 8950 Mentor Avenue
                 Mentor, OH  44060
                 Taxpayer ID Num: 987-65-4321

              Keri Imports                  156,345.00
                 2384 Fifth Avenue
                 New York, NY  10024

Musical Pony-All A/P Accounts
Esc-Create  Ctrl-M Memorize        F1-Help              Ctrl-P Print
```

The Form 940 reports the liabilities owed and deposits made for federal unemployment tax. Form 941 calculates the payroll taxes paid by your company and withheld from your employees. Chapter 8 includes the steps you perform to prepare these reports.

Form 1120, U.S. Corporation Income Tax Return

A corporation uses one of three variations of Form 1120 to report to the IRS on its earnings. Form 1120-A is the short form, which can be used by corporations with gross receipts of less than $250,000. Form 1120-S is for S corporations. Other corporations use Form 1120. QuickBooks can provide the information you need to complete these forms. If you examine the first page of Form 1120, shown in Figure 12-6, you see that it is a business profit and loss statement. You can use the profit and loss statement prepared by QuickBooks to fill it in. Figure 12-4 shows a profit and loss statement that this text uses as an example for completing Form 1120. It is the same one used for Schedule C, but the assumption of the type of business has changed.

Completing Form 1120

With QuickBooks' profit and loss statement, you can now complete the appropriate lines of Form 1120. The following is a list of line numbers and how you can complete them in Form 1120.

- *Line 1* This line shows gross sales and the discount. Place the Retail Sales amount ($304,904.06), Sales Disc amount (–$14,249.99), and the difference ($290,654.07) from your report on this line.

- *Line 2* This line shows cost of goods sold. Place the COGS amount ($154,344.81) from your report on this line.

- *Lines 3 and 11* These lines show your gross profit and total income since no other types of income are recorded. These lines equal the difference between Sales in line 1 ($290,654.07) and the cost of goods sold in line 2 ($154,344.81).

- *Line 12* This line is your gross wages paid to the company's officers. Since this company only has one employee, her pay is shown here rather than on line 13, where other employees that are not officers are shown.

The Tax Form Library, 518 W. Main St., Louisville, Ky., 40202, (502) 589-7466

Form **1120** — Department of the Treasury, Internal Revenue Service

U.S. Corporation Income Tax Return

For calendar year 1991 or tax year beginning .... , 1991, ending .... , 19 ...
▶ **Instructions are separate. See page 1 for Paperwork Reduction Act Notice.**

OMB No. 1545-0123 — **1991**

A Check if a—
(1) Consolidated return (attach Form 851) ☐
(2) Personal holding co. (attach Sch. PH) ☐
(3) Personal service corp. (as defined in Temp. Regs. sec. 1.441-4T—see instructions) ☐

Use IRS label. Otherwise, please print or type.
Name
Number, street, and room or suite no. (If a P.O. box, see page 6 of instructions.)
City or town, state, and ZIP code

B Employer identification number
C Date incorporated
D Total assets (see Specific Instructions) $

E Check applicable boxes: (1) ☐ Initial return (2) ☐ Final return (3) ☐ Change in address

Income

Line	Description		Amount
1a	Gross receipts or sales 304904 06 b Less returns and allowances 14249 99 c Bal ▶	1c	290654 07
2	Cost of goods sold (Schedule A, line 7)	2	154344 81
3	Gross profit. Subtract line 2 from line 1c	3	136309 26
4	Dividends (Schedule C, line 19)	4	
5	Interest	5	
6	Gross rents	6	
7	Gross royalties	7	
8	Capital gain net income (attach Schedule D (Form 1120))	8	
9	Net gain or (loss) from Form 4797, Part II, line 18 (attach Form 4797)	9	
10	Other income (see instructions—attach schedule)	10	
11	**Total income.** Add lines 3 through 10 ▶	11	136309 26

Deductions (See instructions for limitations on deductions.)

Line	Description		Amount
12	Compensation of officers (Schedule E, line 4)	12	32600 00
13a	Salaries and wages ____ b Less jobs credit ____ c Balance ▶	13c	
14	Repairs	14	
15	Bad debts	15	
16	Rents	16	24613 73
17	Taxes	17	2748 00
18	Interest	18	
19	Contributions **(see instructions for 10% limitation)**	19	
20	Depreciation (attach Form 4562) — 20: 4000 00		
21	Less depreciation claimed on Schedule A and elsewhere on return — 21a	21b	4000 00
22	Depletion	22	
23	Advertising	23	3287 42
24	Pension, profit-sharing, etc., plans	24	
25	Employee benefit programs	25	
26	Other deductions (attach schedule)	26	34131 81
27	**Total deductions.** Add lines 12 through 26 ▶	27	101380 96
28	Taxable income before net operating loss deduction and special deductions. Subtract line 27 from line 11	28	34928 30
29	**Less:** a Net operating loss deduction (see instructions) — 29a; b Special deductions (Schedule C, line 20) — 29b	29c	

Tax and Payments

Line	Description		Amount
30	**Taxable income.** Subtract line 29c from line 28	30	34928 30
31	**Total tax** (Schedule J, line 10)	31	
32	**Payments:** a 1990 overpayment credited to 1991 — 32a		
b	1991 estimated tax payments — 32b		
c	Less 1991 refund applied for on Form 4466 — 32c ( ) d Bal ▶ 32d		
e	Tax deposited with Form 7004 — 32e		
f	Credit from regulated investment companies (attach Form 2439) — 32f		
g	Credit for Federal tax on fuels (attach Form 4136). See instructions — 32g	32h	
33	Estimated tax penalty (see page 4 of instructions). Check if Form 2220 is attached ▶ ☐	33	
34	**Tax due.** If the total of lines 31 and 33 is larger than line 32h, enter amount owed	34	
35	**Overpayment.** If line 32h is larger than the total of lines 31 and 33, enter amount overpaid	35	
36	Enter amount of line 35 you want: **Credited to 1992 estimated tax** ▶ **Refunded** ▶	36	

Please Sign Here — Under penalties of perjury, I declare that I have examined this return, including accompanying schedules and statements, and to the best of my knowledge and belief, it is true, correct, and complete. Declaration of preparer (other than taxpayer) is based on all information of which preparer has any knowledge.

▶ Signature of officer — Date — ▶ Title

Paid Preparer's Use Only — Preparer's signature ▶ — Date — Check if self-employed ☐ — Preparer's social security number
Firm's name (or yours if self-employed) and address ▶ — E.I. No. ▶ — ZIP code ▶

Cat. No. 11450Q

Form 1120 to report business results for a corporation
Figure 12-6.

- *Line 16* This line shows rent expense. Enter the amount you show for Rent ($24,613.73) here.

- *Line 17* This line is for taxes the company pays, including payroll taxes (not including the portion withheld from employees' pay) as well as state, local, and foreign taxes.

- *Lines 20 and 21b* These lines show depreciation and the section 179 deduction from Form 4562, Depreciation and Amortization. Enter the depreciation expense ($4000) here.

- *Line 23* This line shows advertising expense. Enter the amount you show for Advertising ($3287.42) here.

- *Line 26* This line is for expenses not claimed on other lines. This includes Auto ($10.67), Total Charges ($4.30), Freight ($12,992.86), Insurance ($5101), Materials ($107.78), Office Supplies ($175.34), Building Repair ($75), Shipping ($2413), Telephone ($3781.12), and Total Utilities ($9470.74) from the report.

- *Line 27* This line shows your total deductions. This is the amount of Total Expenses ($255,725.77) less the cost of goods sold in line 2, assuming your company has no nondeductible expenses.

- *Lines 28 and 30* These lines show your net profit (or loss). Enter the amount from Total Income/Expense, $34,928.30.

This shows only one part of Form 1120, which has another three pages. The remainder of the form requires a variety of information, some of which does not come from QuickBooks; for example, the business's principal activity. For Schedule L of Form 1120 (Part III of Form 1120-A and Schedule L of 1120-S), QuickBooks' balance sheet report will help you complete the balance sheet report on the tax form. The tax code has many regulations that can affect your tax return, so you will want to contact your accountant for assistance.

PART 5

APPENDIXES

APPENDIX

A

INSTALLING QUICKBOOKS

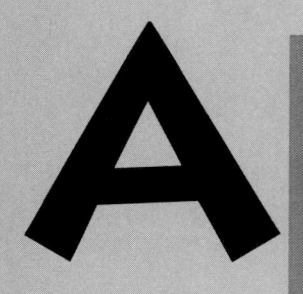

Installing QuickBooks is simple. The installation program decompresses the QuickBooks files on the installation disks and copies them onto your hard drive. QuickBooks requires approximately 3MB of free space on your hard drive. This appendix tells you how to install QuickBooks, register your program, and set up your printer for QuickBooks.

Installing QuickBooks on a Hard Drive

1. Put the first installation disk in the correctly sized floppy disk drive and close the drive door, if any.
2. At the DOS prompt, type the letter of the drive the installation disk is in, followed by **:\install**, for example:

    b:\install
3. Press [Enter] to start the installation program.
4. Select whether your monitor can display colors. If your monitor can display more than two colors, select Yes by highlighting 1 Yes, and pressing [Enter]. If your monitor can only display two colors, such as black and amber or black and white, press the [↓] to highlight 2 No, and press [Enter].
5. Select the drive you are installing QuickBooks from. You will normally be installing from the same floppy disk drive where you started the installation program. Your choices are A, B, or Other. Highlight the appropriate option using the arrow keys and then press [Enter].
6. Select whether you want to install Bizminder. Bizminder is a program that will remind you if there are any pending transactions in QuickBooks when you start your computer. Highlight your response and press [Enter].
7. Enter the name of the directory where you want QuickBooks installed. Press [Enter] to accept the default directory of C:\QBOOKS. QuickBooks will create this directory if it does not already exist. Type another directory name if you wish to install QuickBooks into another directory, then press [Enter].
8. Accept the installation selections or return to a previous selection to make changes. The Installation Summary window lists what drive you are installing QuickBooks from, where on your hard drive it will be installed, and whether you will install Bizminder. Press [Enter] to install QuickBooks, or [Esc] to go back to one of the earlier prompts and change your response.

When the next disk is required to continue the installation of QuickBooks, you are prompted to place the disk in the drive you selected to install from, then press [Enter].

Installing QuickBooks

When the installation of QuickBooks is complete, you are automatically returned to the DOS prompt. A message is displayed, telling you that you can start QuickBooks by typing **QB** and pressing [Enter]. Also, the message tells Quicken users to check Appendix A of the documentation to see how to create QuickBooks files from Quicken files.

Registering QuickBooks

To use QuickBooks, you must register the product. Registering your copy of QuickBooks makes Intuit's product support available to you. Also, if you do not register your copy of QuickBooks, you can only use the program 25 times before you can no longer use QuickBooks. To register QuickBooks, follow these steps:

1. Type **QB** and press [Enter] to start QuickBooks.
2. Type **9** to select 9 Register QuickBooks.

The Please Register QuickBooks Now window prompts you to enter your customer number. You get this number two ways. If you purchase QuickBooks directly from Intuit, your packing slip includes your customer number in the upper-left corner. When you purchased QuickBooks directly from Intuit, Intuit registered that copy of the product for you. If you purchased QuickBooks from your local computer store, call Intuit at the phone number shown on the registration screen. When you call them, you must provide the serial number that appears on your screen as well as your name, address, daytime phone number, and preferred disk size (3 1/2 inch or 5 1/4 inch). When you give Intuit this information, they will give you the customer number. It is also a good idea to write this number on your QuickBooks manual or where you can find it easily, because you will supply this number every time you call Intuit with a question.

3. Type the eight-digit number (do not include the *A* that appears on the Intuit packing slip) and press [Enter].
4. Press [Enter] after reading the message telling you that the registration process is complete.

Your copy of QuickBooks is now registered and you can continue to use QuickBooks as many times as you want.

Setting Up Printers in QuickBooks

You will want to be able to print QuickBooks reports, invoices, and/or checks on your printer. Before you can print, you must set up the codes necessary to use your printer with QuickBooks. To do this, follow these steps:

1. Press [Esc] until you are at the Main Menu.
2. Type **7** to select 7 Set Up/Customize.
3. Type **6** to select 6 Set Up Printers.
4. Type **1** to select the first printer you want to set up.
5. Press the [↓] until your printer is highlighted.

If you do not see your printer, select a compatible one from the list. After selecting a printer, a Setup Printer window lists different fields for the different printer settings you can change. The two most important field settings are the Printer name and Printer Port. The Printer Port field selects how the printer is connected to your computer. The possible selections include PRN, LPT1, LPT2, LPT3, AUX, COM1, and COM2. Use the same setting that you use in other programs that print to the same printer.

6. Press the [↓] or [↑] keys to highlight any field you want to change, press [Ctrl]-[L], and select one of the listed choices.
7. Repeat step 6 for each of the remaining fields.
8. Press [Ctrl]-[Enter] when you are finished changing the printer's settings.
9. Type **2** to change a second printer's settings, if you have one, and repeat steps 5 through 8 for the second printer.
10. Press [Esc] repeatedly to return to the Main Menu.

APPENDIX

BACKING UP AND MERGING FILES

Your QuickBooks files contain all of the financial transactions that you have entered. These files represent an investment of time and energy that will continue to pay dividends every time you access your data. To protect your investment, you should do everything you can to safeguard your QuickBooks files. QuickBooks' backup features let you create copies of your files that you can use to restore your original files should they become damaged or lost.

Other features, such as the merge capability, are designed to let you merge the data from two separate files should you decide to combine two business entities into one or to share a custom chart of account with a new company file that you are establishing.

Backing Up Your QuickBooks Files

Back up your QuickBooks data regularly to safeguard your large investment of time and money against loss or damage.

A regular backing up regimen can help save you time and anguish in the event that a QuickBooks file is destroyed or corrupted. By creating backups of your QuickBooks files you are ensuring that, even if your original QuickBooks file is damaged, your data is not entirely lost. Re-creating the data you have entered in your QuickBooks file may be difficult, or even impossible. You are not only protecting against corruption by viruses or malfunction of your hard drive by creating backups, but also against such real-world problems as fire, flood, and theft, which can just as effectively eliminate your files.

To create a backup of a QuickBooks company, follow these steps:

1. Select 7 Set Up/Customize from the Main Menu.
2. Select 2 Back Up/Restore/Copy Company Files.
3. Select 1 Back Up Company Files. The Select Company to Back Up window will appear.
4. Highlight the company you want to back up using the arrow keys, and press [Enter].
5. Insert your backup floppy disk in a drive. If the drive you plan to use is not the A drive, type its letter before pressing [Enter]. If the disk is not formatted, press [F9] to exit temporarily to DOS, where you can format the disk. You can format the disk by typing **FORMAT A:** and pressing [Enter] (assuming the disk to format is in drive A).

   QuickBooks displays windows indicating which of the company's files QuickBooks is currently copying to the floppy disk. When QuickBooks is finished backing up the company's files, it displays a window saying so.
6. Press [Enter] to return to the Select Company to Back Up window.
7. Repeat steps 4 through 6 to back up another company or press [Esc] until you return to the Main Menu.

Backing Up and Merging Files

Remember to make backing up your files a regular part of your routine. If you do not back up your files on a regular basis, you run the risk of losing data.

Restoring Your QuickBooks Files

Store the backup copies of your QuickBooks files in a safe place away from the computer you normally work on.

If you should ever lose your company files stored on a hard drive, you will need to restore the backup files you have created. *Restoring* the files re-copies them to the hard drive. After restoring the files, you will need to reenter any data entered since you last backed up the files. While this will take some time, it takes much less time than totally re-creating the files. If you usually store your files on a floppy disk, you can just start using the files on the backup disk rather than restoring them.

Follow these steps to restore QuickBooks files:

1. Select 7 Set Up/Customize from the Main Menu.
2. Select 2 Back Up/Restore/Copy Company Files.
3. Select 4 Restore Company Files.
4. Insert your backup floppy disk in a disk drive. Specify the disk drive, if it is not drive A, before pressing [Enter].
5. Select the company that you want to restore to your hard drive from the list presented, by highlighting it and pressing [Enter].

    If the files already exist on your hard drive, you must type **O** to overwrite the copy on the hard disk with the one on the backup disk. Or, type **C** to create a copy of the backup with the name "Restore Copy of," followed by the company name. Then press [Enter]. When QuickBooks has finished restoring the files, it displays a message to this effect.

    The same filename as the original is used, but with a sequential number attached to the end.

6. Press [Enter] to continue.
7. Repeat steps 3 through 6 until you have restored all files from the companies you want to restore, or press [Esc] until you return to the Main Menu.

Merging QuickBooks Files

You may discover that you established too many different companies and you need to combine them, or that you want to use the chart of accounts from one company for another. To do these two things, you merge the two companies' files. When you *merge* two companies, you create a third company that combines the information in the original two. (The original two are not destroyed.)

When you merge two companies, all accounts, transactions, and list items in either company exist in the third company. If a list item appears in both companies, the information found in the second company is used in the merged company. The company settings, information (other than name and address), and passwords of the second company are used for the third company. The names of the balance sheet accounts of the first and second companies must be different, or the merge will not be completed.

Follow these steps to merge two companies:

1. Choose 1 Select/Add a Company in the Customize menu to select the company that you want to use as the first company in the merger.

CAUTION: Which company is first or second can change how the merge occurs.

2. Select 7 Set Up/Customize from the Main Menu.
3. Select 2 Back Up/Restore/Copy Company Files.
4. Select 3 Merge Company Files. The Merge Company Information window appears.
5. Type the name of the company you want to merge the current company with in the Select company to merge with field, then press [Tab].

    This is the second company. You can also press [Ctrl]-[L] to display a list of companies that you can select this company from, then press [Enter].

6. Type the name you want to use for the third company (the one created by merging these two companies) in the Name for resulting company field, then press `Tab`.

7. Type the eight-character name for the third company's files in the File name for resulting company field, and press `Tab`.

8. Change the two dates if you want to restrict which transactions are added to the third company's files. If you do not want to include any transactions, use dates when there are no transactions.

9. When you are finished making entries in this window, press `Ctrl`-`Enter`.

When QuickBooks is finished merging the company files, you are returned to the Back Up/Restore/Copy Files menu. The current company is not changed. You may get a message that one or more of the balance sheet accounts are the same. When this happens, you must alter the account names in one of the copies and repeat the steps until you successfully merge the two files.

APPENDIX

GLOSSARY

It is important to acquaint yourself with various financial and accounting terms in order to understand how QuickBooks supports your financial activities. For your convenience, this appendix contains a glossary of the terms used throughout this book.

You will not want to read these terms from start to finish. Rather, you should use this glossary as you would a dictionary to look up a term that you are not familiar with. The definitions are designed to provide straightforward, concise definitions without all the detail that you find in business school textbooks.

Accelerated Depreciation A method of depreciation that recognizes more expense in the early years of an asset's life.

Account A QuickBooks document where personal and/or business transactions that increase or decrease the amount of money in the account are recorded. Examples include bank, cash, credit card, other assets, and other liabilities accounts.

Account Balance The amount of money in an account.

Accounts Payable Money owed to suppliers for goods or services.

Accounts Receivable Money owed to you by customers or clients.

Accrual Basis An accounting method that records income when services are provided rather than when cash is received. Similarly, expenses are recorded when services are received rather than when cash is paid.

Accumulated Depreciation The total amount of depreciation expense taken on an asset since the time it was placed in service.

Adjusting Entry An entry made in a register at the end of a period to make adjustments to the balance.

Asset Any item of value that a business or individual owns.

Balance The amount remaining in an account after all transactions have been applied.

Balance Forward Applies payments to invoices automatically, crediting the payment to the oldest invoice first.

Balance Sheet A financial statement that summarizes a business's assets, liabilities, and owner's equity at a specific time.

Glossary

Book Value The cost of an asset less the amount of depreciation expensed to date.

Budget A plan indicating projected income and expenses. Budget also refers to a comparison between the projections and actual amounts for each income or expense category.

Cash Basis A method of accounting used for business or tax purposes. Income is recorded when cash is received, and expenses are charged when cash is paid.

Cash Flows The inflow and outflow of cash during a specific time period.

Chart of Accounts A list of the categories used to charge income and expenses for a given company and record the assets and liabilities of a company.

Closing Entries Entries made to close the books at the end of the year. These are not required with QuickBooks.

Corporation A form of business organization that limits the liability of the shareholders.

Credit Memo An invoice that negates a bill or indicates a return.

Current Asset Something that the firm has or owns with a life of less than one year. Accounts receivable and cash are examples of current assets.

Current Balance The present balance in an account. This does not include postdated items.

Current Liabilities A debt with a due date in less than one year.

Deposit An amount of funds added to an account. A deposit is sometimes referred to as a "credit" to the account.

Depreciation The portion of the cost of an asset that is expensed each year on a profit and loss statement.

Diamond Fields Fields on the QuickBooks screen marked by a diamond, which can be completed by pressing Ctrl-L or clicking the field with the mouse to display a list of options.

Double Entry System An accounting method that requires two accounts to be used when recording a transaction. For example, when supplies are purchased, both the cash and supplies accounts are affected.

Equity The amount of the owner's investment in the business. For individuals, this is the money invested in property or another asset.

Expense The cost of an item or service purchased or consumed.

FICA Social security tax paid by employers and employees.

Financial Statements Periodic reports prepared by businesses to show the financial condition of the firm. Major financial statements include balance sheets, profit and loss statements (income statements), and cash flow reports.

Fixed Asset An asset with a life longer than one year. A fixed asset can be tangible, like a building, or intangible, like a patent.

FOB In QuickBooks this abbreviation indicates the shipping location. It also indicates when ownership of shipped goods transfers to the person or company receiving the goods.

FUTA Federal unemployment tax.

FWH Federal income tax withheld from employees' earnings.

Gross Earnings Total earnings of an employee before deductions are subtracted.

Income The money earned by an individual or business. On a cash basis, it is the amount of cash received for goods or services provided. On an accrual basis, it is the amount of income

Glossary

recognized and recorded during the year for services provided.

Income Statement   A summary of the income and expenses of a business. In QuickBooks, you use a profit and loss statement to display your company's income or loss.

Journal   A list of financial transactions in a register.

Liability   The money you owe to a vendor, creditor, or any other party.

Life of an Asset   The number of years that the asset is expected to last.

Long-term Assets   Property owned by the company that will be used for more than one year. Long-term assets that decrease in value with time are depreciated.

Long-term Liabilities   Debts with a due date more than one year in the future.

Memorized Transaction   A transaction that you have asked QuickBooks to remember and recall at a later time.

Net Income   Total revenues less total expenses.

Net Pay   The amount of pay received after deductions.

Net Worth   An amount determined by subtracting the value of financial obligations from financial resources.

Open Invoice   An invoice that has not yet been paid in full.

Open Item Method   A QuickBooks method for applying payments to specific invoices.

P&L Statement   An abbreviation for profit and loss statement; it shows the profit or loss generated during a period.

Partnership   A form of business organization where two or more individuals share in the profits and losses of the business.

Payment The amount paid to a vendor, creditor, or other party.

Payroll SDI State disability insurance payments often referred to as workers' compensation.

Postdated Transaction A transaction, such as a check or invoice, dated after the current date.

Reconciliation The process of comparing a copy of the bank's records for your account with your own records. Any differences should be explained in this process.

Register A record of financial activity for a balance sheet account.

Reverse To enter a second transaction that negates the effect of an earlier transaction. Reversing transactions are used instead of deleting the original transaction, to maintain a history of all financial activities.

Salvage Value The value of an asset at the end of its useful life.

Single Entry System An accounting method that only uses one account to record a transaction. When supplies are purchased, only the cash (or checking) account is affected.

Sole Proprietorship The simplest form of small-business organization. There is no separation between the owner and the company.

Straight-line Depreciation A method of expensing the cost of an asset evenly over its life.

SUTA State unemployment tax.

SWH State income taxes withheld from employee gross earnings.

Glossary

Transaction A financial activity that takes place on a specific date, which has an effect on an account balance.

Transaction Group A group of memorized transactions that can be recalled together whenever you need them.

Transfer A transaction that affects the balance in two accounts at the same time by moving funds between them.

Valuation The current value of an asset.

APPENDIX

D

CONVERTING QUICKEN FILES FOR USE IN QUICKBOOKS

Created by the makers of QuickBooks, Quicken is a popular financial management program used by individuals and small businesses. If you have used Quicken previously for your business, you will want to use your Quicken files in QuickBooks so that you do not have to reenter all your data. QuickBooks will take your Quicken files and create equivalent QuickBooks files, without destroying or altering the original Quicken files.

When QuickBooks creates QuickBooks files from your Quicken files, it makes certain changes to match the QuickBooks formats. You will need to name the new QuickBooks company, then the program creates a QuickBooks balance sheet account of the type closest to the Quicken account type. Accounts receivable, accounts payable, and sales tax payable accounts are opened, with no transactions listed, along with an Open Bal Equity account. Your memorized transactions and groups are copied, but your memorized reports are not, because the report formats are so different. Your Quicken categories and subcategories are mirrored in a list of income/expense accounts. In each transaction, the category is changed to the corresponding income/expense account. Your class list is mirrored in a list of projects. If these changes do not suit how you want to work with the data in QuickBooks, you can make the changes after the new QuickBooks file is created.

Performing the Conversion

Follow these steps to copy and convert your Quicken data for use in QuickBooks:

1. Select 7 Set Up/Customize from the Main Menu.
2. Select 3 Add Company Using Data from Quicken.
3. Type the directory that contains your Quicken data files and press [Enter].

   For example, if your Quicken data files are in C:\QUICKEN, you type **C:\QUICKEN** and press [Enter]. If you have more than one set of Quicken files in that directory, you will need to press the [↑] or [↓] to highlight the Quicken files you want, then press [Enter].

4. Type the name of the company or person that the account is for and press [Enter] in the Enter Company Name window.

   The next window displays the selected filename and directory for the new QuickBooks file. The filename is created from the name of the company you provided, and the default data directory is C:\QBOOKS\QBDATA\ that was created when you installed QuickBooks.

Converting Quicken Files for Use in QuickBooks

5. Press [Enter] twice to accept the filename and data directory, or make your changes and press [Ctrl]-[Enter].

   When QuickBooks is finished creating the new file, it presents a window telling you that the new files were created and that no memorized reports were copied.

6. Press [Enter] after reading the message.

The new file you just converted is the active file in QuickBooks, and its Chart of Accounts window is displayed.

APPENDIX

E

CUSTOMIZING QUICKBOOKS

QuickBooks' customization features are designed to help make QuickBooks more useful for you. You will need some settings, such as the printer setup, in order to print reports, checks, and invoices. You can use other settings to make QuickBooks more functional for you. For example, you can set Bizminder to remind you of tasks to be carried out, or you can set the feature that allows you to use projects as an alternate method of organizing your financial data. Still other settings can be used simply to make

QuickBooks more to your taste, such as those that cause QuickBooks to beep or display reminder messages, or that determine the colors used to display QuickBooks.

Take care in changing the customization features. Changing the settings to match the way that you use QuickBooks and the way that you run your business will help ensure that data is entered accurately and completely and with relative ease. If you use customization features that cannot help you, you will find that QuickBooks is more difficult to use, and you will have a greater possibility of errors.

To access a variety of settings that you can use to customize either QuickBooks as a whole, or the current company, select the 7 Set Up/Customize options from the Main Menu. These customization features establish defaults for QuickBooks to match the way you run your company, thus making it easier for you to keep the books. For all of the windows that you open by selecting from a menu, you can close them and finish making the changes by pressing [Ctrl]-[Enter]. Several of the selections in the Set Up/Customize window are described in Appendixes B and D. Selecting the printers you are using is described in Appendix A.

Customizing the Company for Your Use

Selecting the Customize Current Company option from the Set Up/Customize menu changes the settings for the current company. These settings are not carried over to any other companies, so if you use QuickBooks for more than one company, you can set these for each company separately. These company settings let you tailor QuickBooks to how you run the company.

Company Information

The first option of the Customize Current Company menu, Company Information, enters information about the company. You can enter the name and address of the company and the company's Federal Employer ID number, which is necessary for working with many payroll forms. The company name appears in various reports. The company name and address are included on invoices. The ID number is used in payroll reports.

Customizing QuickBooks

The last two fields are most useful if your company sells products (rather than services) that you must send to the customer. You can enter the location where you normally ship invoiced products from in the Usual FOB location field. This location can be up to 13 characters long, and it will automatically appear in the FOB field in invoices. Examples include Destination and Shipping Pt. In the Usual shipping method field, press `Ctrl`-`L` to open the shipping methods list. Select your most common method of shipping products. QuickBooks will automatically fill the Via field on your invoices with this entry.

Options

The second option of the Customize Current Company menu, Options, establishes settings for a number of features that make entering your data easier. There are 15 features that you can adjust. To change the settings, move to the field by pressing `Tab`, and then type one of the entries in the parentheses.

Invoice Type   The Invoice type field sets the fields that appear in an invoice. QuickBooks has product invoices, professional invoices, and service invoices. You can change to a different type by selecting another type in this field. Changing the Invoice type field does not affect invoices you have already entered.

Open Item/Balance Forward   The Receive payments from customers on Open item or Balance forward method field sets how customer payments for invoices are automatically applied. When you select 2 Invoicing/Receivables from the Main Menu and then 2 Receive Payments, the payments you entered are applied to the invoices written to the customer depending on how this field is set. When this field is O for Open item, all of the invoices have zero in the Payment column until you make another entry. When this field is B for Balance forward, the payment is applied to the oldest invoice through the newest until the payment is entirely applied to invoices.

Days Between Date and Pay Date   The Default number of days between DATE and PAY DATE in Accounts Payable field sets the number of days after the date in the Date field in accounts payable that QuickBooks enters in the Pay Date field. It is a good idea to set this number to the most frequent interval between when you record a bill and when you pay it.

Item Codes/Accounts   The Require item codes on invoice line items field sets whether you must include item codes on all invoice line items so you can later have reports on the items you have sold. The Require account on all transactions field sets whether you must select an account for all transactions. Setting both fields to Y for Yes ensures that certain information appears in all entries.

Sales Tax   The Sales tax collected is payable Monthly, Quarterly, or Annually field sets the pay date for entries in your sales tax accounts payable account. The sales tax collected is recorded in this account as you write invoices that have an item with an item type of Sales Tax. The appropriate setting depends on where your business is located. If Bizminder is installed, Bizminder will remind you when the sales tax bill is due.

Project Tracking   When you set the Project tracking on field to Yes, Project fields appear to the right of Account fields when you enter checks and transactions. Projects provide another method for tracking expenses, by job or project, rather than by type of expense.

Check Printing   The Extra message line on checks field sets whether QuickBooks displays a Msg field to the right of the payee's address on the printed checks. The Change check dates to date printed field sets whether or not QuickBooks changes the date when you print a check if it is different than the date you prepared the check. A Y for this field means QuickBooks changes the date and an N means the check is printed with the date you prepared the check. If you are using voucher checks, the Print full detail on voucher checks field selects the information printed in the voucher area. A Y for this field includes the description, account, and amount information, while an N only shows the description and amount.

Show Accounts   The Show Memo/Account/Both in registers field selects whether register transactions include the memo field, the Account field, or both in the second and third lines of a transaction register. The Show lowest subaccounts/subprojects only field selects whether a subaccount or subproject name also includes its parent

Customizing QuickBooks

account or project name. The Show account Name/Desc/Both in reports field selects whether account names in reports use the account name, the account description, or both.

The last two settings ensure that you do not reuse a check or invoice number. Reusing check or invoice numbers normally indicates that there is some type of accounting error, since there should be only one invoice or check to each number. If these numbers are being reused, you should double-check for the reason immediately, and ensure that there is no fraud occurring.

Passwords

The Passwords option opens the Set Passwords window, where you can set two levels of passwords. QuickBooks supports a high-security password, called the Owner password, and a low-security password, called a Bookkeeper password. A person using the Owner password can change the Owner password and the Bookkeeper password. The owner can also change what level password is required for different activities in QuickBooks by selecting 4 Password Table. People using the Bookkeeper password cannot change the passwords, nor can they change the level of password required for different activities. If you only have one level of password, it must be an Owner password. QuickBooks does not distinguish between upper- and lowercase. You can remove an existing password from the window to remove password protection.

The third field in this window is the Date through which books are closed field. The date entered here differentiates between transactions. After establishing passwords and entering a date in this field, you can establish different security levels for editing or viewing transactions before and after this date. This feature helps ensure that no one will change any old transactions.

After you finish with the Set Passwords window, you must enter the owner password again as confirmation. This time, and all subsequent times, the characters you type for the password appear as squares. Next, you will go directly to the Password Level Assignment window, where you can assign different password levels to different activities, such as adding and deleting transactions. When you want to change the password levels without changing passwords, select 4 Password Table.

Password Table

Selecting 4 Password Table opens the Password Level Assignment window. In this window, you can highlight an activity by pressing the ⬆ and ⬇; then use the [Backspace] to set the level of password protection you desire for that activity. You can choose between None Req'd, Owner, and Bookkeeper to set whether a password is required and which one must be used. The activity you can limit with passwords includes adding and deleting transactions, printing checks and invoices, altering accounts, adding and deleting items from your company's lists, and changing company options.

Once you assign passwords to these activities, you can still select these activities from the menus of QuickBooks. However, when you do, a window appears requesting the appropriate level password. If you assign the bookkeeper password to an activity, you can supply either the owner or the bookkeeper password. You cannot set password assignments until you have set passwords, using the 3 Passwords menu option.

Customizing QuickBooks for All Companies

Other customization changes that you make are made to QuickBooks itself, which means that these settings remain for every company you are working with. Changing these settings adjusts the QuickBooks program to your hardware and lets you make decisions about how the program works. You can also change the colors and screen refresh speed used by QuickBooks.

Options

When you select 1 Options, the Program Options window opens. This window allows you to specify the settings for ten QuickBooks features. To change the settings, move to the field by pressing [Tab], then type one of the entries in the parentheses.

QuickTrainer   QuickTrainer is more useful when you are first learning QuickBooks. As you become more proficient with QuickBooks, you will want to turn this feature off by typing **O** for the QuickTrainer

Customizing QuickBooks

lag field. Otherwise, you must press [Esc] to exit each QuickTrainer screen as you are working if you hesitate in making your entry.

Beep   The Beep when recording and memorizing field sets whether you hear the beep that QuickBooks sounds as you work with the product.

Confirmations   When you work with QuickBooks, you will notice that the confirmation prompts you to select whether you want to record or change an invoice, check, or register entry. You can remove these confirmations by typing **N** for the Request confirmation field.

Bizminder   Bizminder and the message below the Main Menu remind you of upcoming bills, invoices, and transaction groups. The reminders include all the transactions for the current date and for a number of days ahead. The number of days is set by the Days in advance to remind of scheduled bills, invoices, and groups field. The default is 3, so the reminder includes all items to take care of today and the next 3 days.

Another warning—to deposit payments you have recorded—will appear when the Warn to deposit payments received field is set to Y.

You can turn off Bizminder by typing **N** for the Bizminder active field. If you did not install Bizminder when you installed QuickBooks, you can install it by reinstalling QuickBooks, as described in Appendix A.

Lines Displayed   If you have an EGA or VGA screen, you can display more lines on the screen in order to see more of your invoices, reports, and registers. To display more lines, type **Y** for the 43 line register/reports field. When this field has an N, the screen always has the same number of lines in it. For On new checks/invoices, start with the Payee/customer or Date field, you can select whether the cursor starts at the Payee or Customer field, or the Date field when you create checks and invoices.

Mouse   The Double-click speed for mouse field sets a speed for double-clicking the mouse. If you click the mouse slower than that speed, QuickBooks recognizes your action as two separate clicks. If more than one person uses QuickBooks, set this option fairly low to allow for people's differing speeds. You can disable the mouse by typing an **0** in this field.

Screen Colors

QuickBooks offers a variety of screen color combinations. You can change the screen colors to enhance visibility on your monitor, or simply to add variety to your screen. The color schemes that QuickBooks provides are Monochrome, Navy/Azure, White/Navy, Red/Gray, and Shades of Gray. Different monitors will be able to display these color schemes with different levels of effectiveness. For example, Monochrome is most useful with monitors that cannot display shades of gray or colors. Red/Gray is designed for users who are color-blind using color monitors. Shades of Gray is designed for monitors that display only shades of gray, such as liquid crystal displays frequently used in laptop computers, or gas plasma displays. If this setting does not display well on your system, use Monochrome.

Monitor Refresh Speed

For most computer monitors, you do not need to change the monitor refresh speed. However, if you are using a CGA screen, you will want to change the speed setting to slow if interference appears on your screen. This interference is caused by a screen that cannot keep pace with the speed at which QuickBooks sends messages to the monitor.

Setting the Data Directory

You can change the directory where QuickBooks looks for your data files. When you select 7 Change Data Directory, replace the current directory with another one to change the directory of QuickBooks companies and files displayed when you choose 1 Select/Add a Company. This is the same window you see when you choose 1 Select/Add a Company and press F9.

INDEX

A

Accelerated Cost Recovery System (ACRS), 255-256
Accelerated depreciation, 254-255
Account reconciliation, 73-79. *See also* Accounts
  correcting errors in, 86-87
  first-time, 82-86
  monthly, 74
  preparing the printer for, 76
  and previous transactions, 84-85
  process of, 74-76
  service charges and interest, 78
  steps for, 76-79
  and uncleared transactions, 78
  updating the opening balance, 81-82
Account reconciliation reports, 76, 79-81
Account register. *See* Register
Accounting. *See also* Accounts
  cash vs. accrual basis, 283
  glossary of terms, 339-345
  steps for end of cycle, 307
  timing differences in, 284
  using accounting periods, 264
Accounts. *See also* Account reconciliation; Accounting; Accounts payable
  adding to the register, 97
  payroll withholding, 193, 196
  setting up, 24-25
  types of, 5
  using subaccounts, 107-108
Accounts payable (A/P), 220-231
  and cash basis accounting, 231
  Choose Bills to Pay window, 227-228, 230, 232-233
  editing bill entries, 224
  entering bills, 221-223
  Pay Vendors window, 226-227
  preparing and printing checks, 229
  recording payments, 226-231

using Bizminder, 225
Accounts payable register, 229
Accounts Payable window, 222
Accounts receivable, 291-294. *See also* Payments (receivables)
Accounts receivable (A/R) register, 175-178, 180, 183
Accrual basis accounting, 221, 283-285
Accumulated depreciation, 253, 257
ACRS (Accelerated Cost Recovery System), 255-256
Action menu, 17
Add New Checking Account window, 25
Add New Customer Type window, 35
Add New Customer window, 42
Add New Employee window, 40
Add New Expense Subaccount window, 108
Add New Part Item window, 50
Add New Sales Tax Item window, 149
Add New Standard Transaction Group window, 113
Add New Terms window, 39
Add New Vendor window, 45
Aging (overdue receivables), 186-187
Aging report, 293
Aligning checks in tractor-feed printers, 67-69
American Express accounts, 182
Amortization schedule, 240-241
Amount field (Write Checks window), 60
Annual payroll report, 211
Apply Discount window, 171-172
A/R register, 175-178, 180, 183

Arrow keys, using, 94-95, 98, 133
Asset accounts list, 223
Asset depreciation. *See* Depreciation of assets
Assets, 6
 book value of, 253
 entering with depreciation, 257-262
 entering existing, 257-258
 life of, 253
 recording loss of, 260-262
 recording purchase of, 259-260
 recording sale of, 260-262

B

Backing up files, 334-335
Backing up transactions at year-end, 311
[Backspace] key, using, 103
Backup files, restoring, 335
Balance forward payment method, 172-173
Balance sheet accounts, 5
Balance sheet reports, 287-288, 324
Balance sheets, 287-289
Balanced account congratulatory window, 80
Bank statements, 85
Banks, Federal Reserve System authorized, 199
Beep, setting, 357
Bills
 changing the payment interval for, 226
 combining for one vendor, 232
 discounts for early payment of, 224

Index

editing entries of, 224
paying, 9-10
paying in advance, 225
paying credit card, 237-239
recording, 221-223
recording payment of, 226-231
Bizminder utility, 114
   activating, 224-225
   installing, 328
   settings, 357
   using, 225
Bonding an employee, 178
Book value of an asset, 253
Bookkeeper password, 313-314
Budget planning, 121
Budget reports. *See also* Budgeting
   analysis of, 131
   creating and printing, 126
   example of, 132
   filtering transactions for, 128-130
   modifying, 127-128
   preparing, 117-133
Budgeting. *See also* Budget reports
   monthly detail for budget categories, 125-126
   QuickBooks process for, 122-126
   specifying budget amounts, 123-125
   year-end review and next year's budget, 311
Business cycle, 306-307
Business plan, preparing, 119
Business type, selecting, 23

C

Calculator, using, 199

Capital, vs. Owners' Equity, 269
Capital accounts, State rules for, 273
Cash basis accounting, 221
   and accounts payable, 231
   vs. accrual basis accounting, 283-285
Cash basis Profit & Loss statement, 290
Cash flow, analyzing, 295-296
Cash flow report, 12, 295-296
Cash payments, handling, 178
Cash sales, depositing, 181-182
Cash sales invoices, 181-182
Chart of accounts, 5, 266
Check numbering, 10
Check printing fields, customizing, 354
Check register. *See* Register
Check Register Does Not Balance with Bank Statement window, 84, 86-87
Check stock, ordering, 56
Check writing window. *See* Write Checks window
Checking account register. *See* Register
Checks. *See also* Printing checks
   correcting errors in, 72-73
   deleting, 65
   memorized, 111
   numbering, 10
   ordering stock for, 56
   postdated, 59
   preparing, 229
   printing, 10, 229
   printing samples first, 65-70
   recorded in accounts payable register, 229
   sample standard check, 57

sample voucher check, 57
selecting to print, 70-72
standard or voucher, 56-57
voiding, 64-65
writing, 9-10, 55-73
writing payroll, 196-197
Checks to Print field (Write Checks window), 58
Choose Bills to Pay window, 227-228, 230, 232-233
Cleared transaction detail report, 79, 81
Cleared transactions in the register, 92
Closed accounting periods, 313
Closing entry for double-entry accounting, 309
COGS (cost of goods sold)
   determining, 246-247
   recording, 248
   updating, 251
Collections agencies, 187
Collections reports, 187, 294
Colors, customizing screen, 358
Companies in QuickBooks
   customizing, 13, 352-356
   establishing files for, 23-24
   setting up new, 23-26
   starting new, 15
Company lists. *See* Lists
Confirmations, setting, 357
Congratulatory balanced account window, 80
Contractors, filing 1099 for, 320-321
Converting Quicken files for QuickBooks, 347-349
Corporations
   determining equity for, 272-273

Federal tax Form 1120, 322-324
   income taxes for, 310
   retained earnings for, 271
Corrected invoices, 155
Correcting errors
   in account reconciliation, 86-87
   in checks, 72-73
   in invoices, 154-155
   in payments, 177-178
   printer errors, 68
   at reconciliation, 78-79
   in Write Checks window, 63
Cost of goods sold (COGS)
   determining, 246-247
   recording, 248
   updating, 251
Create Budget Report window, 123, 127
Create Cash Flow Forecast Report window, 276, 278
Create Opening Balance Adjustment window, 83
Create Profit & Loss Statement window, 264
Create Summary Report window, 283
Credit card accounts, 236-239
   business vs. personal, 237
   deposits to, 182
   paying bills, 237-239
   reconciliation summary, 239
Credit Card Statement Information window, 238
Credit memos, 155-157, 174-175
Credit policies, 144, 151-152
Ctrl-A, using, 76, 92
Ctrl-arrow keys, using, 48, 100
Ctrl-D, using, 100, 130

Index

Ctrl-Del, using, 104, 156, 178, 224
Ctrl-E, using, 112, 125, 229
Ctrl-End, using, 92, 95, 98, 104
Ctrl-Enter, using, 24, 59, 63, 96
Ctrl-F, using, 99
Ctrl-F10, using, 83
Ctrl-H, using, 177, 224
Ctrl-Home, using, 98
Ctrl-Ins, using, 146
Ctrl-J, using, 111
Ctrl-L, using, 22, 59, 62, 67
Ctrl-M, using, 109, 133, 156, 286
Ctrl-N, using, 43
Ctrl-P, using, 67, 70, 133, 157
Ctrl-Pg Dn, using, 98
Ctrl-Pg Up, using, 63, 98
Ctrl-Q, using, 27
Ctrl-R, using, 63, 72
Ctrl-S, using, 59, 61, 64, 107
Ctrl-Spacebar, using, 160
Ctrl-T, using, 109, 156
Ctrl-V, using, 104
Ctrl-W, using, 63
Ctrl-Y, using, 18, 77, 227
Current Balance field (Write Checks window), 58-59
Current liability accounts, 196
Custom Company Settings field, 63
Custom reports. *See also* Reports
  creating, 275-276
  options for, 280-285
Customer Aging Status window, 186-187
Customer Not Found window, 143
Customer Type field, 33-34
Customer types. *See also* Customers
  adding, 35-36
  deleting, 34-35
  for different businesses, 34
  maintaining lists of, 33-37
  printing lists of, 37-38
Customers. *See also* Customer types
  charging deposits to, 234-235
  credit limits for, 151-152
  getting a list of, 40-44
  maintaining information on, 183-187
  purging records of, 42
  statements for, 183-186
Customize Current Company window/menu, 59, 353-356
  Company Information, 352-353
  Options, 353-355
  Password Table, 356
  Passwords, 355
Customizing QuickBooks, 11-14, 351-358
Customizing the QuickBooks company, 13, 352-356

D

Data directory, setting, 358
Date fields. *See also* Dates
  on invoices, 145, 158
  in the Print Statements window, 185
  in the register, 95
  in the Write Checks window, 60-61
Dates. *See also* Date fields
  customizing, 353-354
  days between date and pay date, 353-354

for filing Federal payroll taxes, 205
on invoices, 145, 158
monitoring payroll due dates, 193
on payables checks, 229
using the Go to Date feature, 102
Debts, short-term and long-term, 219-220
Declining-balance depreciation, 255
[Del] key, using, 103
Deleting a check, 65
Deleting customer types, 34-35
Deleting an invoice, 156
Deleting transactions in the register, 104
Delinquent accounts, 187
Deposit summary, printing, 181
Deposit Summary window, 176, 179-181
Deposits, 178-183
    in accounts receivable register, 180
    of cash sales, 181-182
    charged to customers against damage, 234-235
    invoices that generate, 179-180
    IRS rules for, 201
    recording IRS, 199-202
    transactions created by, 183
Depreciation of assets, 253-262
    accelerated, 254-255
    accumulated, 253, 257
    entering, 257-262
    IRS rules for, 253
    methods of, 253-255
    and original cost, 253
Depreciation expense, recording, 260
Description field (voucher checks), 62
Diamond fields, 22, 32

for accounts, 223
on invoices, 141
and recording payments received, 169
for vendors, 222
Did Checks Print OK? window, 71
Direct payments, 169, 230-231
Directory, setting for data, 358
Discounting, 171-172
    for early bill payment, 224
    as invoice line item, 148
Disks, formatting, 334
Ditto (") key, 59-60, 143
Dot dot (..) wildcard characters, 101
Double-clicking the mouse, 16, 357-358
Double-entry accounting, 309

E

Earnings (in Retained Earnings account), 269-273, 309-310
Employee lists, 39-40
Employees
    bonding, 178
    check preparation for, 229
    paying hourly workers, 199
    preventing theft from, 178
[End] key, using, 98, 133
Ending balance, entering at reconciliation, 78
Ending Balance field (Write Checks window), 59
End-of-year activities. See Year-end accounting activities
[Enter] key, using, 16, 18, 59

Index

Envelopes
   Intuit window envelopes, 73
   printing labels for, 73
Equal sign (=) wildcard character, 101
Equity, 6
   determining, 263-273
   determining for corporations, 272-273
   determining for partnerships, 270-272
   determining for sole proprietorships, 267-270
   profit and loss statements, 263-264
Equity accounts, 264, 266-267, 309-310
Error correction
   in account reconciliation, 78-79, 86-87
   in checks, 72-73
   on invoices, 154-155
   in payments, 177-178
   printer errors, 68
   in Write Checks window, 63
Esc key, using, 15
Expense accounts, 5-6
Expense accounts list, 223
Expenses, prepaid at year-end, 308-309

F

F2 key, using, 66
F3 key, using, 65, 99, 104
F4 key, using, 110
F5 key, using, 17, 286
F6 key, using, 63, 65
F7 key, using, 17, 24, 30, 111
F8 key, using, 128, 142, 171-172, 210
F9 key, using, 67, 71, 78, 82
F10 key, using, 24, 77
Federal income taxes for corporations, 310
Federal payroll taxes, dates for filing, 205
Federal Publication 534, 254, 256
Federal Reserve System, 199
Federal tax forms. *See also* IRS
   Form 1120, 322-324
   Form 940, 322
   Form 941, 199, 206-207, 209
   Form 1099, 215-216, 231, 320-321
   Form W-2, 210-213
   payroll, 194-195
   rounding cents on, 319
   Schedule C, 315-317, 319-320
   table of year-end, 316
   year-end, 315-324
FICA withholding, depositing, 199-200
Fields
   register, 93-94
   Write Checks window, 58-59
FIFO (first in first out) inventory valuation, 249
File formats for reports, 279
File/Print menu, accessing, 66
Files
   backing up, 334-335
   backing up at year-end, 311
   converting Quicken to QuickBooks, 347-349
   merging, 336-337
   restoring backup, 335

saving reports as, 279
Filter Report Transactions window, 129, 280-282
Filtering report data, 280-282
Filtering transactions
   in budget reports, 128-130
   in payroll reports, 210
   special characters used for, 129
Financial management program, 118-122
Financial terms, glossary of, 339-345
Financial transactions. *See* Transactions
Find feature, 99-102, 143
Find window, 99-101
Find/Edit menu, 65
Form 1120, 322-324
Form 940, 322
Form 941, 206-207, 209
Form 1099, 215-216, 231, 320-321
Form W-2, 210-213
Formatting a disk, 334
Forms, Federal tax. *See* Federal tax forms
Forms, State, 195
Forward slash ([/]) key, using, 95
Full Report option, 81
Funding, sources of, 120
FUTA payments report, 214-215
FUTA tax transactions, 203

G

Gift certificates, 234-236
Glossary of terms, 339-345
Go to Date feature, 102

Groups of transactions, 111-114

H

Hardware, setting up, 14
Help, accessing, 27
Help features, 14
Help screen for Main Menu, 14
Historical data, 97
[Home] key, using, 98, 133
Hourly workers, paying, 199

I

Income accounts, 5
Income summary account, 309
Income taxes for corporations, 310. *See also* Federal tax forms
Income/expense report, 299-300
Inkjet printers, printing checks with, 69-70
[Ins] key, using, 103, 154
Installation Summary window, 328
Installing Bizminder, 328
Installing printers, 25
Installing QuickBooks, 327-330
Insurance expenses, prepaid at year end, 308-309
Interest, entering at reconciliation, 78
Inventory
   at beginning and end of periods, 250
   calculating end of period, 251
   determining on hand, 246-252
   entering initial values for, 249

Index

for a manufacturing firm, 247
physical, 248
price extensions for, 249
recording, 248-250
setting account balances, 252
updating, 248, 251-252
valuing, 246-252
Invoice forms, custom, 161
Invoice line items, 144, 146-151. *See also* Invoices
  cash sales, 181-182
  customizing, 354
  discounts, 148
  other charges, 148
  payments, 150
  percentages in, 147
  refunds, 150-151
  sales tax, 146, 149-150
  subtotals, 146, 151
Invoice memo list, 52
Invoice memos, 52
Invoice window, 143-145
  Item Code column, 142
  PO Num field, 143
  using ditto (") in, 143
Invoices, 137-164. *See also* Invoice line items
  correcting errors in, 154-155
  creating, 140-153
  and customer credit limits, 151-152
  Date field in, 145
  dating, 158
  deleting, 156
  entering historical, 153-154
  examples of, 32, 149, 176
  for gift certificates, 235
  matching payments to, 172-173
  Memo field, 145
  memorized, 155-156
  numbering, 152-153
  overdue, 152
  postdated, 158
  printing, 157-162
  printing to an ASCII file, 161
  printing multiple copies, 161
  printing a sample, 161
  reprinting, 161-162
  reviewing, 154
  sales tax on, 146
  selecting paper for, 160
  styles of, 8
  that generate deposits, 179-180
  transactions created by, 146
  Type field, 353
  types of, 138-140
  using diamond fields, 141
  writing, 8
IRS. *See also* Federal tax forms
  deposits in Split Transaction window, 200
  expensing of Section 179 property, 253
  Publication 534, 254, 256
  recording deposits, 199-202
  rules for asset depreciation, 253, 255-256
  rules for deposits, 201
Item Code column (invoice window), 142
Item codes
  customizing, 354
  using, 50-51
Item lists, 146-151. *See also* Lists
  customizing line items, 354

discounts, 148
entering line items, 49
other charges, 148
payments, 150
percentages in, 147
refunds, 150-151
sales tax, 146, 149-150
from sample company, 49
subtotals, 146, 151
table of line item types, 50
using, 144-145
Itemized income/expense report, 299-300
Items/parts/services lists, 48-51

J

Job order costing, 46

K

Keys for entering notes, 44
Keys for moving around in QuickBooks, 28

L

Labels, printing, 73, 162-164
Laser Form Leaders, 69
Laser printers
    printing checks with, 69-70
    voucher checks for, 56
Liabilities, 6
    long-term, 219-220, 239-242
    short-term, 219-220, 231-236
Liability accounts, current, 196
Life of an asset, 253
LIFO (last in first out) inventory valuation, 250
Line items in the item list. *See* Item lists
Lists, 146. *See also* Item lists
    performing maintenance on, 36-37
    printing, 37-38
    standard entries in, 30
    table of uses for, 31
    types of, 30
    using, 22, 30-47
Loans. *See* Liabilities; Mortgage liabilities
Long-term liabilities, 219-220, 239-242
Loss of assets, recording, 260-262

M

MACRS (Modified Accelerated Cost Recovery System), 255-256
Mailing labels, printing, 162-164
Main Menu, 16
    help screen for, 14
    selecting options from, 16
Make Deposit window, 46
Manufacturing firm, inventory for, 247
Matching entries
    finding in the register, 100-102
    finding in report data, 281-282
Memo field
    on invoices, 52, 145

Index

in Write Checks window, 61
Memorized checks, 111
Memorized invoices, 155-156
Memorized reports, 286-287
Memorized transactions, 7, 30, 108-111, 113, 196, 202
Memorizing Report window, 286
Menus, using, 16-18
Merging files, 336-337
Message line (for check writing), 60
Minus (−) key, 95
   for check numbers, 71
   for invoice date, 145
Modified Accelerated Cost Recovery System (MACRS), 255-256
Modified cash basis accounting, 283-284
Monitor refresh speed, 358
Monthly Budget for Account window, 125
Monthly reconciliation of accounts, 74
Mortgage liabilities, 239-242
   amortization schedule, 240-241
   making payments, 241
   principal repayment, 239
Mouse
   double-clicking, 16
   setting speed for, 357-358
   using in the register, 98
Multiple copies of invoices, 161

N

New QuickBooks company
   setting up, 23-26
   starting, 15
Nondepreciable assets, entering, 258
Notes, adding to customer list, 42-44
Numbering invoices, 152-153

O

Open Bal Equity account, 249, 258, 264, 266, 271-273
Open item payment method, 172-173
Open item/balance forward, 353
Opening balance, updating, 81-82
Opening Balance Does Not Match Bank window, 82
Ordering check stock, 56
Overdraft charges, 74
Overdue receivables, 152, 186-187
Overpayments, handling, 174-175
Owner password, 313-315
Owners' equity, 5, 269

P

Paper, for printing invoices, 160
Par value of company stock, 272-273
Partial Page Printing window, 72
Partnerships
   determining equity for, 270-272
   retained earnings for, 271
Password Level Assignment window, 314, 356
Password Required window, 315
Password Table, 313-314, 356
Passwords, 312-315
   adding, 312-313

customizing settings for, 355
    using, 314-315
Pay date
    accounts payable, 222
    customizing, 353-354
    sales taxes, 232
Pay Vendors window, 226-227
Payables. *See* Accounts payable (A/P)
Payables register, 229. *See also*
    Accounts payable (A/P)
Payables reports, 294-295
Payee field (Write Checks window), 59
Paying bills. *See* Bills
Payment Methods list, 46
Payment summary report, 228
Payments (receivables), 167-178
    balance forward vs. open item,
        172-174
    cash, 178
    changing the default method, 174
    correcting errors in, 177-178
    discounting, 171-172
    entries created by, 175-177
    handling overpayments, 174-175
    invoice line items for, 150
    matching to invoices, 172-173
    overdue, 186-187
    processing, 8
    recording, 167-178
    terms for, 38-39, 144
Payroll, 191-216. *See also* Payroll
        reports; Payroll taxes
    hourly workers, 199
    IRS deposits, 199-200
    memorizing transactions, 202
    monitoring due dates for, 193
    QuickBooks system, 192-204

QuickPay package for, 192
    register entries for, 197-198
    split transactions, 197-198
    State unemployment tax
        transactions, 203
    using transaction groups, 202
    using your own chart of accounts,
        193
    withholding accounts, 193, 196
    workers' compensation payments,
        204
Payroll checks, 196-197
Payroll forms, 194-195
Payroll reports, 204-216. *See also*
        Payroll
    examples of, 208, 211-213
    filtering, 210
Payroll taxes, 321-322. *See also* Payroll
    dates for filing Federal, 205
    register entries for, 234
Percentage line items (invoices), 147
[Pg Up] and [Pg Dn] keys, using, 98, 133
Plus ([+]) key, 95
    using for check numbers, 71
    using for invoice date, 145
PO Num field (invoice window), 143
Position Number field (Write Checks
        window), 69
Postdated checks, 59
Postdated invoices, 158
Prepaid Expense accounts, 308-309
Price extensions (inventory), 249
Price field (for product invoices), 144
Principal repayment (mortgage), 239
Print Checks window, 66, 70
Print Customer Mailing Labels
        window, 163

Index

Print Invoices window, 158, 160
Print Statements window, 185-186
Printer position number, 67
Printers
   preparing for reconciliation, 76
   problems and solutions, 68
   setting up, 25
   setting up for QuickBooks, 330
   using inkjet or laser, 69-70
   using tractor-feed, 66-69
Printing a budget report, 126
Printing checks, 10, 65-73. *See also* Checks
   customizing fields for, 354
   with inkjet or laser printers, 69-70
   printing a sample first, 65-70
   selecting checks to print, 67, 70-72
   with tractor-feed printer, 66-69
Printing the deposit summary, 181
Printing invoices, 157-162
   to an ASCII file, 161
   and dating or postdating, 158
   making multiple copies, 161
   printing a sample, 161
   reprinting, 161-162
   Select Invoices to Print window, 160
   selecting paper for, 160
Printing a list, 37-38
Printing mailing labels, 73, 162-164
   for best customers, 164
   for selected customers, 163-164
   specifying a Zip code, 163-164
Printing reports, 279-280
Printing statements, 185-186
Product Invoice window, 8
Product invoices, 8, 139-140, 144. *See also* Invoices

Professional invoices, 8, 138-139, 144. *See also* Invoices
Profit, calculating, 247
Profit & Loss statement, 318
   creating, 263-265
   customizing, 288, 290-291
   using cash-basis accounting, 290
Program options, 12-13, 356-358
Program Options window, 13, 356-358
Project field, 93
Project list
   from sample company, 47
   working with, 46-48
Project report, 299, 301-302
Project tracking, 93-94, 97
   setting, 354
   using Custom Company Settings, 63
Projects
   creating, 47-48
   reorganizing, 48
   using, 105-106
Protecting data with passwords, 312-315
Pull-down menus, 17-18
Purchase order numbers, 143
Purchasing an asset, recording, 259-260
Purging customer records, 42

Q

QBDATA subdirectory, 15, 23
QBSAMPLE file, 26
Quarterly Federal tax Form 941, 206-207, 209

Question mark (?) wildcard character, 101
Quick Keys, 15
    table of, 29
    using, 18
Quicken, and QuickBooks, 4
Quicken files, converting to QuickBooks, 347-349
QuickPay payroll package, 192
QuickTrainer feature, 14, 27, 356-357

R

Rate field (for invoices), 144
Receivables. *See* Payments (receivables)
Receive Payments window, 9, 168-171, 178, 181
Reconcile Register with Bank Statement window, 77-78, 81-82
Reconciliation summary reports, 76, 78-81, 239
Reconciling an account. *See* Account reconciliation
Refund line items (invoices), 150-151
Register
    adding accounts to, 96-97
    assigning projects to transactions, 105-106
    cleared transactions in, 92
    for a credit card account, 237
    displaying, 91
    entering data in fields, 94
    entering historical transactions, 84-85
    entries for payroll, 197-198
    entries for payroll taxes, 234
    entries for sales taxes, 233
    finding matching entries, 100-102
    Go to Date feature, 102
    historical data in, 97
    maintaining, 90-97
    making entries in, 89-114
    recording transactions, 94-96
    reviewing entries, 97-98
    revising transactions, 102-105
    sample entries in, 92
    sample manual, 6, 91
    scrolling through, 98-99
    Show Accounts field, 354-355
    table of fields used in, 93
Register window, switching to, 63-64
Register window scroll bar, 92
Registering QuickBooks, 329
Reminder feature (Bizminder), 114
Report Options window, 128, 283
Reports
    aging, 293
    balance sheet, 287-288
    budget, 117-133
    cash vs. accrual basis, 285
    cash flow, 12, 295-296
    cleared transaction detail, 79, 81
    collections, 294
    custom, 275-302
    data to use for, 276
    file formats for, 279
    filtering data, 280-282
    filtering payroll, 210
    of FUTA and SUTA payments, 214-215
    itemized income/expense, 299-300
    memorizing, 286-287
    options for, 10-11, 280-285

Index

payables, 294-295
payment summary, 228
payroll, 204-216
payroll summary, 208, 211-213
printing, 279-280
printing to a text file, 280
Profit & Loss, 263-265, 288, 290-291, 318
project, 299, 301-302
receivables, 291-294
reconciliation, 76, 79-81
reconciliation summary, 79-81
sales, 291-293
sales tax, 294-295
sample annual payroll, 211
sample budget, 132
sample payroll, 208, 211-213
saving as files, 279
standard, 275-302
State and local quarterly tax, 209
summary, 295-297
table of types and uses, 277-278
1099, 295, 321
transaction, 297-299
uncleared transaction detail, 81
viewing, 279
wide-screen, 131, 133
Reports menu, 17
Reprinting invoices, 161-162
Restoring backup files, 335
Retained Earnings account, 269-273, 309-310
Revenue, 6

S

Sales report, 291-293
Sales Tax item type, 354
Sales tax report, 294-295
Sales taxes, 231-233
  on invoices, 146, 149-150
  register entries for, 233
Schedule C (Profit or Loss from Business), 315-317, 319-320
Screen colors, customizing, 358
Scroll bar (register window), 92
Scrolling through the register, 98-99
Searching the register, 99-102, 143
Section 179 property, IRS expensing of, 253
Select Invoices to Print window, 160
Select List window, 30
Selling an asset, 260-262
Service charges, 78
Service invoices, 8, 138-139, 144
Set Check Number window, 71
Set Passwords window, 312-313, 355
[Shift]-[Enter], using, 141
[Shift]-[Tab], using, 59, 131
Shipping method list, 51-52
Short-term liabilities, 219-220, 231-236
Show Accounts field (register), 354-355
Slash (/) key, using, 95
Sole proprietorships
  determining equity for, 267-270
  retained earnings for, 271

Schedule C for, 317
[Spacebar], using, 38, 71, 179
Specify Monthly Budget Amounts window, 124
Split Transaction window, 61, 64, 107
   with IRS withholding, 200
   a payroll transaction in, 198
Split transactions, 61, 106-107
   payroll, 197
   for selling an asset, 262
   on voucher check, 62
Standard check sample, 57
Standard entries in lists, 30
Standard Memorized Transaction List window, 110
Standard reports, 275-276, 278-280
Standard Transaction Group List window, 112
Starting your first QuickBooks session, 15
State and local payroll forms, 195
State and local quarterly tax reports, 209
State rules for capital accounts, 273
State unemployment tax transactions, 203
Statements (customer), 183-186
Stock (company), par value of, 272-273
Straight-line depreciation, 254-255
Subaccounts, using, 107-108
Subprojects, 48, 106
Subtotal line items (invoices), 146, 151
Summary reports, 208, 211-213, 295-297
Supplies, ordering from Intuit, 56

SUTA payments report, 214-215
SUTA tax transactions, 203

T

[Tab] key, using, 18, 59, 131
Tax forms. *See* Federal tax forms
Tax transactions. *See also* Federal tax forms
   dates for filing Federal payroll, 205
   FUTA and SUTA, 203
   payroll, 234, 321-322
   sales, 231-233
   state unemployment tax, 203
1099 form, 215-216, 231, 320-321
1099 report, 295, 321
Text file, printing a report to, 280
Theft of cash, preventing, 178
Tilde (~) wildcard character, 101
Timing differences in accounting, 284
Tracking projects. *See* Project tracking
Tractor-feed printers, 66-69
Transaction to Find window, 99-101
Transaction groups. *See also* Transactions
   changing, 112-113
   defining, 111-112
   establishing payroll, 202
   recording, 114
   working with, 111-114
Transaction history, accessing, 177
Transaction History window, 177
Transaction reminders, 114
Transaction report, 297-299
Transactions, 6, 92-93. *See also* Transaction groups

Index

assigning, 105-106
cleared, 92
created by invoices, 146
deleting, 104
filtering for budget reports, 128-130
memorized, 7, 30, 108-111, 113, 196, 202
recording, 5-7, 94-96
reinstating, 104-105
reversing, 105
revising, 102-105
splitting, 106-107
voiding, 103-104

U

Uncleared transaction detail report, 81
Unemployment tax transactions, 203
Updating inventory, 248, 251-252
Updating the opening balance, 81-82

V

Valuing inventory, 246-252
Vendor lists, 44-46, 222
Vendor type codes, 45
Vendor Type list, 44-46
Viewing reports, 279
Voiding checks, 64-65
Voiding transactions, 103-104
Voucher checks, 56-57. See also Write Checks window

completing, 61-63
Description field, 62
with split transaction, 62

W

Wide-screen reports, 131, 133
Wildcard characters, 101
Wildcard searches, 101
Window envelopes, 73
Windows, using, 18
Workers' compensation payments, 204
Write Checks window, 58
    Amount field, 60
    Checks to Print field, 58
    Current Balance field, 58-59
    Date field, 60-61
    Ending Balance field, 59
    entering data, 59-61
    fields in, 58-59
    getting an extra message line, 60
    making corrections, 63
    Memo field, 61
    Payee field, 59
    Position Number field, 69
    printing checks from, 66-69
    switching to Register window, 63-64
    using ditto (") in, 59-60
Writing checks. See Checks; Write Checks window
W-2 forms, 210-213, 321

Y

Year-end accounting activities, 305-324
  backing up transactions, 311
  closing, 307-310
  maintenance tasks, 310-315
  password protection, 312-315
  for prepaid expenses, 308-309
Year-end tax forms, 315-324

QUICKBOOKS COMMAND CARD

Keys Available from Most Locations

Keypress	Result
Backspace	Deletes the previous character
Ctrl-←	Moves left one screen on reports or to the previous word in a field
Ctrl-→	Moves right one screen on reports or to the next word in a field
Ctrl-A	Adds or selects an account
Ctrl-Backspace	Deletes the current field setting
Ctrl-C	Displays the calculator
Ctrl-E	Edits description for selected item in a company list
Ctrl-End	Moves to the last check or invoice
Ctrl-Enter	Finalizes the current window or transaction
Ctrl-F	Displays window to enter text to find
Ctrl-F1	Displays Help index to select a topic
Ctrl-Home	Moves to the first check or invoice
Ctrl-L	Displays a company list to select a field's entry
Ctrl-M	Memorizes the current transaction or report
Ctrl-Pg Dn	Moves to the next check or invoice
Ctrl-Pg Up	Moves to the previous check or invoice
Ctrl-Q	Activates QuickTrainer if available
Ctrl-T	Recalls a memorized transaction or report
Ctrl-Z	Repairs a file that you have highlighted
Del	Deletes the current character
End	Moves to the end of a field
End, End	Moves to end of the check or invoice
End, End, End	Moves to the last check or invoice
Enter	Moves to the next field
Esc	Backs out of the current activity
F1	Displays help information
F10	Finalizes the current window or transaction
Home	Moves to the beginning of the field
Home, Home	Moves to the beginning of the check or invoice
Home, Home, Home	Moves to the first check or invoice
Ins	Switches between inserting and overwriting characters
Pg Dn	Moves down one screen

QuickBooks for Profit: Making the Numbers Work　　　　　©1993 Osborne/McGraw-Hill

Keys Available from Most Locations *(continued)*

Keypress	Result
Pg Up	Moves up one screen
Shift-Enter	Moves to the next section on a check or invoice
Shift-Tab	Moves to the previous field
Tab	Moves to the next field
↓	Moves down one transaction or line
↑	Moves up one transaction or line

Keys Available in the Main Menu

Keypress	Result
Ctrl-B	Backs up a company
Ctrl-E	Backs up the current company and exits
Ctrl-G	Selects the company to make current

Keys Available for Entering Checks, Invoices, Payments, and Bills

Keypress	Results
Ctrl-D	Deletes the current line
Ctrl-Del	Deletes the current check, invoice, or transaction
Ctrl-F	Finds transaction
Ctrl-H	Displays transaction history of current transaction
Ctrl-I	Inserts the current line
Ctrl-Ins	Inserts an item in the list while entering data in a window
Ctrl-J	Displays memorized transaction groups to add to register
Ctrl-N	Displays Notepad for customers or vendors
Ctrl-P	Prints checks, invoices, payment summaries, and account registers
Ctrl-R	Switches to the check, accounts receivable, or accounts payable register
Ctrl-S	Opens split transaction window in a register or moves to voucher area on a check
Ctrl-V	Views the selected customer's or vendor's record
Ctrl-W	Switches to writing checks or invoices
Ctrl-X	Displays transfer account information
Ctrl-Y	Switches to reconciling checking account, receiving payments, or pay vendors window
Ctrl-↓	Finds next matching transaction
Ctrl-↑	Finds previous matching transaction